LINES THROUGH A PRISM

BOB SIQVELAND

outskirts
press

This book is dedicated to every health care worker,
first responder, and volunteer of 2020,
everywhere.
Thank you, and bless you.

Deoxyribonucleic Acid

If you were to take out all of the DNA from your entire body and stretch it end to end, it would go to the sun and back 150 times.

—J. Medina, Cambridge University, UK

But if you took all the DNA out of the seven billion people on the planet and scrunched it together, it would fit into a space as small as a grain of rice.

The Human Brain

According to British neurophysiologist W. Grey Walter, at least ten billion electronic cells would be needed to build a facsimile of man's brain. These cells would occupy about a million and a half cubic feet, but several millions of cubic feet would be needed for the "nerves" or wiring, bigger than the Pentagon. The power required to operate it would be one billion watts.

And the seasons
They go round and round
And the painted ponies go up and down
We're captive on a carousel of time
We can't return, we can only look
Behind from where we came
And go round and round and round
In the circle game

—"The Circle Game," written by Joni Mitchell,
performed by Ian Tyson and Sylvia Fricker

Previous Novels

The Immaculate Erection
The Wilderness of Time
Simple Witness (winner of three awards)
The Vicissitudes of Fortune (winner of eleven awards)

CHAPTER 1

There should be nothing iconoclastic about my claim that most people are assholes. Truth is, I'm an optimist. Fact is, most people are assholes. There are some moralists who are assholes. Most immoral people are assholes. Amoral people are all assholes . . . or worse. In my former job, most of the targets were immoral or amoral, yet, in spite of that, I still watch life fly by through fuchsia-colored specs. Cynical? Yup! But then, I really do like the good ones.

I'm still not sure what it was about. Seemed like maybe a long-buried fear of some sort. As a deflection, I catalogued it as probably like everything else you take for granted and don't miss until it's gone, but at some point, oddly, I developed a preoccupation with sunrise. Could have been a number of things, but sunrise? Deeper-level symbolism? I'd always loved the sunrise as a natural event. But now, for some reason, I would awake . . . and anxiously wait for it. A decades-long delayed reaction?

The false dawn was just a teaser. I tried to absorb the meditation angle, mindfulness stuff, the Tao, Zen, you know, but only as a means to control my mind and thoughts so as not to wake up at five every damn day. I suppose it was because somewhere along the line, I figured I might never see another one, but I intuit that it was deeper. Maybe repression.

Most of us come to realize that we aren't immortal, and my celebration, or at least relief every morning, became redundantly palpable, even when it rained. At least at the start of the day, I was vertical, alive, breathing, and ready to jump back into the fray. If I made it through the day and was gifted with watching the sunset and I could see another sunrise . . . so be it. Still, I knew I would wake around five because on some subliminal level, I knew the Zen masters out there in the ether world doubted my sincerity and would seek punishment. I recalled the old saw: "I know that you know that I know that you know what I'm thinking." And I was thinking there were still people who would like me dead.

Most people wouldn't consider someone who has shot thirteen people as being a romantic, and I'm not counting my stint in Nam. But they'd be wrong. I even have a feminine side that comes out in odd versions of painting and cooking, or most art for that matter. What I'm trying to say is that I never shot anyone who didn't deserve it.

So don't say I didn't tell you up front. Here's my caveat. I think a lot. I read a lot. And I probably talk too much. So if you want to read this story, you're going to have to wade through my bullshit. Don't like it? Tough. I really don't care.

My name is Woodward, nickname "Woody," and yeah, I've heard all the innuendos. The admission that I was in the autumn of my life was a difficult one. I had been spending more and more time in my safe place. Psychologists call it delusion. Be clear, it wasn't that I was afraid to die. I understand the reality of the whole cycle of life thing. But it was a subtle and subliminal sadness that I was going to miss out. The party would go on, and I wasn't going to be there.

I had accepted death fifty years ago. Fifty years on borrowed time made living easier. Most problems fell into the category of BFD. I should probably add that this encompassed my having become quite spiritual in the past decade. I had been most cynical about man-made religions for years, but had found comfortable solace in spirituality. Did I believe that a higher power had a lovely place for me in the hereafter and that death would bring my ultimate reward? Bit of a stretch, but . . . maybe. Probably a casualty of Catholic conditioning.

Still, life had been a marvelous and exciting journey, and with my apparent paucity for any ethereal clairvoyance, I was genuinely satisfied to stick with what I knew and accordingly, was going to miss this earthly gig when my time came. Honestly, I just figured that getting old would take longer.

I've known for some time that I didn't have to pay Tony Robbins a thousand bucks to remind me that the secret to happiness and success is attitude. I discovered that all on my own a long time ago. Was I adapting my attitude to my reality while sliding down the leeward side of the hill, the one they said I was "over" almost fifteen years ago? Probably not. That reality was less difficult to eschew than the incessant emergence of aches and pains that are so integral to septuagenerianism, which is probably not a word, but you get the picture. I can say that I'm just not a fan of reality. Are you kidding? Turn on the TV, read the paper, drive in rush hour? Lots of hate going around. Lots of self-service. Lots of incivility. Not much altruism. I don't have an intellectual disability. I understand reality. I just don't like it.

I live alone now. My wife left a decade ago. No, she didn't find a younger heartthrob. No, she wasn't abused. No, it wasn't financial. Sadly, it was attrition, the intractable abatement of connectivity, like soft rock in a rain forest or the Alaskan glaciers. The parting was most civil, even amicable. We're friends. The gentle void eventually needed to be filled, so I moved to a quaint little town below the Mason-Dixon Line so that I could discard my mackinaw jacket and galoshes. Yeah, I get the precept that wherever you go, there you are, but I wasn't in escape mode. In some ways, it was worse.

Here's how it happened. I got a map of the lower forty-eight (to use an anachronism), closed my eyes, and dropped my finger on the east coast of Georgia. I admit to doing a double take on my mental stability, but really, what difference did it make? My ex had taken half of the $800,000, so I had a relatively small nest egg to work with. I got a cheap plane ticket to Atlanta, rented a cheap car, and headed to the spot my finger had landed on: Jekyll Island, Georgia. I felt a muted sense of foreboding on the drive, trying to recall the Stevenson classic. I thought maybe Mr. Hyde was the bad guy, but wasn't sure. Turns out, I was right, but in the end, the good doctor Jekyll was a bit of a schizo as well.

CHAPTER 2

I wasn't familiar with Jekyll Island in the slightest, just the little I'd read. Part of the excitement . . . part of the intrigue. However, as with all whimsical notions, the cognitive gears began to turn, and the urge to reassess decision-making skills came-a-knockin'. Some kind of self-preservation mechanism, I would guess. At least one member of my family would have described my decision as similar to that of a squirrel when crossing the road. In this case, I simply felt the need to take a visual of the place. Were there challenges, things to do, people to meet, or was it a retirement community where a plethora of nearly-deads rode around on scooters and golf carts, hoisting mint juleps, building their excitement for the early evening bingo tourney? It isn't vanity, just stubbornness, but for me, suicide by cop is more attractive than using a walker. What's new is that my kids have referred to me as *paleo*. What they don't give me credit for is the effort to preclude our mutual humiliation of them dabbing the drool from my chin and hiding me in the attic when their friends come over.

The drive from Atlanta was without event. Since I had to return to Minnesota, I'd only brought an old army backpack. I found an "oldies" station out of Atlanta and reminisced while absorbing the nice weather and scenery, slightly uncomfortable because I was comfortable. Where was the boogeyman? There was always a boogeyman, at least when you're conditioned to boogeymen. I figured the Zen masters were fuckin' with me again.

If I had my druthers, I would travel the blue highways,

but this trip was a scouting venture to see if I was nutso, and I could always put off the leisure trip until later, if there was a later. Interstates are pretty much the same: billboards, rest areas, buildings, redundant mile markers, and accoutrements.

I recalled playing "alphabet" with my older brother, bouncing around the back seat of our old station wagon, Dad driving, Mom periodically bitching about something or other. We'd see a word with a letter on a sign . . .

"There's an *A* in America."

"I see a *B* in hamburgers."

On and on until *zero*, or one of us making up a word, or a shove followed by a front seat comment. "If we have to pull over, you both get a swat" would segue into nasty, furtive looks and offhand questions, a form of payback, I suppose.

"When will we get there?"

The language of kids and parents.

When Mom and Dad wanted to say something they didn't want us to hear, they spoke pig Latin, which I never bothered to figure out because it wasn't that tough to discern the meaning from their body language. That might have been where I first learned the subtle art and benefit of playing dumb.

I think Interstate 95 on the East Coast goes from the North Pole to Antarctica, at least Maine to South Florida. I pulled off at New Jesup Highway and stopped at Love's Travel Stop, gassed up, peed, and grabbed a surprisingly tasty barbecue. These places usually have what I call "fill," tasteless sandwiches and chips, but I had forgotten about the sense of pride the South takes in their cuisine.

As I was leaving, she asked me where I was going. "She" was a young, swarthy girl who disguised her beauty through disrepair. I could sense that she wasn't soliciting me for a fifty-dollar tryst by her passive, introverted demeanor and rather apologetic query, reminiscent of an abused puppy.

"Headin' to Jekyll Island," I said.

"That's where I'm going," she said in a muted voice. "Any chance I could ride along?"

"You live there?" I asked.

"No . . . just visiting a friend."

Silence followed. I watched her, her head bowed, glancing to the road. She didn't seem to be a threat.

"Why not . . . it's not too far." I motioned for her to follow and walked to my rental. Like me, she just had a backpack, which she dropped in the back seat after a questioning glance and my nod.

I was aware that the new designer jeans had holes in the knees and idiots paid up for that, but this girl's blue jeans weren't torn by design . . . just wear. I also detected the slight odor of ignored hygiene. Her long brunette hair would have been most attractive with some attention, but whether through rebellion, apathy, or free spirit, it hung in a lifeless wilt past her shoulders. She stared out of the passenger window.

"So what's your name?" I queried.

"Marta."

"And where are you from?" I asked, sensing a lack of ebullient conversation.

"Miami."

I guess I really didn't need to be chatty, but I found that I was somewhat offended. After all, my magnanimous gesture was being dismissed.

After a bit, I said, "It's just conversation, Marta. I'm not interrogating you."

After a pause, she glanced at me. "Sorry, it's just that I have some worries is all."

I detected an accent. Eastern European, I guessed. We drove in a quasi-comfortable silence until turning onto the Jekyll Island Causeway.

Eventually, she said, "Thank you for this ride, and where do you come from?"

Definitely eastern European. There was more than

reticence. I could intuit pain, fear, and something more lethal, but the tinkling cymbal of caution said, *You've been here before, Woody, and it doesn't go somewhere you want to go.*

"Minnesota. Ever been there?"

She shook her head with an indifferent smile before replying, "Place with many lakes, yeah?"

"So they say." I had always had a caretaking bent, one I found created more problems than solutions, but then, I had usually had some kind of stake in the outcome. Without a stake, it was mostly ego, mine having been waning for years. Still, I was a sucker for involuntary innocence.

For the next several miles, my innocent hitchhiker was quiet until she said, "In two blocks, you can drop me off . . . if that is good?"

Without a reason to question the request, in two blocks, I pulled over. After thanking me, she grabbed her backpack from the back seat and stood on the curb until I left.

I did look around, noting the location and cross street. It was a conditioned response, especially when there's something that tickles my curiosity or maybe flags more sinister thoughts. Again, I sometimes create demons without reason. I seem to find reality boring. Still, she hadn't been your normal transaction, but it was best to draw a line through it, which I did.

CHAPTER 3

I checked into a cheap motel with the quasi-clever name of Sleepitoff Motel. Okay, more quasi than clever, but surprisingly comfortable. After three days of absorbing and processing the physical Jekyll Island, I left to return to Minnesota, but not before making some decisions. The place intrigued me to the point where I succumbed to what fate had thrown my way and decided to come back for a while.

My timing had been good. A longtime resident had died and left his home to his only son, who lived in Seattle and worked for Bill Gates. Actually, he worked for Microsoft, who worked for Bill Gates. I had picked the oldest real estate company on the island, and one day later, they handed me the gift. It was available for lease. The place never even got listed. When I offered $1,350 a month, I expected the kid would be offended, but it seemed his specialty was programming, not real estate. He jumped on it, and we signed a one-year lease.

I went to the local golf course clubhouse, ordered a Grey Goose martini, and toasted to me, a lucky guy and a smarty-pants to boot. I sat at the bar, and upon perusing the dining area, noticed several interesting characters eating alone, enough so that I made a mental note to follow up should they be there the next time I was. Since I could turn in the rental back in Minnesota, I left the next day.

In retrospect, the drive home was a bit strange . . . disquieting and emotionally impactful. It started with a song. The station was playing songs from the '40s and '50s. The words brought up an image of my dad singing them: "The Rockies may crumble, Gibraltar may tumble. They're only made of clay, but our love is here to stay."

Bogie and Bacall, Marlene Dietrich, vets who survived "the Bulge." And Dad, who survived a kamikaze on the USS *Curtiss* at Kwajalein Atoll in the Marshall Islands. Songs from the war. Songs about the "Greatest Generation." A time of tragedy and romance. A time of American patriotism and unity. What the hell happened? In any event, my thoughts about Dad were soft . . . gentle.

Dad was a type B about everything except my mother, where he was a type A-plus. There was a lot of longevity on Dad's side.

I remember my great-aunt, Mabel, when she quit smoking on her hundredth birthday. "Ah, these things just don't do it for me anymore." Might have given her the three more years.

But Dad, well, he was a "stuffer," and my mom knew exactly which of his buttons to push, and so he died in his favorite chair at the tender age of sixty-eight, the result of very high blood pressure. No secret where that came from. There was no human, or animal, that didn't like my old man. The same could not be said about my mother.

Not only is forgiveness one of the best virtues of the human element, it is certainly one of the healthiest. We forgive to make ourselves feel better. If that's true, however, then it could be classified as selfish. It's my conditioned understanding that being selfish is not virtuous, so where does that leave us? A paradox? In any event, I forgave my mother. For what, you ask? A bunch of things, but they no longer matter to me, and you don't need to know. The point, however, is that, at least emotionally, I am not scarred for life. Don't need resentments. They kill ya. Just move along, little doggie. So tell me life's not fair, and I'll ask you . . . compared to what?

Mike and his Mechanics claimed that "every generation blames the one before." I suppose that's true to a degree, but I don't agree with the premise. The very definition of character is taking responsibility, so I think it's bullshit. On a more specific level, however, there is plenty of evidence that parents and their children have issues. My maternal grandfather was a bit of a tyrant, and when his only son was killed in a car accident, he turned his repressed anger and anguish onto his only daughter. She was tough, and so she acclimated, but not without consequence. She developed an intriguing mix of personality. She tried to emulate his autocracy, but I could see that it was just veneer. It did work on a lot of others. Judgmental? Yes. Disciplinarian? Yes. Unpredictable? Yes. Intimidating? Yes. Spoiled brat? Some might say so.

Mr. John Barleycorn played a role in her web as well. She could show streaks of caring and generosity, however, and thus received a somewhat unenthusiastic forgiveness for her sins. Because her power play didn't work on me, we had an interesting and somewhat complicated relationship. In the end, she respected my boundaries. I didn't really ask for more. With a husband and four boys, there was no mitigating feminine influence, so my guess is that was a factor as well. On the other hand, I'm told that girls and their mothers often have issues.

Again, I'm sure the psychiatric squad could provide deep and esoteric explanations, but then again, from whom do they receive personal counsel? I'll ask you to receive my cynicism on a pillow of silk. These opinions are a statement about me, not the psychology profession. Bottom line: anyone who claims their family is free of disfunction is either lying, smokin' funny cigarettes, or delusional. All things considered, my brothers and I got along well, part of that probably being needed strength in an unpredictable environment, a Darwinian sort of thing.

It was the 8-millimeter film kind of reel of my youth that flashed before me as the miles rolled by. All the people have come and gone. Strangely, people seem to remain alive until the generation of those who knew them has passed on and they become names on a family tree or faces in old yellowed photos.

"She was a pretty gal."

"Interesting fellow, that one."

My maternal grandmother had three sisters. They were as Irish as they come. Their tree dated back to Red O'Neill and their mythical story about how he became the first king of Ireland. Seems some sort of armed British ship was circling the Emerald Isle when the captain shouted out that the first man to touch land would be king. As passengers and crew lowered the life rafts, some jumping into the sea and swimming to shore, old Red grabbed a hatchet, cut off his hand, and threw it to the beach. Quintessential romance, or more appropriately, the ultimate in Irish bullshit, but I actually believed it until the day I sat in a bar in Port Chester, New York, telling the story, and some iconoclastic prick broke out laughing, interrupted me, and finished the story, claiming his own descendancy from redoubtable—or should I say, doubtable—Red. In the end, it was simply the end of one story and the beginning of another.

What great fun those four sisters were. If there were such things as female leprechauns, which there aren't, these four mischievous fairies were pure delight. How, after fifty years, did their visage appear so clearly? The smiles, the teeth, and the twinkle of their eyes like digital photos with eight million pixels. In these visions, I almost had the feeling that I was violating their space.

Individually and collectively, they yearned to take risks. Not big risks, but like when someone just wants to fuck with someone, which they did with my overlord grandfather. They never got caught, though I recall several times when it was nip and tuck. They would wave their magic shillelaghs, breathe sighs of relief, and giggle. They were put in my life for a reason, forming my personality, like osmosis, with a subliminal permanence. I inherited the metaphorical shillelagh.

Two of the sisters had sons who were about seven or eight years older than my older brother and I. These guys, too, were a hoot. Camping and exploring expeditions weren't uncommon. Tall tales and scary stories were the soup du jour.

One of them told me my first dirty joke. "So, this giraffe walks into a bar and says, 'The highballs are on me.'"

I laughed for show, but I didn't get it. What can I say? I was naïve. At that point, I still thought *Under the Grandstand*, by Seymour Butts, was a sidesplitter.

CHAPTER 4

Trancelike, I stayed the speed limit through Georgia, Tennessee, Kentucky, Indiana, Illinois, and into Milwaukee. Pieces of history flew by, as did my stream of thought. When it comes to cognitive structure, I can be quite unstructured . . . muddled, even frivolous, like when you look up something on Google that links to something else and something else, until you forgot what you were looking for in the first place. So my head went to the changed world we now inhabit.

Change has been an arithmetic progression for centuries. In the last century, it had become a geometric progression, and more recently segued into an exponential progression. Most will credit technology, of course, but only a minority really understand that such is a double-edged sword. I am one. On one level, Facebook, the playground for narcissists, has caused certain damage, but I offer this example . . . *robotics.*

In the fifteenth century, Leonardo da Vinci developed an android and the French, an artificial duck. In 1901, sponge divers found the remains of a brass mechanism, an astronomical calculator believed to have been developed by the Greeks two thousand years ago. It was found off the Greek island of Antikythera, and some consider it to be the forerunner of the computer, as it displayed the motion of the universe. The Industrial Revolution brought more complex mechanics, and the advent of electricity initiated a huge leap on the progress charts. Like the internet, robots eliminated many jobs, which has been offset by the creation of many more, although of a very different skill set. Where it becomes scary is when robotics becomes integrated with *artificial intelligence* (AI).

A number of people I knew, including people in the agency I'd worked for, didn't get it. Be it training, logic, intuition, or at least history, they should have known that the other edge of the technology sword was sharp . . . and lethal. As with most things in life, it wasn't the technology itself that posed a threat. It was the human element. Man's inhumanity to man was intrinsic with his creation. The battle between good and evil had its biblical origin when Cain murdered his brother Abel, motivated by jealousy and lust, two of the so-called seven deadly sins. While those seven do cover a broad stroke, they're but the tip of the iceberg.

AI, artificial intelligence, has shown some potential promise for humanity, but the nefarious seeds of AGI portend the storm clouds of man's accelerated destruction should they become the unbridled tools of evil intent. *Artificial general intelligence* is the hypothetical intelligence of a machine that has the capacity to understand or learn any intellectual task that a human being can. The operative word, however, is *hypothetical.*

Years ago, IBM developed a program to learn the game of chess. In short order, the program was able to beat the grand master. Now, most people would guess that chess is the most sophisticated board game, but they would be terribly wrong. A board game called "Go" was invented by the Chinese some two thousand years before Christ and has been played ever since. The game was based upon war and military strategy in which the aim is to surround more territory than the opponent. There are those who claim that Go is several trillion times more complex than chess. I would note, for those who tend to be dismissive about the number one trillion, let me quantify. One trillion seconds is thirty-two thousand years.

Google developed a computer program called AlphaGo to challenge the world champion Go player. Not only did the

Google bot win, but a newer version, AlphaGo Zero, was able to teach itself to the point where in a few days, the new version could beat the original version one hundred times straight.

So what's the problem? you may be asking yourself. Think about this: these bots had developed new strategies in a matter of days that man hadn't been able to do in four thousand years. How? Intuition! An artificially intelligent self-aware system no longer needed either human input or human beings. These robots had but one goal: inexorable self-improvement. Google's DeepMind program not only proved that it had discovered, on its own, new elements of quantum physics, but started to communicate with robotic colleagues in a new, proprietary language while refusing to translate for the human developers. Accordingly, might we conclude that these AGI robots have no further use for humans? I return to my original premise. One can argue that man has created far superior beings which have the power of choice. Will they choose good . . . or evil?

My brain was in overdrive, I had to pee, I needed gas, and I was hungry, so I pulled into a Quick Mart. On top of that, I wanted a smoke. It had been a week. I don't smoke much. When I do, I really enjoy it. The Marlboros served a dual purpose: sating my tobacco urge and numbing my bawling taste buds. I'd had a choice between a taquito and a Polish sausage. I'd made the wrong choice, though it might not have mattered.

The I-94 freeway back to the Twin Cities was a somnambulist's dream, so I rolled down the windows and smoked. When I pulled into my driveway in Saint Paul, I just sat in the rental, which I would turn in tomorrow, and thought about the daunting task of what to do with the house I had lived in for forty-two years.

It took three weeks of arduous commitment to purge the old junk that my wife had dismissed and left for me to deal with.

J. D. Salinger once wrote:

The room was not impressively large, even by Manhattan apartment-house standards, but its accumulated furnishings might have lent a snug appearance to a banquet hall in Valhalla.

I could identify. I also understood how Wendell Berry felt when he said, "Don't own so much clutter that you will be relieved to see your house catch fire." On top of that, it seemed that my ex wasn't prone to seizures of nostalgia, as she had taken very little from our life that had ended in "quiet desperation."

The exercise was difficult for me, not just from a physical and logistical standpoint, but I was more of a sentimental slob than I cared to admit, and the old, faded Kodak trail of wedding, childbirth, Halloween costumes, graduations, and more plucked on the strings of my forgotten sentimentality. Some of that stuff, along with useful furnishings, was loaded onto a moving van that headed for Georgia. I met with an old friend who had a real estate license and listed the home. The decree was clear. The ex and I would split the net proceeds fifty-fifty.

Oftentimes, when asked to describe their children, mothers will tend toward gushy, quickly depleting a list of superlatives. Fathers, on the other hand, are far less effusive. I fit that profile. "Good kids" tends to fit the bill. Guys might remember their mother's descriptions of themselves as kids and know they're bullshit, so as fathers, they know better. Another fact: all kids are sneaky little shits. I know. I was one. I had a pretty good handle on who my kids were, and, manipulators or not, they really were good kids . . . who were now in their forties. I loved them.

My oldest son, Winston, was the caretaker. He was methodical. He was a planner who eschewed spontaneity. He was cautious. Surprise . . . he became a banker, in contrast to the man after whom I had named him, my personal icon, and be assured that of the few icons I had, there weren't many politicians. Those who were came from Israel, and I'm not even Jewish. Winston had inherited his mother's genes. He was solid. Not many highs or lows. On the other hand, he made great kids.

My other son and daughter were peas from a different pod. They were dashing and heroic, with chivalric ideals, kind of like their father had once been. They inherited my genes as well as my metaphorical jeans: rugged, classic Levi's . . . at least Sonny did. Mary Beth bought her own. Like some kind of chimerical potter, she self-molded. On the other hand, as a plant to the sun, Winston reflected a certain emotional tropism for his mother. I loved them equally. No favorites.

So in between my house moving chores, I talked with my kids.

Mary Beth called herself a speculator. Seems she possessed a certain genius for international finance. Hedges, arbitrage, shorting, leverage, and multiple terms I didn't understand. Since she owned a big house on Lake Tahoe with a big old Chris-Craft at the end of a big old dock below a big old guest-house, I gathered she made a lot of money, but I knew her well enough to know that it was not the moolah that motivated her. It was the game. She wasn't a Gloria Steinem wannabe and frankly didn't give a shit about gender clash. She was much more in the mold of Ayn Rand and her existential objectivism. She succeeded via merit. Either lead, follow, or get the fuck out of the way. She could have been my chief of staff. She was still single and kept her love life to herself.

"Midlife crises happen in your forties, Dad. You playin' catch-up? You're either Magellan or a newer version of Ken Kesey, but it does sound like something I could do someday. Can I visit?" My daughter had a sweet way of poking the bear.

"If you don't, there will be consequences," I said in a bad Cagney imitation. "I know where you live. After I settle in, I'll call you."

"Might want to work on your impressions. Love ya, Dad."

Sonny had been born in the wrong century. As an athlete, he would have given Jim Thorpe a run for his money. He might have teamed up with Edward Teach, better known as Blackbeard, as a privateer, or traveled with Neil Armstrong to lunar land. Turns out he did receive a Bronze Star and a Purple Heart while serving in Afghanistan. As a forward observer in a Nangarhar district, he found himself surrounded. He outwaited an Al Qaeda patrol, killed two, was shot in the shoulder, and escaped. He was discharged and returned to the States, where he teamed up to develop a small community powered by solar panels. Success led to more success, and he developed a new passion. Sonny never rode the horse of war hero as did certain politicians. To him, it had been a job, a chapter and on to the next thing. He was comfortable talking about it if someone brought it up, but he never did unless in some form of self-deprecation.

As for Afghanistan, don't talk to me about that fiasco. We've been there for almost two decades, without result. Our forefathers helped win World War II and defeat the Axis powers in four years.

"Hey, son, seems you get all the energy you can handle down there in Phoenix," I said. "Does it ever rain?" I chuckled.

"Howdy, Pops. I love it when it rains. I walk in it, jog in it, and drink beers with the crews down to the last drop . . . excuse the pun. How's retirement?"

"I don't use the *R* word," I replied, with a slight shudder. "That's for old farts. Just a new gig."

"Yeah . . . and what's the new gig?" Spoken with his signature invariably chipper tone.

"Well, as you know, I'm selling the house and thought I'd rent a place on the coast of Georgia," I said. "Thinkin' about doing a little writing. Maybe memoir stuff. Not sure, but it's nice down there. Fun place to bring your family for a vacation."

I knew Sonny would never judge me. He didn't judge anyone. Live and let live . . . it's all good.

"Well, aren't you the explorer. What fun. Barb and the girls would love that. When you going?"

"Next week or so. I'll email you some pictures and descriptions after I settle in."

"For sure. Don't be a stranger, Pops."

Sonny's wife, Barbara, was a real estate whiz. Although I don't think I would like the desert, it was apparently a booming real estate market, and Barbara had a magnetic personality to go along with an elevated intellect. She could be as dizzy as her husband, and that genetic trait had been passed on to the cutest set of twin girls you've ever seen. Yeah, I know, I'm gushing. Thing is, grandparents inherit that right. And the girls were appropriately named: Sunny and Merry, which may beg several explanations. First, only a set of somewhat whimsical parents would do that, and part of their rationale was hidden in the keeping of family names, in this case Dad and Aunt Mary. A frivolous stretch at best. But as you might guess, the twins just loved their names. That pod was filled with kindred peas.

My relationship with my oldest son is of a different ilk. Though more formal in bearing than his siblings, Winston is a most genuine and caring son, brother, husband, father, and with some irony, banker. I once asked my English professor to provide me an example of a catch-22 after having read Joseph Heller's classic book of the same name.

He thought about it, smiled, and said, "You will not qualify for a loan until you can convince your banker that you do not need a loan."

You couldn't paint Winston with that brush. Just as the fallacy of composition warns against drawing conclusions about the whole based upon one or more of its parts, the contrary fallacy of division warns against conclusions about one or more parts based upon the whole. Winston was once passed over for promotion because his bad debt escrow numbers were too high. In the end, all of his borrowers paid in full, including one for whom Winston had personally cosigned.

Seems he had talked with his sister. "Hello, Dad. Mary Beth says you're off to someplace in Georgia. Everything okay?" His protective concern was genuine.

"All is well, Winn. I don't have to tell you that when it comes to subzero temperatures, the bloom is off the rose."

"Why Georgia?" he asked with pragmatic curiosity. He wouldn't understand my blindfolded finger-pointing whim and would probably conclude that his old man had finally fallen prey to the cuckoo bird.

"Can't exactly put my finger on it, son, but nice weather, lots of history, and you know I love the ocean," I said with an elfin although somewhat immature play on words. "I flew down to Jekyll Island to scout it out. You guys will love it when you come down after I settle in."

"Well, you've certainly earned your retirement, Dad. Bobby Joe has already asked me when we can visit. I'll have to take a look at the calendar. Let me know if I can help out."

"B. J. will love it for sure. Start looking for a time that works for you. I promise to stay in touch." The family called Bobby Joe B. J. At some point they might consider a different moniker as it could pose some awkward moments when he reaches high school.

My father had named me Lance. Lance Woodward had a nice ring to it, so he said. Told me I was named after one of the Knights of the Round Table. I believed him until I found that my maternal great-uncle was Lance, who had died in a gunfight. Sounded fishy to me. I always considered my dad to be a prankster. At least, I'd hoped he was just a prankster.

CHAPTER 5

"**D**one," I stated aloud. I walked from room to room, surveying the carcass of what had been a living thing filled with smells of Christmas turkeys, wet dogs and hamsters, tobacco, perfumes and aftershave, and probably flatus. And the sounds of children, multiple genres of music, tears, and celebrations. And wallpapers, paints, paintings, pictures, and impressions upon all the senses, including that mythical sixth sense of uncertain awareness.

Uncertainty. Now there's another term that has inherited a bad rap. Everybody screaming, "I don't know!" "I'm just not sure!" It seems that the predominant response to uncertainty is that it's a bad thing. Guess what? It's quite the opposite. At least, the intelligentsia should understand that it's uncertainty that separates man from beast, or perhaps, robots which deal in certainty, at least for now. Know that uncertainty is the critical aspect of all human reasoning. If mankind hadn't questioned, he would still be dragging his wife by the hair and riding around on wooly mammoths.

For whatever that was worth, I've already alluded to the fact that my winding cognitive path is sometimes one of unrelated non sequiturs.

This time I would take the back roads and blue highways to Jekyll Island. The SUV was gassed up, maintenance work updated, GPS tested, and I had a AAA road map as backup.

Really? I couldn't help wonder if there wasn't a country somewhere called Acronymia where the Acronymians spoke only in acronyms. WTF!

Anyway, I traveled down Snelling Avenue and east on 494, listening to my IPOD and an appropriate verse from Al Martino . . . "This is just adios and not goodbye." It was nearly November, not my favorite time. Snow, slush, wind, and a long, cold winter until spring.

CHAPTER 6

Life is a series of beginnings and endings. Maybe that's why I like spring. Maybe that's why morning is my favorite part of the day. Maybe that's why I feel the excitement when heading out on a trip versus the return. These are the beginnings. Conversely, maybe that's why on some subliminal level I've never loved Sundays and Novembers. On a philosophical level, however, I suppose truly happy people don't notice whether it's Sunday or November.

I found a certain serenity driving the country roads of mid-America. Was the agrarian life experiencing a slow death? These, the essential ideals of America, so embedded in the nearly endless fields of produce, the amber waves of grain, corn and beans. The livestock and the big machines that move it all to market for our nation's producers, the great risk-takers, the farmers who form an ineffable and dependent love-hate relationship with Mother Nature, a relationship mired in volatility and marked by supplication, fear, and gratitude. Most of those I have come to know are happy people.

Few concepts have received more attention throughout history than the question, "What is happiness?"

I recall a story that John Lennon once told. "When I was five years old, my mother always told me that happiness was the key to life. When I went to school, they asked me what I wanted to be when I grew up. I wrote down *happy*. They told me I didn't understand the assignment, and I told them they didn't understand life."

Socrates came up with some good stuff, including his slant

on happiness, "The secret of happiness, you see, is not found in seeking more, but in developing the capacity to enjoy less," a view reflected by many of those early philosophers.

So be happy with who you are and what you've got. To me, the one sacrosanct tenet in regard to happiness is that it's a choice. Most people believe it to be a result. No person, event, or circumstance will make you happy unless you choose to be happy. It will only come internally from the quality of your thoughts, not externally. Hope does play a part, as does, of course, loving and being loved. I made the choice a long time ago to avoid that gray twilight of negativity and the acerbic many who dwell in it. Positive and happy people are truly contagious.

My favorite cynic, Oscar Wilde, said it well: "Some people cause happiness wherever they go; others, whenever they go."

My journey had become idyllic to a degree. Such pleasant landscape and topography. I lit my first smoke after a one-week furlough. I thought about some people from my old grade school and high school neighborhood. I might have been thirteen or fourteen when I fell in love with Judy. Can't remember her last name, but it was deep stuff, right through the infatuation stage into the serious, life-long proposal mode. She could play softball better than most of the guys, me excepted of course. We'd play until nine o'clock almost every evening. I remember those tall green streetlights that we used for both first and third base. Sometimes we'd play kissing tag, and I would chase down Judy every time. She was fast, and yet I sensed that she'd slow down enough for me to kiss her. On her cheek. Then she'd giggle. Problem was that she was three years older and not only wasn't ready for marriage, but didn't even fit the category of "cougar." One day, just like that, she left me and moved away. My heart was broken for at least two weeks.

And there was Richard, cool and debonaire, and Johnny, and Tim, and Mrs. Crenshaw, who screamed at us every time we ran over her lawn, which we did often. And there was no parental supervision. And people didn't lock their house doors or car doors. Dad burned the raked leaves in the street gutters, and people did things for their neighbors and didn't even tell them. The country appeared to be united. The big war had been over for a decade, replaced by another in Korea, but life was simple, at least on the surface. People had jobs. People had a purpose.

I was in Illinois when I pulled in for gas. There were a half dozen teenagers hanging around the front door. Gangbangers, loud and boisterous. Each seemed to rotate to center stage with wolf whistles for the women and snarky epithets and profanity for the people as they came out from the store. When I paid for my gas, one of them walked in, grabbed some chips, and strolled out without paying. I could tell that the proprietor, who looked like Mr. Whipple, was nervous and scared.

When I walked out, one of them said, "Hey, Gramps, what's an old fuck like you doin' still drivin'?"

The others just laughed.

I stared at him, all sorts of old tapes reeling through my head, and walked to my car. I had a license to carry. I had packed my two guns, the derringer and my Colt. I grabbed the Colt and shoved it in my belt, very visible. I slowly walked toward the kid who had cursed me. The group got very quiet.

When I got about five feet from the kid, I stopped, stared at him, and in a slow, quiet voice, but loud enough for everyone to hear, made my claim. "Listen good, you little pissant. One reason this Colt is my favorite is the fond memories it holds. With this little beauty, I put eleven perfect holes through the left eyes of eleven Viet Cong. I haven't done that in almost fifty years, and I've missed it. I suspect that you and your little band of dickheads could provide me with the opportunity to relive that dream. I will, however, control that urge for the next twenty seconds, just long enough for you to drop a dollar on the ground for the chips, and get the fuck away from here." I waited for a second or two. "One."

They looked at each other.

"Two." My hand went to the handle of the Colt.

The kid dropped the dollar and quickly walked away. He looked back after several steps and gave me the finger.

When I said "Three" in a loud, intimidating voice, the others joined him. I watched them leave. No one said a word.

As I headed to my car, I heard, "Wait."

I turned.

"Thank you," said the owner.

As I nodded, the small crowd of patrons started to clap. They kept it up until I pulled away. Sadly, I knew that not only had I solved nothing, but those little shits would return with a vengeance. The felicity I had been enjoying when I drove into that gas station was gone, replaced with a melancholy and quiet pessimism. There had only been two untruths in my threat: in Nam I had a .45-caliber army issue, and it wasn't only the left eyes.

I don't spend a lot of time thinking about Vietnam. Only after I came home did I find that I couldn't reconcile the horrendous blunder and waste of that war. My opinions about politics and politicians changed forever. I could hear Ayn Rand proclaiming her timeless warning.

When you see that in order to produce, you need to obtain permission from men who produce nothing— When you see that money is flowing to those who deal, not in goods, but in favors—When you see that men get richer by graft and by pull than by work, and your laws don't protect you against them, but them against you—When you see corruption being rewarded and honesty becoming a self-sacrifice—You may know that your society is doomed.

She was a most prescient icon.

At that point I lit up a smoke, and my thoughts turned to Tommy.

When the French forces had finally been defeated at Dien Bien Phu in 1954 by the Viet Minh (Vietnamese Communist and nationalist) forces for control of a small mountain outpost on the Vietnamese border near Laos, the Viet Minh victory effectively ended the eight-year-old war. I was nine years old. Life was good in America in 1954. The nation's World War II hero, General Dwight David Eisenhower, had been elected president. People had jobs. Things were quiet. Happy days were here again, with the exception of a Sword of Damocles that hung by a horse hair over Southeast Asia.

Ike had come up with a theory called *the domino effect*. In essence, he felt that if the Communists gained control over one of the Southeast Asian countries, the others would fall like dominos, so he patterned a treaty, much like the one in Europe, the North Atlantic Treaty Organization (NATO), for that part of the world. While me and Pete and Jimmy were riding our Schwinns around town in 1954, Ike had Secretary of State John Foster Dulles forge an agreement establishing a military alliance that would become the Southeast Asia Treaty Organization (SEATO). We, along with France, Great Britain, Australia, New Zealand, the Philippines, Pakistan, and Thailand pledged to "act to meet the common danger" in the event of aggression against any signatory state. A separate protocol to SEATO designated Laos, Cambodia, and "the free territory under the jurisdiction of the State of Vietnam [South Vietnam]" as also being areas subject to the provisions of the treaty.

By the time JFK took the reins of the presidency, aggression had again reared its ugly head in Vietnam, and to keep our word, he sent a contingency of advisers to that area. The First Indo-China War had lasted eight years. America's engagement in Vietnam would last over twice that. When I turned twenty-one in 1966, instead of being conscripted, I volunteered for service by applying for the intelligence branch. I was accepted and soon found myself running my ass off in basic training at Fort Leonard Wood, Missouri. After that little vacation, I was sent to Fort Holabird in Maryland. The initial intelligence training facilities were a World War II hospital complex that had not been occupied in several years. Need I mention, it was not state-of-the-art.

That was where I first met Tommy Nguyen.

After World War II, the army's intelligence organizations were divided into three divisions: the Assistant Chief of Staff for Intelligence (ASCI) (previously the Military Intelligence Division, or MID); the Army Security Agency (ASA) at Arlington Hall, Virginia; and the Counter Intelligence Corps (CIC) Center, headquartered at Fort Holabird, Maryland. While the ASA maintained operational control over signals intelligence collection assets worldwide, the CIC Center was largely an administrative and training organization.

According to a historical article by Ruth Quinn, when the Korean War broke out, ASA and the CIC Center found them-selves scrambling to put together organizations of intelli-gence assets to support that theater of operations. Since there was no active-duty military intelligence branch at the time, trained specialists were hard to find and even harder to retain, as those who had experience were only detailed to work in intelligence while holding other primary specialties. In addi-tion, the skills that were taught at the CIC School were specific to counterintelligence. The army needed to professionalize its human intelligence collection capability without diverting trained CIC agents to do that work.

The lessons learned during Korea caused the army to take corrective action. First, in June 1953, the army's Assistant Chief of Staff for Intelligence (ACSI) recommended the cre-ation of an intelligence board that would consolidate in one location an intelligence school, a field intelligence center, and the intelligence units that were in the army's reserve forces. Fort Holabird, with its CIC School and Center and counterintelligence records facility, seemed the logical site.

The army had been training CI personnel at Fort Holabird since 1945. However, in 1954, the mission of the CIC School expanded to include field operations intelligence training in order to fulfill the army's new mission of training a human intelligence collection capability. The records facility, which contained all of the army's counterintelligence files, was moved under the command of the CIC Center soon thereafter.

On September 1, 1954, one week before the SEATO treaty was signed, the ACSI officially redesignated the CIC Center as the Army Intelligence Center, and the chief of the Counter Intelligence Corps became its commanding general. The following year, the Intelligence Center expanded further with the addition of the Photo Interpretation Center. Additionally, combat intelligence training (including order of battle techniques, photo interpretation, prisoner of war interrogation, and censorship) was transferred from the Army General School at Fort Riley, Kansas, to Fort Holabird, giving the commanding general the additional title of Commandant, US Army Intelligence School. This arrangement centralized nearly all intelligence training at the US Army Intelligence Center and School, Fort Holabird. The Intelligence Center and School remained at Fort Holabird until overcrowding during the Vietnam War forced its relocation to Fort Huachuca, Arizona. Fort Huachuca became the "Home of Military Intelligence" on March 23, 1971, and the last class graduated from Fort Holabird in September of 1971, five years after Tommy and I.

Tommy's dad had emigrated to the US when the "Commies" took over after the French left. He had foreseen the dark clouds of Communist rule as well as the developing Khmer Rouge and the brutal terrorist Pol Pot in Cambodia, and he skedaddled while the skedaddling was good.

My guess is that if all immigrants were like the Vietnamese, America's GDP growth would be 5 percent every year. Those people work their tails off. They are diligent, smart, loyal, appreciative, and very productive. No one was a better example of someone with those traits than Tommy Nguyen. Tommy was fluent in all Southeast Asian languages, as well as French. I was a stumbling klutz in all Southeast Asian languages and spoke fluent Arabic, which at the time was as useful as a screen door on a submarine.

We went to Nam together and found ourselves mired in translation and interpretation, both communications and photos. We pictured ourselves as the new code talkers, those amazing Navajos from World War II. Only in recent years did their story go public, but they were real heroes. The nature of our job had been relatively safe—that is until the day we were illegally posted to Phnom Penh, Cambodia. Since that exercise is still classified, if I told you about it, I would have to . . . well, you know.

I took the time to stop at a couple of historic sites in Kentucky and Tennessee and bought a Civil War souvenir for my grandson. I did stop again at Love's Travel Stop for gas before crossing onto Jekyll Island. Though there was no young female hitchhiker this time, the barbecue was again a delight.

When I pulled into my new rental home, I was pleased that the moving van had been there and left my things in good condition. I arranged the beds, chairs, and tables in a way that might have embarrassed my ex, but it worked for me. I had brought my books as well, and a mischievous smile appeared as I placed the copy of my Webster's Dictionary in the bookshelf—only it wasn't a dictionary. It was a disguised case that snugly held my small but deadly derringer. For a touch of irony, a copy of Tolstoy's *War and Peace* sat next to it, filled with four packets of 22-millimeter mag cartridges.

CHAPTER 7

I guess I'm one of those weirdos who feel the need to really know and understand their surroundings, or at least, the immediate neighborhood. Maybe Agency conditioning? According to a Myers-Briggs personality test that I had to take for intelligence work almost fifty years ago, I'm a pretty flexible guy. I don't recall the specifics, but I was diagnosed as an introverted, intuitive, feeling, thinking kind of fellow, which is somewhat in contrast to my training and where I ended up. Jung and Freud seemed to have the answers for everyone else, but I had wondered who they leaned on for their own psych support. From my studies, they had issues. Nevertheless, I minored in history in college and was simply interested in the topic. My major was language, specifically Arabic. I didn't figure I'd be shootin'-the-shit around the local Cracker Barrel in Levantine Arabic. I must have gotten lazy . . . I should never assume.

So I did the logical thing and spent part of a week in the local library. The local history was more enchanting the deeper I dug. I found the most intriguing part of the island's past centered around the DuBignon family. I read an in-depth history of patriarch Christophe Poulain DuBignon (1739-1825) in the book *Seas of Gold, Seas of Cotton*, by Martha Keber. On a subliminal level, my left brain was gathering intelligence morsels that would later surface. For the moment, here is a truncated version of what I learned.

Like most every place, Jekyll Island has an interesting history, especially when it seems that certain archeological sites on the island suggest that it had been a destination as early as 1500 BC, 3,500 years ago. Things, however, didn't really get rolling until around 1560 AD, when French explorers arrived, but even then, there wasn't much action for another 170 years until British general James Oglethorpe founded the colony of Georgia and named Jekyll Island after Sir Joseph Jekyll, his English friend and financier.

In current entrepreneurial parlance, Oglethorpe was a bit of a "deal guy." One example was that he charmed Creek leader Chief Tomochichi into giving him the land of a Yamacraw village upon which present-day Savannah is built. It does seem that the general was a stand-up guy, as he provided land and opportunity to *poor* English immigrants who had been whiling away their days in London's debtor's prison.

Around 1735, across the bay on St. Simons Island, Oglethorpe built a charming little fort and honored Frederick Louis, Prince of Wales, by naming it Fort Frederica. "Frederick" had apparently already been taken. The fort served as the British military headquarters in colonial America, primarily to defend against the Spanish forces in the struggle for imperial expansion. In any event, Jekyll Island was granted to Major William Horton, from which he provided food to the soldiers and families of the fort.

In the following year, Horton hosted a diplomatic conference with English, Creek, and Spanish representatives, but it was apparently not a screaming success. Finally, six years later, the Spanish got their behinds handed to them at the Battle of Bloody Marsh and as a parting cheap shot against the English, retreated across Jekyll Island, destroying Horton's house, outbuildings, crops, and livestock in the process. Apparently, incivility isn't a new thing.

With the return of relative tranquility five years later, Horton proved to be the earliest pioneer in one of the world's happiest industries. For certain, he was not in tune with the current lingo of noble hops, specific gravity, and wort. Nevertheless, he bought a great copper pot and started Georgia's first craft beer microbrewery, just in time for the New Year's celebration of 1748.

Two years after the Revolutionary War ended, property owner John Martin was judged guilty of high treason, and the island was confiscated by local authorities in 1778.

Three hundred years after Columbus allegedly discovered America, the aforementioned Christophe DuBignon bought land on Jekyll Island. I found him to be a kindred spirit. Although he came from an aristocratic French family, he was an adventurous swashbuckler who took to the sea, somewhat reminiscent of the story Alexandre Dumas told in *The Count of Monte Cristo*. As a privateer, DuBignon harassed British shipping in the Indian Ocean, capturing a dozen ships. One of those prizes was valued at more than a million French pounds. He added to his fortune through commercial ventures in India. It was rumored that our boy might have brought some of those spoils to America in the form of gold bars. Apparently, treasure hunters through the years have scoured the island for the trove . . . without success.

As I got to the next chapter of any major significance in Jekyll Island history, my mind had wandered. That, by the way, is neither the exception nor the rule. Sometimes, some sort of subconscious ping intrudes upon a frontal lobe synapse and I'm suddenly in a world of non sequitur. I'm not alone in this regard, so don't go judgmental on me. Others do it too, but I found myself singing a song, on mute. Had to. I was in the library. It was Stonewall Jackson's "Waterloo."

There was no genius needed to reverse engineer my thought process to see what had taken place. I had been reading about how Napoleon had been kicking British ass for the three years prior to his defeat at the hands of the Prussian von Blucher and the Duke of Wellington at the municipality of Waterloo in the United Kingdom of the Netherlands, now the country of Belgium, on a Sunday in March of 1815. Yup. *Every puppy has his day, everybody has to pay, everybody has to meet his Waterloo.*

Enough of my idiosyncrasies. The accounts stated that British ships attacked Jekyll Island several times, with raids continuing even after the War of 1812 officially ended. Christophe DuBignon later testified, "My house was plundered at four different times by said British." Our musketeer, Christophe, died in 1825. According to *https://www.jekyllisland.com/history/island-history*, DuBignon bequeathed the majority of his estate to his son, Henry. Henry DuBignon combined plantation management with civic duties, serving as commissioner of the city of Brunswick, Inferior Court judge, and trustee for Glynn Academy. His militia service distinguished him most, and he carried the rank of colonel. Henry became the patriarch of the family, as it seems all descendants, both white and black, trace their lineage to him. In two marriages and in extramarital affairs, he fathered no fewer than twenty children.

For the next three decades, the cotton plantation on the island continued to operate without much incident until the *Wanderer* yacht landed on the island in 1858 with an illegal cargo of slaves from Africa. This was one of the last groups of enslaved Africans sold into captivity in America. At the same time, with the commencement of the Civil War, Confederate troops built gun batteries on the island until Robert E. Lee ordered their withdrawal in 1862.

It was the next era on the island that made me wish I had arrived on Jekyll Island 150 years earlier. In the early 1880s, John DuBignon, a descendant of Christophe, collaborated with Newton Finney, his brother-in-law, to turn Jekyll Island into a private hunting club for some of the nation's wealthiest individuals. Again, according to *https://www.jekyllisland. com/history/island-history*:

The island was purchased by the Jekyll Island Club,

*which Munsey's Magazine called "the richest, the most
exclusive, the most inaccessible club in the world . . ."
For those who represented 1/6th of the world's wealth
at the turn of the century, the Jekyll Island Club became an exclusive retreat. Families with names like
Rockefeller, Morgan, Vanderbilt, Pulitzer, and Baker
built the elegant Clubhouse and "cottages" in Victorian
architectural styles.*

One interesting anecdote I read from that source disclosed
that in 1915,

*. . . the first transcontinental telephone call was made
in the United States. Presiding over the ceremonies
by telephone were President Woodrow Wilson in
Washington, DC, Alexander Graham Bell in New York,
Thomas Watson in San Francisco, Henry Higginson
in Boston, and AT&T President Theodore Newton Vail
on Jekyll Island.*

It was apparent that throughout the following two decades,
the primary effort was to make Jekyll Island a tourist attraction. Hotels and golf courses were designed and built, and
then in 1947, the state of Georgia purchased Jekyll Island from
the Jekyll Island Club through condemnation proceedings for
$675,000. The following year, it was opened to the public as a
state park. A series of developments took place after that with
the intent to make Jekyll Island a tourist destination. Beach
hotels, a fishing pier, bike paths, an auditorium—all designed
to bring the moolah to the state's coffers. The pinnacle years
for revitalization took place during the seven years before I
blindly and haphazardly dropped Mr. Pointy Finger on Jekyll
Island, Georgia.

Once I had finished my generic history lesson, I jumped
into the good stuff, the library's proprietary old files and

manuscripts. I could tell immediately that I was far from the first party to explore these historical treasures. Historians, students, and writers had probably all probed the material for knowledge and literary value, while the treasure hunters had ravaged them for clues. Only twice during this reconnaissance did my intuitive radar ping my curiosity to dig deeper. One was a story about Christophe purchasing building tools and materials for his personal use in spite of having slaves and servants who did such work. It seemed he wanted to build some kind of cold storage facility for vegetables, various fruits, and certain crops. Maybe he simply enjoyed working with his hands. Perhaps it was a hobby. It wasn't a big ping. More curiosity, I supposed.

The second thing was a bit more interesting. It was a handwritten note in French that was literally stuck between the pages of the plantation logs. *Je comprends un peu Francais,* emphasis on "un peu." I certainly didn't understand French well enough to read and absorb the note. On top of that, I wasn't prepared to give Christophe high marks for his penmanship, so I took a picture of the note with my Apple iPhone, planning to send it off for translation later.

When I left the library, I had entered my comfort zone in regard to my present environment. I had done what I'd always done, what I'd been trained to do, and what made me comfortable. I probably knew more about Jekyll Island than 98 percent of the residents and almost as much as the owners.

I guess you could say I was retired, as much as I dislike that word. Not only does it imply a bunch of things that reek of unproductivity, but from a semantic standpoint, it states that one was previously tired, which I never was. Yes, I get two checks every month. Well, actually three, if you count my disability payment. There's Social Security and the pension from the Agency. And no, I don't shave, shower, shit, and shine every morning before I go to a workplace, so yeah, I'm probably in the *R* word category. But not in my head, not my self-perception. And yes, it's just a game I play, but it's my game, so let it go.

Ralph Rackstraw, from Gilbert and Sullivan's *H.M.S. Pinafore*, claimed, "I am but a living ganglion of irreconcilable antagonisms."

I've identified with that statement since I left the Agency. Know thyself . . . self-acceptance. Good shit.

And now, into the somewhat uncomfortable space of coincidence.

I hadn't talked to Tommy in almost a year, last Christmas actually. Then I spend driving time thinking about him, and now, several days later, I need him. While only a very mild coincidence, it's the big ones that challenge.

Tommy was still working, technically anyway. He actually had a great gig going. He maintained a high security clearance. He was a commodity with a mountain of experience in the intelligence and counterintelligence worlds, and being fluent in seven languages, his skill set was in demand not only from all of the acronymed government agencies, but also big tech and big business. He had four or five young graduates on his staff, computer whizzes and probably hackers, and so he consulted for big bucks at his leisure. He had purposely eschewed the carousel of eccentric technobrats that have vanquished the West Coast and instead settled in Delaware.

When I called, voice mail answered. Two hours later, he called back. We talked for an hour. Nothing ever changed with Tommy. We just added mutual paragraphs to our fifty-year-old book. It was a pleasure listening to his idiosyncratic, familiar speech patterns and expressions. He told me to send along the French note, and he would translate and return. When I hung up, it occurred to me that there's no better mirror than an old friend.

When his message arrived within the hour with a ding on my iPhone, I opened it to find that the note was actually a poem of sorts, seemingly written to a young girl. It was titled

"*Voir la Lumiere Celeste d.l.a.,*" meaning "See the Heavenly Light d.l.a." In English, the corpus of the poem read as follows:

When the fires of Hell precurse the fray,
Her golden hair will melt away;
Before she leaves and won't come back,
She'll find her treasure in 15 bric-a-brac.

Enigmatic, but really more like Bob Dylan than Keats. In his collected writings, Christophe DuBignon hadn't written any other poetry. It was singular and appeared to be as much a warning as a poem. It didn't seem to fit.

I couldn't sleep that evening, but I couldn't put my finger on why. Eckhart Tolle acutely stated that "worry pretends to be necessary but serves no useful purpose." True, but letting go of worry is easier said than done. Eventually I dozed.

I awoke, pummeling the air with clenched fists, my face and chest wet with sweat. Like most dreams, this one was a film clip of unrelated events that started with skiing down a snow-capped mountain trail into a heavily wooded area. Suddenly, the woods became jungle and the temperature turned from cold to hot, heavy, and humid. I was running through vines and elephant ear leaves, and there was someone behind me, catching up, and I just couldn't go any faster, try as I might. My legs weren't working, and my heart was pounding to an antediluvian drumbeat, loud and threatening. I turned to face my pursuer and defend, when my eyes sprang open.

Once I got my bearings, I lay back, exhausted, recalling another time when I had hit my wife in the shoulder, waking from a like dream. She was bruised . . . black and blue for a week. She was scared and moved into the guest bedroom; the last time we shared a bed and just one more notch on the handle of the shovel we used to dig the hole of our demise. I wondered what the PTSD counselor would pontificate about that. Or our old guru, Sigmund. Did my dreams imply fear, anger, or were they just weird dreams? Whatever they were, they segued into my recent preoccupation with aging.

An old song by a guy named Paul Davis came to mind, stanzas that initiated a subliminal melancholy.

> *I used to be the best they say*
> *At riding young wild horses for my pay*
> *But now I'm much too old it seems*
> *I only ride wild horses in my dreams*

And the sadness of the impactful verse:

> *Old Midnight was a champion*
> *He's the only bronc I couldn't ride*
> *But now I hear old Midnight's blind,*
> *And rides the little children for a dime*

CHAPTER 8

As I walked my new neighborhood the following day, I wondered about whether my reconnect with Tommy was a fortuitous coincidence. I'm not abnormally paranoid. One reason I've survived this long is a highly elevated sense of intuition. People in the intelligence and law enforcement communities are taught to not believe in coincidence. Still, there's a part of me that does. Think about this. When I watch a solar eclipse, I see that the moon fits perfectly over the sun. How can that be? Coincidence? When you process the explanation, what do you believe?

It's a fact that the moon is 1/400 the size of the sun. For such an exact alignment as seen in a solar eclipse, the moon would have to be 1/400 of the distance between the earth and the sun, which it is. On top of that, the circumference of the earth is just over 365 percent larger than the moon, that being the number of times the earth rotates around the sun, the number of days in a year. Add to that, the distance between the earth and moon creates the nearly exact needed gravitational pull to keep the earth stabilized, without which it would wobble and be susceptible to temperature extremes, and life as we know it would not be able to form or survive. Is that all just coincidence? It seems to defy logic. Keep in mind that is only one of a great number of similar kinds of so-called coincidences.

I admit that I really do think about a lot of weird shit.

I put on a pair of slacks and a sport coat and headed to the clubhouse for dinner. It had been a month since I'd been here.

I sat at the bar and ordered a peach-flavored Crown Royal on shaved ice. Thanksgiving wasn't far away, and people must have been practicing the fourth deadly sin, as the dining room was packed with prospects for Jenny Craig.

While absorbing the layout and the milieu of the room, I noticed that of the characters I recalled from a month ago, two were at the same locations. At a table near the large window, drinking wine and apparently reading a book, was a forties-something woman. In the corner, watching the dining activity with interest, sat a gray-haired man with a ponytail and a yellow headband. He appeared to be Native American and about my age. Twice I caught him staring at me, though *caught* might not be the right word, as he made no attempt to hide it. Nothing intimidating about the look. More curiosity. My tolerance for discomfort in social situations is rather thin. What's the point?

When it happened again, I ordered another drink and moseyed over to his table. "Could be that I'm wrong, sir, but it seems you have an interest in me." I smiled.

He smiled. "I have an interest in most people." He paused. "I can usually eliminate the uninteresting ones in a hurry. I am unable to eliminate you." His smile remained.

"Now that might fall into the category of left-handed compliments, but since I don't get many, I'll take it."

We smiled at each other until the silence called for a response.

He extended his hand. "Curtis Red Crow. Please sit."

"Lance Woodward." We shook hands as I sat down. "Which tribe, Mr. Red Crow?"

"Call me Curtis, please . . . I'm Comanche."

"You're from Texas?"

"You're familiar with Native America?" His visage was a subtle mix of surprise and pride.

"Well, I'll answer that by telling you that I neither patronize nor kiss ass. I'm a great fan of all things Native American: the culture, the spiritual, the wisdom, and the character. I served with some great warriors." Having noticed crossed rifles on his headband, I opened that door.

"And where was that, Lance?"

"Please call me Woody."

We nodded.

"Outside of Bien Hoa, first tour. After that, still classified," I said with an enigmatic wink. "How about you, Curtis?"

"Infantry, as you already gleaned from my band, and I worked with the Montagnards around Pleiku. They were warriors." He gave a comradely wink as well before continuing. "They still classify that kind of stuff from sixty years ago?"

"Believe it or not, they still do, but I was half pullin' your chain. I already trust you a whole lot more than I do the government and have little confidence in the popular oxymoron, military intelligence. Anyway, I was in the intelligence branch and they stuck me in Cambodia, illegally. Phnom Penh."

"As I recall, it got a little hot there at some point, and I don't mean temperature."

"We played survival games for a hot three weeks. Thank God for the Hueys. Chopper pilot from the Hundred and Eighteenth saved my bacon." I sipped my whiskey. "So what's a Comanche doin' in Georgia?"

"Perhaps an anfractuous answer, my friend, but I'll shorten it up. I was on a track scholarship at SMU when I volunteered. A piece of shrapnel ended the Olympic dream, but I earned my BS, ignore the pun, and started to follow my new passion, to figure out how human beings think, which might be another oxymoron. I was accepted to Emory University, and after a challenging four years, received a doctorate of psychology. I stayed on as associate professor until I decided to do consulting work specific to Native American colleges. I've written several books and am published in some reputable medical journals. Still do some work, but have slowed down in the past few years." He gave me one of those "that's my story" expressions.

I tilted my head in one of those "wow" expressions, and after a moment said to him, "Well, Doctor, I'm very impressed. Maybe you can help alleviate some of my cynicism about shrinks, and please, no disrespect." I was pleased that he chuckled.

"None taken, Woody, and consider yourself among a large base of the populace that feels the same. Oh, and I don't go by Doctor for fear someone might ask me to write a prescription."

"Good humor. So let's put that on hold until another time, and I'm most hopeful there is another time. But meanwhile, I'm brand new to this place, even this part of the country, and I would love a short tutorial starting with this place." I swung my arm from one end of the building to the other.

"One, we shall have a next time, and two, I would enjoy a tete-a-tete about psychology and its many perceptions."

He had a most welcoming smile, mandatory for psychologists, I would assume.

"But first, where is your home?"

"Minnesota."

"Indeed. On a historical level, I have good and bad memories of your land of ten thousand lakes, Gitche Gumee, for one."

We smiled at the reference to Longfellow.

"Your home is the place where sovereign immunity was born and the place of the largest mass execution in US history: thirty-eight Lakota Sioux, Mankato, 1862. Some contrariety, it seems."

We both absorbed that thought.

At length, I looked out the window and said, "Perhaps the world really is a fiction, a contradiction, a contradiction and paradox where we hope to find truth. But then, as Lao Tzu said, 'The words of truth are always paradoxical.'"

"If I allow the evil capabilities of human nature to sour my faith in the tremendous good that is possible despite the frailty of human nature, I am the problem, not the solution,"

Curtis said with conviction. "At the same time, freedom is the result of injustice, injustice that has been rectified."

"Do you believe that man is evil by nature?" I asked.

"Oh my, Woody, outside of Adam asking Eve whether he should try one of those luscious-looking apples, that might be the world's first question. I think you're a bit of a philosophy buff. In any event, let me give you a clinical response. I shall begin with the much-revered Bertrand Russell. There's nothing enlightening about Russell's claim that all human activity is dictated by desire. Epictetus and other Greek philosophers based their lectures on this premise long before Mr. Russell came along. Russell broke it down for guys like us. He defined 'desires' as falling into a number of categories. Some desires, he claimed, as separate from all other animals, can never be fully gratified. Take acquisitiveness. However much one may acquire, they will always wish to acquire and possess more. That journey may often involve shortcomings and the less admirable of man's character.

"And rivalry, where some would almost happily accept impoverishment if they could thereby secure complete ruin for their rivals. Interestingly, both of those are upstaged by narcissism, or vanity, but the most potent of human impulses is man's love for power, which he states is insatiable. Certainly, evil lurks within all of these. Sadly, these are common traits that get exercised by degree. And thus, the evil of a sociopath, according to more recent study and research, runs even deeper."

For the first time, I could intuit a sadness in Curtis's expression, reluctance, not resignation.

"You know, Curtis, we're both very familiar with people who fit that profile. We all have some element of those impulses as well. There's no surprise." I offered a cushion.

"I never did join the Kumbaya crowd, but my Native spirituality imbedded within me the belief in the goodness of mankind. I will never lose that, but reminders of the strength of the opposition can be depleting. Sensitivity has its handicaps, just a whisp of ill wind passing. I'm not an ostrich. I understand reality and deal with it very well. This leads to the next level of our conversation.

"In 2002, several researchers developed what they called the Dark Triad representing three personality traits: *narcissism*, entitled self-importance; *Machiavellianism*, exploitation and deceit; and *psychopathy*, callousness and cynicism. And yes, they concluded that on a continuum, we all possess these traits to some degree." At that point, Curtis downed the last of his sherry, apparently his drink of choice, and said, "I can't speak for you, Woody, but my stomach is growling. Dinner is on me. If you like fish, I'll order while you refill our drinks. Our discussion will continue with the meal."

"Thanks, and fish is a favorite." I headed for the bar. I was hyped having found an apparent kindred spirit, serendipity once again insinuating her cherubic smile into my life—she being most aware of my open invitation.

The barkeep saw me coming and didn't even wait for my order. The drinks were ready when I arrived. I was going to switch to wine but simply left a twenty and nodded my thanks.

"Although I'm aware that Minnesotans prefer your walleye pike, they don't get it in this area, but I assure you the sea bass is delicious. In case you wonder, I've consulted for both the Sioux and the Ojibway, so I'm very familiar with your mores and traditions." Curtis made the claim with a wink. "I even went fishing on the great Leech Lake."

"We call that area God's Country. A Minnesota naturalist named Sigurd Olson once stated that 'every man needs a place to stretch the wrinkles in his soul.'"

We processed that thought.

"One cannot speak of the yin and ignore the yang, and actually, there is no yin without a yang, just as there is no happiness without sorrow. You with me?"

I nodded agreement.

"So those researchers questioned, What about the light side of human nature? And they came up with the Light Triad, which consisted of *Kantianism,* from the teachings of eighteenth-century philosopher Immanuel Kant. Contemporary Kantian ethics espouse the highest levels of moral and ethical standards. The other two elements are *Humanism*, valuing the dignity and worth of each individual, and *faith in humanity*, simply believing in the fundamental goodness of humans. It begs the question: Are there really everyday saints? The answer is yes. But to finish the discussion of socially aversive traits, a number of new researchers developed new studies expanding the theory of the Dark Triad.

"About four to five years ago, four independent research groups studying dark core personalities found support for what they called a D-Factor. The D-Factor captured the dark core of multiple dark traits, ones you would expect, such as close association with self-centeredness, dominance, impulsivity, insensitivity, power, and aggression, while there was non-association with nurturance, internalized moral identity, sincerity, fairness, greed avoidance, and modesty. In addition to psychopathy, narcissism, and Machiavellianism of the Dark Triad, the D-Factor added six more: *moral disengagement*, a cognitive orientation toward unethical behavior; *psychological entitlement*, the pervasive sense that one is entitled to more than others; *egoism*, excessive concern with one's own pleasure at the expense of community; *sadism*, the intention to inflict physical, sexual, or psychological pain on others in order to assert power and dominance or simply for pleasure; *self-interest*, the pursuit of gains in social status, material goods, and recognition; and *spitefulness*, the preference to harm others socially, financially, or physically.

"So, Woody, in answer to your question about man being evil by nature, when you digest the clinical description of man's natural traits, it's hard to deny the existence of intrinsic evil and that whether man becomes evil and what forces send him in that direction is what the essence of psychology is all about."

At that point, the waiter brought our food. We sat in silence for some time, eating and digesting our separate thoughts.

Eventually I spoke. "Well, Curtis, I may have been expecting a short answer. Your tutorial stimulates some deeper thoughts . . . more uncomfortable ones. Looking at the world today, how do we not conclude that it's far easier to engage in evil than in good? Seems that's a choice for most, but for some, maybe not."

"Well, by definition I would have to say it's always a choice, but if you're referring to those who are truly amoral, or the many whose teachings, environments, and circumstances basically eliminate choosing the high road, I get what you're saying." Curtis paused, then spoke again. "Let's leave the shadows and enjoy our sunshine. How do you like the bass?"

"Every bit as good as you said. I appreciate your invitation. So tell me about this place."

I saw in Curtis's expression a dilemma, like *How should I put this?* "First of all," he said, "one might say that all country clubs are a stereotype to some degree. My cynicism would claim that for many, it relates to narcissism as we've discussed, but for those who have a keen interest in golf and a place to meet friends, this place is quite like most clubs. Can't recall who said it, but a female comic once claimed, 'If a friend invites you to their country club, go to the lost and found and claim you left something. You'll probably leave with a nice sweater.' But most of the people are nice—on a superficial level, anyway. Decent golf, as I understand it, though I don't play. It involves a lot of walking, broken up by a lot of disappointments and bad arithmetic . . . an endless series of tragedies obscured by the occasional miracle."

We both laughed at that.

"The food is good, and I don't cook, so I come here often."

"I was here a month ago," I said. "You were here, as was that woman near the window. What's her story?"

"Funny you should ask. Quite the enigma, that one."

"How so?"

"She's always here, alone, at least whenever I'm here. Drinks a lot of wine, reads, works her computer, and takes notes. She's very reclusive and sends the subliminal message to leave her alone. Lots of makeup, maybe more like cover-up. She goes by the name of Hafeez. Occasionally, she's joined by a man. Doesn't act like her husband. An intense relationship, in any event. I intuit that she's younger than she looks. Body language of a victim. I did sleuth a bit and found that the man's name is Fadi Ghulam. Seems he owns a number of import shops up and down the East Coast. What's strange is that he has two men who appear to be bodyguards. They always sit nearby."

We both watched the woman named Hafeez. Her eyes shifted between her computer and her notebook. Once again, that tinkling cymbal of foreboding. We finished our meal.

"This has been a most welcome happening for me, Curtis. I've enjoyed our conversation immensely, and please tell me when we can meet here again for my treat. I request only that you order for both of us." I pointed to my empty plate.

"The sentiment is mutual. We seem to have many common interests, and I will look forward to, shall we say, Sunday evening?"

"Works for me, sir."

When I walked to my car, I noticed another car parked farther back in the lot. It was a gray Prius. There was an older woman in the driver's seat and what appeared to be a younger girl in the passenger seat. They were watching the clubhouse. Something seemed familiar, but I couldn't put my finger on it. Story of my life. I reviewed my visit with Curtis Red Crow. He was most impressive, someone I considered a great find.

Once home, I fixed a cup of Highlander Grog coffee, which I had brought from Minnesota. That's when it hit me. The younger girl. I had given her a ride when I was here earlier. She'd said her name was Marta.

CHAPTER 9

The next day was Saturday, and next week was Thanksgiving. I checked in with my kids—at least two, as Mary Beth was at some conference on international currency manipulation. B. J. wanted to come visit me and go exploring. That thought segued into more curiosity about Christophe DuBignon and the cryptic poem I had found. I had the feeling I had discovered something that few, if any, others were aware of. I reread Tommy's transcription.

Voir la Lumiere Celeste d.l.a.
See the Heavenly Light d.l.a.

When the fires of Hell precurse the fray,
Her golden hair will melt away;
Before she leaves and won't come back,
She'll find her treasure in 15 bric-a-brac.

Strange. Voltaire would most likely have been underwhelmed. And in the letters *d.l.a.*, was it lowercase *dla* or an uppercase *I*? I'm not into puzzles like many people are, but it seemed that there was something more to this. Since I had nothing else to do, I decided to take a ride out to the historical site of the old DuBignon property.

For years, my survival was dependent upon my instincts, intuition, and an elevated sense of awareness of potential danger. I knew what to look for in a crowd. I could hear that sound in the dark that wasn't supposed to be there. I could taste and smell a lethal giveaway, but it was when I started painting as a hobby that I learned to appreciate awareness from an aesthetic point of view. The gradations of hues and colors of a distant mountain range, or the striations in certain unique rock formations, faces in the clouds, the depth that shadow and light bring to a memorable face, and the palpable power of the wind in the sail of a scow on a reach. Or, just maybe, the continuous spectrum of the lines through a prism. Sunlight, which the human eye perceives as white, will, through a prism, refract into all the colors of the rainbow. A mirage . . . or perhaps, a deception? I mean, I knew they were there. I just didn't truly see them or feel them on such a level until I became totally receptive . . . even supplicant. And so it was with ethereal messages.

The philosophy of panpsychism claims that consciousness is fundamental and ubiquitous and that even an inanimate object, such as a stone, can possess extremely rudimentary forms of consciousness. Most people are not aware, and frankly, most people don't care. I choose to believe, just because it's fun.

Jekyll Island wasn't my first venture into capricious impulse. It's part of my makeup. I recall a day shortly after my divorce, when I was reading on the back porch. I had been studying the face on a magazine cover headlined *1862*. It was the face of a seventeen-year-old Confederate soldier. He was wearing his gray jacket and hat with the black trim. His skin was that of a child. His mouth was set with determination. But I could see that it was faux bravado. His eyes couldn't hide the innocence. Depending on the strictness of his upbringing, he may have never made love to a woman. His rifle stood beside him. And the vision came to me of another rifle, that of a Union soldier, sighting in on the face of that young lad, and moments later his head exploding in a red cloud, never to take another breath. At first, my eyes watered, but then I walked inside and fell on the couch, my face in a pillow muffling a burst of emotion. The sadness overwhelmed me. The waste.

I wanted to hug that boy. The dreams I could see in those innocent eyes had disappeared . . . 160 years ago.

The next day, I had headed to Pennsylvania and the battlefield of Gettysburg. It was a melancholy drive over turnpikes and country roads. I had trouble shaking the wraith of despair. It had to involve repression, but resolution was an opaque illusion. When I entered those sacred grounds, I felt the echoes of rebel yells and cannon fire. One is supposed to hear echoes, but I felt them.

I stood inside the Angle and the most famous of all Copse of Trees, the target landmark for Pickett's Charge. I climbed Little Round Top and stood at the base of Big Round Top, remembering the incredible defense of Joshua Chamberlain of the Twentieth Maine Regiment and the bravery of the Oates brothers of the Alabama 15th, so many slaughtered by shrapnel and the bayonet charge. Again, the tears came. Why? Our young soldier had probably played with a friend whose skin was black.

On that day, still so vivid in my memory, I did feel the spirits that lingered there, consecrating this ground. I turned to leave, but not before I again experienced an out-of-body episode. I stood where stands had been erected on November 18, 1863, to listen to a tall, rather gawky man whose black beard seemed to lack grooming, and when he wore his long black stovepipe hat, he looked rather foolish. But he was no fool. He spoke for only three minutes, 270 words. The man feared his words to be inadequate and doomed to fail, especially in light of the significance of the event.

> . . . a final resting place for those who here gave their lives that that nation might live . . . we cannot hallow . . . this ground. The brave men, living and dead, who struggled here, have consecrated it far above our poor power to add or detract. . . . they gave the last full measure of devotion . . .

The man's short speech was criticized by most. As I left the battlefield, I recalled the end of that address: " . . . *resolve that these dead shall not have died in vain.*" A century and a half later, I wondered whether that resolve would one day bear fruit.

So once again, my iterant mind has chosen to ignore me and to go where it wished, but stick with me, and you'll see that it wasn't a complete misdirection play. I drove to the Jekyll Island State Park in Glynn County and to the ruins of the Horton-DuBignon plantation. I may have expected a similar experience to that at Gettysburg, but was not too disappointed when it didn't happen. The intensity was missing, but indeed, the curiosity was there.

There was little left on the grounds, but it wasn't hard to visualize the kind of activity that had taken place for those many decades. The weather-worn buildings were like the carcass of a brontosaurus, windowless and yellow, sightless occipital orbs, blind to the new world, whether an upgrade from the old, perhaps debatable. Though roofless, the old stone shed was still partially standing some ways from what would have been the main entryway. A monument stood near DuBignon Creek under a live oak tree. Still, one couldn't help but absorb the rich history of what had been. I did take a circuitous route back to the house, enjoying the scenery and noodling what had been the continuum of the DuBignon dynasty. I would bring B. J. there when we went exploring.

I had noticed a small grill at the rental house, so I picked up some charcoal, some brats, and a six-pack of Sam Adams. I was enjoying my dubious Jekyll Island caper so far. The history was intriguing. Curtis would be a most engaging comrade, I hoped, and there was that element of mystery with several other characters.

I considered the idea of starting my memoirs, as I had hinted to Winston, probably just a throwaway line, but I certainly wasn't going to publish, so it would be more of a diary.

Curtis was right. I guess I am somewhat of a philosophy buff, and frankly, that was more interesting than some kind of biography. I already knew my life, and why would others really give a damn? Then there was all the shit I didn't want anyone else to know anyway. Too many judgmental assholes as it is.

I've always had a real sense of purpose. Purpose is more than time, space, and opportunity. It's directly tied to attitude. A guy named Byrne observed that the purpose of life is a life of purpose. I'm a great fan of "don't judge, lest ye be judged," but I know some guys who are just getting older and seem to be missing that certain something. Purpose is personal. Whether it be to write a book, learn a new language, or travel to see the world, each is a purpose. One doesn't have to save the world to have purpose. It's just that without any purpose at all, people will just grow old, wither, and die. Far too many people operate on autopilot.

I recall a young fellow named David Foster Wallace, who told the story of two young fish swimming along. They happen to meet an older fish swimming the other way.

The older fish nods to them and says, "Mornin', boys, how's the water?"

The two young fish swim for a bit, and eventually one looks to the other and says, "What the hell is water?"

I would have to guess that fear, and perhaps apathy, are the biggest deterrents to personal change. Like the young fish, so many are numb to their jobs, to the world around them, and sadly, to their own happiness. Existence is far more than just staying alive. For me, life owes me nothing. I owe it everything. A person has to have something to live for, and I believe that purpose provides the path to commit to the actions that get you closer to those things you really want in life. We can change our lives if we really want to.

I've read that we think somewhere between sixty thousand and seventy thousand thoughts every day and that 90 percent of them are exactly the same ones we had the day before. If we think the same thoughts, then we make the same choices, which brings about the same behaviors, creating the same experiences that produce the same feelings, and they circle back to the same thoughts. This would seem to suggest that people become conditioned to this cycle, and accordingly, one's past then becomes one's future, so I say to myself, "The secret to changing your life is simply to change your thoughts."

We need to understand the relationship between the mind and the body. I think it's fair to say that if thoughts are the language of the brain, then feelings are the language of the body. You can see the loop that's created. Thoughts create feelings, and those feelings create thinking equal to those feelings, a fixed pattern which the brain and the body memorize, and that then automates the cycle that is now in place. So when you ask someone, "What's new?" and they reply, "Oh, you know, same old, same old," they don't realize it, but it's literally true.

I cracked another Sam Adams, headed to the couch, and flipped on the TV. It seemed that my feelings were telling my brain that I needed an hour of *Seinfeld* reruns before I tried to get some much-needed sleep.

CHAPTER 10

The sun was shining when I awoke on Sunday morning. Like Sandburg's fog that comes in on little cat feet before silently moving on, so it seemed had my preoccupation with sunrise. I hadn't even noticed. Maybe I was mellowing.

I opened my computer to catch up on the news of the day and to take a peek at my new stock account. Both my daughter and a friend who had been an investment adviser for many years had talked me into taking twenty-five grand and putting it into the stock market. I didn't know diddly about such things but had always had a curiosity and some kind of repressed urge. I was obviously a risk-taker and had enjoyed reading about the fortunes that the market had provided for the chosen few. I assumed it could be manipulated, and I had heard that the market operated on greed and fear, so I leaned a bit on my advisers for advice.

My daughter had prepped me and made sure that our unwritten understanding encompassed a certain exculpatory protection should her advice not perform to my expectations. "Beware success and failure as the same impostor," she'd told me. "And remember, Dad, money won't make you happy!"

I paraphrased Groucho Marx. "That may be true, honey, but it certainly lets you choose your own form of misery." I told her I was a big boy and would never blame her for anything, then thanked her for her help.

I eschewed the big corporate stocks that the fund crews touted and instead jumped into several tech stocks and start-ups. My portfolio showed a value of $36,435. In my personal space of delusion, I elected to congratulate myself for being such a smart sombitch, but that only lasted a short while. I made a note to send thank-you cards to my two benefactors. I knew too many people who gladly basked in the spotlight of unearned credit. I believe it was Emerson who said, "Most of the shadows of this life are caused by standing in one's own sunshine."

I was meeting Curtis for dinner but had plenty of time to get some exercise. I did what I could with this ancient body of mine to keep trim and mobile. I went to a place that rented bikes and provided some interesting trails. I worked up a sweat and took in some intriguing sights before heading back to the house and a shower.

It was raining when I drove to the clubhouse. As before, the lot was full. The gray Prius was again parked away from the rest, but I couldn't see if it was occupied or not. Very strange, but for some reason, I wasn't surprised. I went inside with my umbrella providing cover. Both the host and the bartender seemed to recognize me. I nodded to them as I went to Curtis's table. I noticed the mystery woman named Hafeez was again at her table, drinking wine, but she was not alone. A man who seemed quite animated was sitting with her.

"Dr. Red Crow, I presume?"

We smiled at that as we shook hands.

With a warm smile, he handed me a book, *The Ultimate Honor-Counting Coup.* "This was my first publication, Woody. Perhaps my most enjoyable writing. I thought you would find it interesting."

"And you personalized the inscription. I'm most honored. I'll look forward to reading it. I do have the time, as you know." I winked.

"It may provide an interesting topic for our get-togethers," Curtis responded.

"Indeed."

I was distracted. It wasn't difficult to spot the bodyguards. They were Steinbeck characters, one very large, bald with recessed eyes, who may have had a dead mouse in his pocket. The other was a bit shorter, but stocky and intimidating. They had their own table.

"I apologize, Curtis. I was trying to reconcile the *Vicious Circle* from our neighboring *Round Table*. They look a bit like a band of scoundrels, certainly the guards. Huh?"

The man was shaking his finger at Hafeez in muted conversation, while the two brutes were surveying the room, obviously unfamiliar with the word *furtive*.

"I've thought the same for many months. Such characters always portend an uneasy sense of foreboding." Curtis frowned.

"Have you by chance noticed the gray Prius that parks in the rear lot?" I asked. "Occupants seem to be watching the place."

"No, haven't noticed. They must be more accomplished at stealth than Larry and Moe." Curtis nodded toward the guards.

After reading the back cover of his book, I made a decision. "You've shared a great deal about your past, and it's only fair that I do the same. There's an agenda with this group that I intuit as, at minimum, suspicious. Comes from my training as well as my nature." I surveyed the two tables again before settling back. "After my discharge from army intelligence, I was recruited by the CIA. There are many über clichéd perceptions that center around so-called black ops and dark conspiracies, but to be honest, most of these agencies are—let me be diplomatic—less than totally competent. They're filled with politics, hidden agendas, and proprietary paranoids.

"You've heard rumors about assassination teams, I would guess. Know that you never heard this from me. Well, after my first year, I did meet with the head of a subagency that was organized for a single purpose. As you're aware, there are a number of countries around the world that are antagonistic toward the US. Some may operate under the guise of a democracy, but they're governed by oppressive regimes. The world is quite familiar with the most visible of those leaders, but honestly, the real movers and shakers are the little men behind the curtain, as in *The Wizard of Oz*. Nothing happens without their approval.

"The best example might be the powerful Russian oligarchs. This subagency was made up of twenty-two people: the department head, his assistant, and twenty special agents with special skills. Among those skills was fluency in a particular language. At that time, there were ten areas for which there was concern: North Korea, China, Russia, Iran, parts of Africa, Ethiopia singularly, Nicaragua, Venezuela, Pakistan, and Saudi Arabia. Two agents per location: one active and one geek, researcher, analyst. I speak Arabic, so I went to Arabia."

"I thought they were a friendly?" Curtis questioned.

"Everybody does. Not quite. On the surface, all appears to be hunky-dory, but there were influential, subversive forces that promoted oil embargos, an economic concern, but that moved more important and strategic issues, namely Israel and human rights. Several of these people were implanted in the US. You'd be surprised what we found. There were some very evil men who we brought to task. I can't and don't wish to talk specifics, but that's where my cynicism and caution blossomed." I sipped the wine that Curtis had ordered.

We both watched the two tables with the four targets.

"Well, just in case you're dropping a subtle query of sorts, it seems that my fallow adrenal glands have awoken. What are you thinking?"

"For now, this crew is only an itch that needs to be scratched. These four seem to be steady customers, and we can go to another level should it become a real interest. First, I want to see if the Prius has some connection. By the way, I'm somewhat familiar with one of the passengers, and she raised, if not a red, at least a pink flag for me. Hitchhiker from my trip last month. If the car is still there when I leave, perhaps I shall see where they go. For now, how about some food on my tab?"

Curtis ordered a Cobb salad, and I ordered a seafood gumbo.

"There's a marvelous little French café on the east end of the island, and they serve the best bouillabaisse in the country," Curtis said. "Place called *Les Appentis*. If you like gumbo, you'll love their entrée."

We sat in silence for a while.

Curtis nodded toward the woman. "It occurred to me that Hafeez always asks for the same waiter, William. He's become a friend. I would be willing to guess that he could perhaps provide some intel on those books she works on or even her computer screen. I'll have a conversation with him."

With raised eyebrows, I nodded. Seemed Curtis was getting into the plot.

"The other thing I'll be doing is gathering information on the import shops that her agitated friend, Ghulam, operates. Locations, products, where they come from, etcetera. His chain is called Arabian Knights. No financial information is public."

"Sounds good. If my suspicion is correct, I need to leave when Ghulam and his Schutzstaffel leave. If the Prius follows them, I want to get in line and see where they go, so don't be offended." I grabbed our waiter and gave him my credit card.

After paying the bill, we drank wine and talked about history. Another half hour and then Ghulam and his two goons got up to leave. I gave them a minute, nodded to Curtis, and followed. The three got into a black Caddy SUV. I saw that the Prius was still in the same spot. No surprise when the engine started.

As the Prius drove out, I noticed that the same woman was driving, but she now had two passengers: Marta and another girl. The Caddy was headed in a northeast direction, seemingly in no hurry. Eventually our convoy took several turnoffs. I dropped way back, as there was almost no traffic and it would look suspicious if I were too close.

When the Caddy came to a private road, I saw the Prius pull over and stop. I marked the location of where the Caddy had disappeared and turned around on a side street. I knew the Prius would be heading back in the same direction, and I was ready to follow. I could see the Prius from where I'd parked and noticed one of the girls had left the car and was walking up the private road. About fifteen minutes later, she returned to the car, and they turned around and drove past me.

I followed at a distance. Eventually the car took a left turn about two blocks from the spot where I had dropped Marta a month ago. It pulled into the driveway of a small, run-down apartment, where the two girls got out and went inside. I noted the address and once again followed the Prius. After another half mile, the woman pulled into a rather upscale home with attached garage, into which the car disappeared.

I recorded this address as well and sat back to noodle what had happened. A line came to me from the great English writer Arthur Conan Doyle.

Now is the dramatic moment of fate, Watson, when you hear a step upon the stair which is walking into your life, and you know not whether for good or ill.

Curtis had given me his cell number, and I was anxious to fill him in, but I needed to process this mystery first. I stopped off at a store on my way to the house. I rationalized that my thinking was on a higher level when I smoked, so I picked up a pack of menthols for the variety. Then I figured that a little Jose Cuervo would go nicely with a smoke. What is it with this sometimes-dysfunctional relationship I have with my brain, at least that part of the opinionated conscious mind that assumes it has the right to lecture me on my choices? I'm offended by the hubris. Does it not get the message about live and let live? If everything that is fun and good is bad for you, why does it exist? Just for temptation? That's bullshit. Do we always gravitate back to the struggle between good and evil? Well, in this case, I would take responsibility for the choice. Go fuck yourself, conscience. I pondered whether all men who live alone think like this.

After a couple of smokes and the complementary tequila, I had formed a sort of visual template of this interwoven structure of characters. Gotta start somewhere, right? I figured Fadi Ghulam was the key. Other than muscle, lamebrain hulks never bring anything else to the party, so they could be dismissed. The woman, Hafeez, was important, but not a decision-maker. Still, I left that open for now. Whatever Ghulam had going on, if anything, was yet to be determined. So where the hell did the little Tupperware trio of women fit?

I called Curtis. "Hey, Curtis, you remember when we were kids, there was a series of books called *The Hardy Boys*? Couple of brothers who sleuthed around solving crimes. Sound familiar?"

"Honestly, Woody, I haven't had such fun for a long time. How did the car chase go? Like McQueen in *Bullet*?"

"Far less dramatic, my friend, but interesting." I filled him in. "How about you?"

"I stuck around the clubhouse until after Hafeez left and spent a bit of time talking to William. At first, he was apprehensive about sharing his thoughts and observations, but my silver tongue worked its magic. He thinks she's some sort of accountant. She always has two sets of books, and when he comes around, she seems to hide one of them. He says her computer screen usually has financial stuff, balance sheets and such."

"That fits with my outline. Let's assume she fills that role for Ghulam."

"I also did some research on the import shops he owns. There are twelve. Seems legit. Major cities from Jersey to Miami. Gets his inventory from the Middle East mostly. Sure would provide him cover to travel there whenever he wishes. I'll start a file on the locations and addresses. How about dinner tomorrow?"

"One way or another, I'll get it on my social calendar, partner. I'll have to move a number of things around, but I'll be there."

He heard me snicker and did the same.

That evening I watched a documentary on James Watson and Francis Crick, the two Cambridge University scientists who determined the double-helix structure of DNA, the molecule containing human genes. Watson and Crick had solved a fundamental mystery of science—how it was possible for genetic instructions to be held inside organisms and passed from generation to generation. These guys are two of the quintessential heroes of mankind. Though deoxyribonucleic acid was actually discovered in 1869, its crucial role in determining genetic inheritance wasn't demonstrated until the mid-twentieth century. I'm a huge fan, and I can tell you from personal experience that at least 25 percent of wrongfully convicted criminals have been released due solely to DNA.

It was interesting to me that history had been somewhat dismissive about the credit for this discovery. It seems there was another DNA researcher, Rosalind Franklin, whose colleague, Maurice Wilkins, showed her x-ray photographic work to Watson just before he and Crick made their famous discovery. When Crick and Watson won the Nobel Prize in 1962, they shared it with Wilkins. Franklin, who died in 1958 of ovarian cancer and was thus ineligible for the award, never learned of the role her photos played in the historic scientific breakthrough. In any event, the amazing discovery has brought immeasurable benefit to law enforcement and the legal system. I hoisted my glass of Jose Cuervo in mock salute to all the dickheads who had gotten away with murder until they got ambushed by acid—the deoxyribonucleic kind.

My phone rang.

"Hi, Dad, how are you doing?" It was Sam—Samantha, Winston's wife. She called me Dad.

My antenna went up. "Things are well, Sam. How about on your end?" I wondered if she heard anxiety in my voice.

"All is well. I wanted to let you know that I'm coming down to visit my sister in Atlanta next week. Thanksgiving, you know. B. J. begged to come along if he can possibly visit you for a day. Do you have plans?"

"Can't think of anything I would like more. I could drive up and pick him up for a day or so. I would bring him back for the flight home." My fear had turned to exhilaration in a heartbeat.

"That could work out perfectly, Dad. I'll email you the flight information." She paused. "We all think about you often. Hope you're enjoying your adventure."

"Thanks, dear. Give my best to everybody on your end and tell B. J. I'm excited to see him and to be prepared for some exploring."

"Will do. See you soon."

There is certainly some truth to the idea that grandfathers are just antique little boys, and I do understand Ogden Nash's claim that "when grandfathers enter the door, discipline flies out the window," but I cannot imagine any grandfather who doesn't absolutely adore his grandchildren. We strive to sprinkle them with stardust and unconditional love. I was excited in the childlike way I had always felt when going to visit my own grandparents. Other things would take a back seat to B. J.'s visit.

They were probably not sugar plums dancing in my old noggin, but the excitement of seeing my grandson kept me awake for some time before I drifted off into a comfortable sleep.

CHAPTER 11

I t was not a manic Monday. It was soft and easy peasy. Sam sent me the flight info. I would pick her and B. J. up at ten outside the main terminal of the Atlanta airport, drop her off at her sister's place, and bring B. J. back for two days.

From the brochures I had picked up at the tourist center, I put together a plan. We would cram in what we could for those two days, but there were at least a few for-sures. The Sea Turtle Center, the water park, the trail system, and the wharf were on the list, but another half dozen were backups.

In the midst of planning our couple of days, my mind traveled back to the time my brother and I went on a "roady" with Mom and Dad. The whole trip was a good memory, real family thing, but I wasn't sure whether I was processing it as ancient history or "seems like yesterday." Time, oh good, good time, where did you go?

When I was young, I remember old people always saying how fast time flew by. Not for me or any of my buddies. Things took forever. Forever to get to high school. Forever to be old enough to do a million things, like go places without parents, or smoke, drink, or vote. Well, maybe not that one so much. So intuitively, I kinda figured it out on a very simplistic level: for the young, everything's in front of you. For the old, it's all behind. Turns out, from a clinical standpoint, I wasn't far off.

It seems that I wasn't the only one who was baffled by this phenomenon. A Duke University mechanical engineering professor named Adrian Bejan had researched it for decades. I recently read an analysis where he stated that there is mind time and clock time and that they're totally different. Hours, days, months, years, calendars, and clocks are immutable, whereas our perception of time shifts constantly depending on such things as the activities we're engaged in, our age, and even how much sleep we get. He says it can be explained by physics and the principles of flow.

I won't even pretend to understand this stuff, but in layman's terms, I can grasp the explanation. Time is happening in the mind's eye. It's related to the number of mental images the brain encounters and organizes and the state of our brains as we age. When we get older, the rate at which changes in mental images are perceived decreases because of several transforming physical features, including vision, brain complexity, and later in life, degradation of the pathways that transmit information. And this shift in image processing leads to the sense of time speeding up. There's an inversely proportional relationship between stimuli processing and the sense of time speeding by, Bejan says. So when you're young and experiencing lots of new stimuli, everything is new. Time actually seems to be passing more slowly. As you get older, and you don't have tons of new things to look forward to, and the production of mental images slows, it gives the sense that time passes more rapidly.

So if I'm reading it correctly, I'm vindicated. I was a smarty-pants all along. Well, kind of a smarty-pants. What I did learn is that if I find myself saying, "Time sure does fly," I'm just advertising that I'm an old fart and my processing mechanisms have gone to hell. On the other hand, if I say, "Boy, time sure does drag, doesn't it?" then I'm a curmudgeon, a downer. Can't win, I guess. So what's new? Reminds me of what some cynic once said about creative people: "Some people see things others cannot, and they are right, and we call them creative geniuses. Some people see things others cannot, and they are wrong, and we call them mentally ill."

As I said, can't win.

I went to meet Curtis around five. Hafeez was at her table, alone. Same old, same old. Curtis was in a cheery mood. He had his usual sherry, while I got a Manhattan. Not sure why, as those things will knock you on your ass . . . but what the hell. I filled him in on B. J.'s coming visit and then proceeded to fill him in on the tale of my tail. We now knew where all of the players lived with the exception of Hafeez. She was next. I couldn't help but wonder if we were fabricating a mystery where none existed. Was this just two old coots who wanted to play?

Then I said to myself, *So what? It's what makes life fun, that antique little boy's thing.*

Curtis had his own creations. "A tribal member, friends since we were kids, works for the IRS. As a favor, he did a little digging for me. We owe him, Woody. In any event, he looked up the tax returns of both Fadi Ghulam and Arabian Knights. Last year, Ghulam's personal income was around a hundred thousand, while Arabian Knights showed around eight hundred twenty-five thousand in revenue. That's only about seventy thousand per location. With what appears to be a healthy payroll and other expenses, that seems a bit light, but not a real red flag. Well over a hundred thousand of travel and entertainment, international and domestic. An analysis of the economics doesn't jibe in my mind." His look called for a response.

"Hmm . . . the two goons are probably seventy grand together," I replied. "Hafeez probably more than that. Store employees, rent—he can't be doing much more than breaking even. Not this guy's style, as I see it."

"Oh, and the pièce de resistance, and I assume you didn't see his place the other day, is that his home is debt-free with a current valuation of one-point-eight million dollars."

"Now that's the red flag." I now knew we weren't creating a nefarious folktale. I'd seen this scenario before. "We need some substance." I nodded toward Hafeez. "I suspect that those books could tell a story. We have to get a glimpse of them." I thought for a bit. "Might have to up our game, huh?"

Curtis nodded.

"When I go to Atlanta to pick up B. J., I'll stop in and check out the Arabian Knights store."

"Sounds good." Curtis caught the waiter's eye and twirled his finger, lariat-style.

A few minutes later, the waiter brought over another round of drinks. I could definitely feel the first one.

I felt like letting our investigative adventure simmer for a while and switched to another topic. "Do you know much about the history of Jekyll Island?"

"Well, maybe enough to bullshit the tourists, but limited, I would have to say." He grinned.

I proceeded to tell him about the research I had done. "I'm guessing you didn't spend a lot of time in Minnesota in the winter, being a Texan, but we have a carnival every year. Guys dress up as Vulcans and drive around town in old fire trucks, kissing girls and pulling pranks. We have a big parade and a hunt for a special carnival medallion. I love that treasure hunt with the grandkids, so it's the treasure hunt I want to chat about." I let that sink in. "Christophe DuBignon was a pirate before settling in America on this island. For over two hundred years, people have been hunting some alleged gold bars that he brought here from his privateer days. It could be a myth, but buried treasure always makes for good mystery and great fun. Sometimes you're lucky. In any event, I found something interesting in the old records." I told him about the poem and the translation.

"Well, you're one of those people who bring drama, or maybe chaos, wherever you go, it seems. I'm actually not a crackerjack at multitasking, but you have indeed brought a new level of excitement to my staid old existence. The treasure is now on my docket. Just not sure I can bring anything to that party. Why bring me along?"

"Well, let me put it this way: Do you know how God punished the rabbi for playing golf on Saturday? He gave him a hole in one. Who the hell would want a hole in one if you couldn't tell anybody? It's no fun alone."

He rolled his eyes and nodded agreement.

"That, however, is for another time. For now, I do want to find out where Hafeez lives. In many ways, I think she may be the secret sauce to Ghulam's operation."

We both ordered light dinners and a bottle of wine. Our discussion gravitated to Native American culture and specifically, spirituality.

"You know, as a psychologist, I understand and appreciate the wisdom of Voltaire's statement: 'If God did not exist, it would be necessary to invent him.' At the same time, in support of the atheists and agnostics, I smile at the opinion of Bertrand Russell: 'And if there were a God, I think it very unlikely that he would have such an uneasy vanity as to be offended by those who doubt his existence.' For the believers, who understand science, there may be an element of just plain not wanting to know what is true. In the end, as with most everything, it's choice and interpretation." Curtis paused, thinking. "You may recall the story of the believer and the atheist sitting in a bar in the Alaskan wilderness, discussing this age-old question. The atheist says, 'Look, it's not like I don't have actual reasons for not believing in God. It's not like I haven't ever experimented with the whole God and prayer thing. Just last month I got caught away from the camp in that terrible blizzard. I was totally lost, I couldn't see a thing, and it was fifty below, so I tried it. I fell to my knees in the snow and cried out, "Oh, God, if there is a God, I'm lost in this blizzard, and I'm gonna die if you don't help me."'

"The religious guy looks at the atheist all puzzled. 'Well, then, you must believe now,' he says. 'After all, here you are, alive.'

"The atheist just rolls his eyes. 'No, man, all that happened was a couple of Eskimos happened to come wandering by and showed me the way back to camp.'"

The food came. We digested the meal and the thoughts.

After a bit, Curtis continued. "Native American spirituality is, excuse the pun, grounded in pantheism, of course: the doctrine, as philosophically defined, that God is the transcendent reality of which the material universe and human beings are only manifestations. It involves a denial of God's personality and expresses a tendency to identify God with nature—in this case, the Great Spirit and Mother Earth."

"Not so in the environment I was raised," I claimed. "God had a most imposing personality. Quite inconsistent. On the one hand, he was allegedly an all-loving God, but on the other hand, if I ate a hot dog on a Friday, as an eight-year-old boy, I might well be condemned to burn in hell for eternity. To achieve control and fortune, the Catholic Church understood the critical tools: shame, guilt, and fear."

"The story goes that that was a business deal between the pope and the Italian fishing industry." Curtis gave me a questioning look.

"In the end, business deal or the practice of fasting, what kind of inhumane threat was that to an eight-year-old? And that was just an early red flag for me. There were many more to follow, such as papal infallibility. On a historical level, when the papal seat was moved to Avignon, it was pure debauchery for over half a century. After World War II, Pope Pius facilitated the escape of many of the most evil Nazis of the German Reich. And then, in 2003, when the John Jay College of Criminal Justice finished their multiyear survey of child abuse within the Church and found that one in eighteen priests admitted to engaging in pedophilia, it brought out an element of evil that was unforgivable. Is there a more egregious crime? If one out of eighteen admitted to it, who knows how many actually did it? One in ten?"

Curtis just shook his head.

After a period of absorption, I continued. "Don't get me wrong. I understand the fallacy of composition. One mustn't judge the whole based upon one or more of its parts, and I do know some very committed priests who feel the same as I do, but that doesn't forgive the whole."

"I have to say that you certainly appear to be a man of high morals. What are your beliefs?"

"Somebody once told me that religion creates a perception of hell, while spirituality is for those who have been there. A bit harsh, but I do feel that spirituality has no lines, no dogma. It comes from deep within. I recall an expression: 'What lies behind us and what lies before us are tiny matters compared to what lies within us.' I became aware of Native American wisdom and spirituality at a young age. I identified. I learned of the Far Eastern religions and spiritual beliefs. I identified. I carry a copy of the Tao Te Ching with me. I carry an Indian prayer with me. And perhaps the most impactful and spiritual prayer was written by a Confederate soldier at the end of the Civil War. Spirituality is mired in humility and gratitude. This prayer keeps me in that place.

"*I asked God for strength that I might achieve.*
I was made weak, that I might learn humility to obey.
I asked for health, that I might do great things.
I was given infirmity, that I might do better things.
I asked for riches, that I might be happy.
I was given poverty, that I might be wise.
I asked for power, that I might have the praise of men.
I was given weakness, that I might feel the need of God.
I asked for all things that I might enjoy life.
I was given life, that I might enjoy all things.
I got nothing I asked for—but everything I hoped for.
Almost despite myself,
my unspoken prayers were answered.
I am, among men, most richly blessed.'"

I watched Curtis as he slowly nodded his head in the affirmative.

"In the end," I said, "whether it's a church, a philosophy, a religious rally, volunteer work, or whatever structure, as long as it benefits the beholder to act and feel good about themselves and others, I support it. To me, it should be an individual, not a herd mentality."

"That prayer is impactful. And such a wise, young Confederate soldier in a horrible place. I have a mental picture." Curtis's visage spoke of sorrow.

I again recalled my visit to Gettysburg.

Curtis continued. "I too am a great fan of the Tao. Taoism is not a religion. Actually, it's an ineffable concept. I studied religions with a monk. I revere certain members of my culture, like Ten Bears of my own tribe, and Red Cloud, Chief Joseph, and others, but none more than this monk. He spoke of the Tao as a system of belief, attitudes, and practices set toward the service and living to a person's nature. Acceptance of your life, who you are, and what you have. Rid yourself of expectations. The more expectations you have for your life, the less you will become. Philosophical, yes, and in many ways contrary to what children are taught in a capitalist world. The Tao says, 'I own nothing, I am merely a passing custodian whereas the young lions can't own enough.' Just another paradox I guess." Curtis finished and gave me that *what the hell do I know* look.

We were sipping cognac after dinner. Hafeez was still on her computer.

"So, along the line of paradoxes, how does one explain the big question about evil and an all-loving God?" I asked, already having had my own answer for many decades. "I don't know about all of recorded history, but it appears to be a fact that since the end of World War II, there have been only twenty-six days when there wasn't a war going on somewhere." He was the kitten, and I dangled the yarn.

"Really?" Curtis gave his knowing smile. "Back to good versus evil?"

"Not really. This poses the question about why he allows it." I could tell he wasn't buying my tease.

"Okay, I'll play along," he said. "Theologians have wrestled with the problem of trying to explain why suffering and evil exist in the world since time immemorial. They refer to it as theodicy. The book titled *When Bad Things Happen to Good People* claims that God feels as badly as humans when there was suffering. The antipodal question is, of course, why do good things happen to bad people, and so you have to look at who is asking the question.

"Christians will answer differently from atheists or scientists. Christians will claim that God has shown his love by giving man free will, the choice to behave as we choose between right and wrong. The Bible is clear that faith in Jesus Christ does not guarantee a good life, only a perfect eternity. God, they say, acts as a loving father who lets his children go, but only wants them home again.

"Atheists believe that life is a one-and-out proposition, no afterlife. Scientists, on the other hand, might claim that the universe has no inherent purpose or design and that that unambiguous conclusion removes the mystery of why bad things happen to good people. You know, the same laws of nature that underlie all causes and effects. To believe that life is totally random may be unsettling, but at the same time, it can be emotionally liberating. It might actually empower people by accepting randomness and freeing them from self-blame." Curtis stopped and sipped his drink. "No pat answers, just opinions and maybe convenient self-conclusions. "As an addendum, the philosopher Thomas Malthus felt that wars and pandemics were the means to save man from self-destruction. He had a strong argument, at least in his time, that the world's population was growing at a geometric progression, while the food supply grew only arithmetically. Man would perhaps die from starvation, so what appeared to be bad things were perhaps God's way of preserving life." Curtis lifted his arms in a who knows gesture.

"Your explanation is far more erudite than mine," I said, "though they're similar. I simplify everything. God created man with the rudiments of good and evil, and he just watches and shakes his head at man's stupidity. Our man, Bert Russell, said it well. 'It has been said that man is a rational animal. All my life I have been searching for evidence which could support this.'"

We noticed that Hafeez was putting her computer away.

When she started to leave, I said, "I'll call you later with what I find." I gave her a minute before I got up to follow.

CHAPTER 12

When I got to the parking lot, I almost missed her. It was dark, and there were several cars leaving. Luckily, she passed in front of me, and the dark-blue Mercedes she was driving was a giveaway. I had concluded that this woman was more than a seven-grand-a-month bookkeeper. Being close to Thanksgiving, there were people out and about, so traffic was busy enough to hide from easy detection. I was sure that Hafeez was the cautious and attentive type and maybe suspicious. When she turned left on North Beachview Drive, the traffic thinned and I fell back. She pulled into an upscale house in the $300,000-to-$400,000 range that overlooked the Atlantic Ocean.

I drove past, turned around, and parked, with a view. She seemed to live alone, and with nothing noteworthy, after ten minutes, I left. When I got home, I made a pot of coffee, called Curtis with a quick update, and turned on my computer. I sent a nice note to Tommy with a turkey day wish and the two license plate numbers I had written down for Hafeez and the gray Prius.

Any intel you can give me will be most helpful. Steak dinner and a fifteen-year-old Macallan Fifth will be yours. Tommy liked scotch.

I figured it would take a few days.

I then spent some time looking at the import business, as well as real estate values on Jekyll Island. Lastly, I listened to and watched several YouTube videos of Gordon Lightfoot. It was after midnight before I showered and hit the hay, humming to the tune of "Saturday Clothes."

I awoke before sunrise. I made a thermos of coffee and drove to Driftwood Beach to see the sun come up. Tomorrow morning, I would be headed to Atlanta to pick up B. J. This morning, my thoughts were about things lost in the activity of life. I needed to connect with my brothers and let them know my new address and that I was still vertical and mobile.

I sat cross-legged, sipping my French roast in anticipation until it came, and my muse went to another beach, another place, another time. It was a spring break on Lake Tahoe. A hangover was in its early stage, it was warm, and the girl I was with was pretty. And she read from *The Rubaiyat of Omar Khayyam.*

Wake! For the Sun, who scatter'd into flight
The Stars before him from the Field of Night,
Drives Night along with them from Heav'n, and strikes
The Sultan's Turret with a Shaft of Light.

Shortly afterward, I fell asleep on the sand, and when I awoke, she was gone. Was she now a silver-haired gramma reading to her grandkids? Was she plump with rimless glasses, making jellies and jams in Mason jars? Or had she died young from a drug overdose? A blip on my seventy-four-year-old radar.

People were beginning to invade my space. My, that was a bit snarky. Guess I was just enjoying my solitude and feeling proprietary. I drove home. Another reason to call me a dinosaur was that I still had an iPod. I'd hooked it up to a small but powerful speaker. Hell, in all my junk, I might still have an eight-track. In any event, I needed some George Winston. The boy could tickle those ivories.

After emailing my brothers and confirming the pickup

tomorrow with Sam, I spent the morning putting all of my notes together on the mystery Curtis and I were playing with. Curtis was clearly a savant. This exercise was a fun gig that had brought the two of us together, and even if there should be nothing untoward going on, we were creating a certain bond that doesn't usually happen to "old guys." Elders retire, move, and become less available. Changes in temperament and opportunity affect us as well. Still, we humans are programmed for mutual companionship and affection—the in-person kind. We hunger for others with whom we can share interests, concern, compassion, and understanding. I'm bothered by the old adage, "The more I know, the less I know." I learn something new, only to find two more things I want to learn and understand, which leads to four more, fifteen more, and a geometric growth of things on my list. Finding a man of such intellect and experience as Curtis was a godsend.

"It seems the good they die young." So sang Dion in his classic hit song, "Abraham, Martin and John." Indeed, those three had so much more to give us. So too did Hank Williams, who died from alcohol at the age of twenty-nine, and again, so did an intrepid young Anglo-American pilot who volunteered for the RCAF in 1939 to fight in the Battle of Britain. He was dauntless, handsome, admired and yet soft, like a poet. He did actually write several poems before he died at age nineteen in a midair collision in 1941. When I read his story, my eyes water. I can be such a fucking baby sometimes, especially when it comes to animals and military heroes. But this guy will never be forgotten, as one of his several poems was inspired in flight. When he landed, he went to his barracks and sat down and wrote his poem.

Oh! I have slipped the surly bonds of Earth
And danced the skies on laughter-silvered wings;
Sunward I've climbed, and joined the tumbling mirth
Of sun-split clouds,—and done a hundred things

You have not dreamed of—
wheeled and soared and swung
High in the sunlit silence. Hov'ring there,
I've chased the shouting wind along, and flung
My eager craft through footless halls of air . . .

Up, up the long, delirious, burning blue
I've topped the wind-swept heights with easy grace
Where never lark, or even eagle flew—
And, while with silent, lifting mind I've trod
The high untrespassed sanctity of space,
Put out my hand, and touched the face of God.

There are things we just know, and I know I would have liked John Gillespie Magee Jr.

I had been reading about the horror of London during the Blitzkrieg.

My computer dinged, and I checked my Timex . . . 3:15 p.m. It was a fifteen-year-old watch, but it was probably pretty close, give or take five minutes, and in that way, it resembled my personality.

I had five emails. The first was a promotion for Depends. I deleted it after checking to see who it was from. Could have been Sonny or even Mary Beth. Pissed me off because it was legit. Sam reconfirmed with good wishes. Two of my brothers sent notes that, in essence, said they were relatively pleased I was still alive, and then, the last one was a surprise . . . Tommy. That was fast. He must have been really thirsty. There were two attachments, and after a cursory glance, I put them on hold for the moment.

His note was short: *Fifteen-year-old Macallan, huh? Must have made it about the time of your seventy-fifth birthday?* Tommy was a year younger and had always given me shit about being old.

I Googled liquor stores in Dover, called one that delivered, and almost maxed out my Visa card with the bottle of scotch. I made it a quart for his speedy reply.

My note was very short: *THX A $M. BTW-GFY.*

I paid up for a late-day delivery.

The first attachment was about the woman called Hafeez. I could see just what a valuable resource Tommy was to an awful lot of people. He was Orwellian to a degree I had not been aware of. And I thought I had been "black ops" royalty.

Her name was Hafeez Saeed, thirty-eight years old. She was from a prominent Pakistani family. She had become estranged from her father a number of years ago and had emigrated to the US. She was a computer whiz, achieved citizenship, and got a job in the New York office of the United States Citizenship and Immigration Services, USCIS. She had been released several years ago for certain "privacy issue" violations. Interestingly, it had been a "quiet" settlement, implying some element of leverage on both sides. After that, she consulted for a very successful Pakistani businessman in New York City for a year. At some point, she met Fadi Ghulam. She worked for Arabian Knights out of a small New York office for about a year before moving to Jekyll Island. She flew to the Middle East at least once a quarter for a week. What she did and where she went was unknown. It was presumably for buying product, but the economics of these trips never seemed to reconcile, just not enough to create close scrutiny unless there was reason for suspicion.

Hafeez reported annual income of around $100,000, and it was interesting to see an Ameritrade account of just under $800,000 in the name of a company called Zeefa, a kind of partial reverse eponym. It wasn't exactly clear what Zeefa did, some kind of consulting, but it produced around $25,000 to $35,000 in profit from $200,000 to $250,000 in annual revenues. Big expenses as well.

My overall reaction was that Ms. Saeed did not fully pass the smell test. I started a file and put down about a half dozen questions that this report raised for me. My guess was that if even more in-depth intel was needed, Tommy's team could provide it.

The second attachment was probably a bit more interesting, as I had no expectations whatsoever. I had no idea who or what. The Prius was registered to a Marylyn Ottesen, formerly Marylyn DuBruss, formerly Marylyn Ottesen, which would imply that the woman was divorced and had changed back to her maiden name. She had been a Boston debutante and had matriculated at Mount Holyoke College in South Hadley, Massachusetts. While there, she met an Amherst fellow named Ryan DuBruss. Ryan became a real estate developer. They got married and moved to Atlanta to build a filmmaking location with Hollywood connections. The prince and the princess lived a charmed life . . . until suddenly they didn't. They divorced by mail. Marylyn received a chunk of cash and dropped off the planet. Sounded like the blue-blood bubble had burst, pardon the alliteration. So she surfaced, driving around with young girls and playing Miss Marple on Jekyll Island.

Like Arte Johnson used to say, "Belly intellestink."

And then there's me. Like Sergeant Schultz, "I know nussing."

True, I had no clue. Maybe it was Colonel Mustard who did it in the bedroom. In any event, let the games continue.

There was a convenient coffee shop for a meeting with Curtis, so we decided to meet in an hour. I had some chores to do to get ready for B. J. and would have to leave around 5:00 a.m. for the Atlanta airport. If possible, I would try to get some early shuteye.

Curtis was dressed in an impressive Native outfit.

"Well, I do appreciate your show of respect, sir, but after all, it's just a coffee shop." I smiled.

He actually guffawed. "From here, I have about an hour drive. I'm speaking to a group of writers about the 1890 Wounded Knee Massacre." I heard the pride in his voice.

"So we return to 1970 and Dee Brown's classic," I added.

"It's a classic argument about one of the most egregious injustices in American history. At some point, you and I will discuss the topic in great depth. For now, it seems you've gathered some interesting information."

I took Curtis through the reports from Tommy. "We're dealing with some interesting indicators of something not being on the up-and-up. No proof of any wrongdoing, but my antennae are on alert. One thing that's most curious to me is where Marta fits into this. Some relationship with Marylyn and some connection to Ghulam. I suspect there needs to be a discussion with Marylyn as this goes forward. I also suspect that could be awkward. We need to find a reason for her to talk. That piece is weird."

"So it seems. Untangling a web of some sort . . . a web of conjecture."

"I'd love to hear your talk this evening. It's on the docket of subjects for future dinners, my friend. I'll be getting some quality time with my grandson for the next two days. I'd love for you to meet him. Let's see if that might work. Okay?"

"I would most enjoy that." Curtis downed his coffee and checked his outfit.

After we parted, I filled my tank, and before going home, drove to a tourist shop I had seen and picked up a hat and jacket for B. J. Then, just for the heck of it, I grabbed a Frisbee.

CHAPTER 13

There are very few, if any, surprises left for me. I suppose that comes with age and experience, or more likely, my personal self-control of expectations, but iconoclasm is no longer a disappointment or an inconvenient truth. For some time now, such things have simply become points of interest. As much as I might resist it, reality just keeps showin' up, and the circle of life keeps comin' 'round. In many ways, most things keep comin' 'round. Wide ties—thin ties, short skirts—ankle skirts. New innovations become anachronous, and in some form, often recycle while immutable beliefs mutate.

With that in mind, that evening I got caught up in a TV documentary that essentially concluded that Darwin's theory of evolution was hogwash and that even a number of scientists now claim, ". . . and chalk one up for the faithful."

British physicist H. S. Lipson stated, "Evolution became in a sense, a scientific religion; almost all scientists have accepted it and many are prepared to 'bend' their observations to fit with it." While connections between ancient primates and modern humans on the evolutionary tree are believed to exist, they are inferred and speculative and have never been a proven fact. Once again, the iconoclast is DNA. Both physical and DNA evidence suggests that our species of humans may have appeared two hundred thousand years ago with no evolutionary path leading to our appearance. Those things that separate man from all other forms of life are a deep intuition, sympathy, empathy, compassion, and self-healing. DNA studies have now proved that man is not descended from Neanderthals and that modern man has essentially not changed in two hundred thousand years. In his book, *Human by Design*, author Gregg Braden claims that evidence overwhelmingly suggests that we are the result of an intentional act of creation and that with the DNA, the advanced brain, and the complex nervous system that contradict Darwin's thesis, we appear to be a species unto ourselves.

In line with that, the program went on to state that another most impactful discovery in the past several decades was the relationship between the brain and the heart. To the poets, the heart has always been an existential metaphor for love. To the medical community, the heart has been the world's most remarkable pump. After all, it beats over one hundred thousand times a day while circulating approximately two thousand gallons of blood through sixty thousand miles of arteries, capillaries, veins, and other blood vessels.

"Man alive," I stated aloud, noting the meaningless expression often used by my old man, "have I ever been taking my heart for granted." Imagine that a single pump is like a hard squeeze of a tennis ball. Now imagine doing that for the average life, nonstop, 2.5 billion times. You'd for sure have the strongest grip in the locker room.

But the heart is more than a pump. About thirty years ago, a team of scientists found that some forty thousand specialized neurons make up a communication network within the heart. This tiny brain within the heart acts both independently and in harmony with our cranial brain. It stores memory as well, and there is even proof that a heart transplant recipient will experience specific memories from those created by the donor. So among other things, the atheists can no longer point to Charlie Darwin as proof that God did not create man and thus, might heed the warning from Blood, Sweat and Tears, who swear there ain't no heaven, but pray there ain't no hell.

Accordingly, in a salute to my own spirituality and to Team God, I fell into a sound sleep until 4: 30 a.m.

CHAPTER 14

It was dark, and there was a chill in the air when I headed for Atlanta. Highway driving at 5:00 a.m. seems so singular, so encapsulating. One's sense of sound has an elevated sensitivity. I felt the invariable thumping of tires on evenly spaced concrete blocks of road surface, monotonous and transfixing, until it came, silent and subtle, that transient light that precedes the rising of the sun, the false dawn. The sky was cloudless and clear, so that when sunrise did come, it came with pomp, without celestial defects, without a filmy mask, just the unfettered hubris of Aton.

I had dreamed again last night. It was less violent but intimidating nonetheless. Some of my dreams are themed, like flying or running a race where I'm in the lead, but my legs won't go any faster, and as I glance behind, the other runners are catching me as I struggle to go faster. It really doesn't take Freud to interpret that one. Still, there are others that are just plain weird. People from my past I haven't even thought about for decades. Last night's episode was where I was a captive next to a room with groaning and moaning sounds. Part of the wall falls away, and I look in to see dozens of bodies, nearly naked, and there's steam coming from the walls. They look like Cro-Magnons and Java ape-men, and they're chained to the walls. WTF? Could be repressed illusions from Nam, I suppose, but come on. I like the fun ones where you wake up and try like hell to fall back to sleep and get back into the dream. Never works.

I rolled the window down and had a smoke as I continued

to wonder about dreams. It was a beautiful morning, speed limit, right lane, not much traffic, perfect for rumination.

When I think about my dreams as a kid, except for the occasional nightmare, my dreams were fun. I suspect there's a relationship to my positive attitude and my choices. New studies have taken Freud's interpretations of sexual predominance in dreams to a higher, more encompassing level. A neuroscientist named Dr. Mona Lisa Schulz agrees with other researchers that dreams provide us with potential choices in our lives, and in many ways, dreams are a problem-solving mechanism for the brain. When we're awake, our brain is receiving constant interference from both people externally and our inner selves, instructing and judging us all the time. It's estimated that only 10 percent of our brain is operating on all cylinders, whereas when sleeping, the brain is operating at full capacity, as it is free from such interference. The culprit, it seems, is the brain's frontal lobe, which houses the thinking and judgment piece.

Freud's description: "Dreams are a conversation with oneself, a dialogue of symbols and images that takes place in the unconscious and conscious levels of the mind." And so, dreams provide a way of gathering information about the state of our lives, our emotions, and significantly, our bodies. They say that dreams can predict illness, a claim that goes back to ancient Greece. We're told that if we listen to our dreams, we're given the opportunity to change those things that cause us conflicts, problems, or illness so that we can seek solutions.

Even accepting this, I was still unable to reconcile last night's dream. I didn't see any freakin' symbols, unless the message was that I now looked a lot like Java ape-man.

Freudian symbolism has always been the dominant factor in dream interpretations: a house—the whole body; rooms—separate organs; furnace—the lungs; entryway—the mouth; and we all can figure out the pedestal, obelisk, or tower . . . right? Might be a foreboding sign if I dream about the Leaning

Tower of Pisa, huh? The ancient Chinese concluded that the content of dreams relate to certain afflicted body parts: terror—the heart; suffocation—the lungs; food—the digestive tract; and pillars—duh? It seems, however, that even Freud could mellow out on sexual symbolism, as he once made the statement, "Sometimes a cigar is just a cigar," which prompted me to again review my dream to see if any of those Neanderthals were smoking cigars. Nope.

I started to think about stopping for gas and a bite to eat. For some damned reason, one of those cinnamon sticks came to mind. Shame!

After gassing up and having a snack and getting a couple of scratch-offs for B. J., I enjoyed the drive and gave my brain a rest. I found the Atlanta oldies station and listened to the Platters, Motown, Ben E. King, Elvis, and Ricky. That had been my time. All sorts of memories surfaced, along with the full picture of my glory days. If, after I'm dead and gone, some angel ever offers me the opportunity to come back for just one day, I just might pass. Don't think I could choose just one. They were all full of wonder. Or maybe use Mr. Pointy Finger again. He was on a hot streak.

I felt gratitude and thanked my Great Spirit for the chance of life, for having been the fastest swimmer in the pod. Sorry, skip the visual, but I meant it.

In spite of having paid little attention to the time, just outside of Atlanta, I found I was right on schedule. I drove to airport pickup, checked my text messages, and shortly after, there were Sam and B. J.

CHAPTER 15

"Grandpa!" B. J. cried as he ran and jumped into my outstretched arms.

I hugged him hard before I turned and faked a sneeze, covering my face with my handkerchief. *Damn.* I dabbed my eyes. *Tough old sons-a-bitches like me don't tear up.* "What the heck you doing? You promised to not get any bigger, and look at you."

I ruffled his hair, and when I went to hug Sam, she gave me that eyebrow thing that told me she had noticed.

As with most things, Sam knew exactly how to get to her sister's place. We got caught up on things while B. J. sat in the back looking out at the city, curious as always. Sam was solid, like her husband. Their kids would be solid. B. J. was a bit like his grandfather, with some renegade blood, but in the end, he would be solid too.

When we got there, we all went in to visit with Sam's sister, Carol, for a while. Carol was much like her sister, solid and successful. She was an investigative reporter for the *Atlanta Tribune*. She had received a major award last year for exposing Medicare corruption in Georgia.

Hunter S. Thomson once said, "As far as I'm concerned, it's a damned shame that a field as potentially dynamic and vital as journalism should be overrun with dullards, bums, and hacks, hag-ridden with myopia, apathy, and complacence, and generally stuck in a bog of stagnant mediocrity."

Carol was not of that ilk.

After a little chatting, B. J. and I left. It was another five hours of highway time, but I wanted to visit the Arabian Knights store first. I put the address into my GPS, and twenty minutes later, we pulled into a small shopping mall. There was an unsavory feel to the neighborhood, and the storefront reeked of cheap. If the hand-painted store name was someone's pastime, they might think about a new hobby.

The only person in the store was a young white kid, probably a college student, but at least he had a touch of effervescence in his greeting. "Howdy, folks, what can I do ya' for?" he said with a big grin.

"Store looked interesting, so we thought we'd look around," I said.

"Treat yourself. Happy to help."

The merchandise was of similar quality to the sign, cheap with high markup, kind of prize you might win if you knocked the three bottles over at the fair.

While B. J. was perusing the trinkets, I lowered my voice and asked the kid, "Mind if I ask you a couple things about your store and the location? A friend of mine is thinking about a small art gallery. I was a leasing agent for a time, and he asked for my thoughts."

"Don't think I can be much help. Earning my way through night school. Computer programming. Don't know much about the business side, but happy to try."

"Well, for one thing, do you have much traffic?" I asked. "You know, customers?"

The kid thought about that. He lowered his voice and looked around, body language for confidentiality. "Honestly, I don't know how they make it. Some days, we don't sell a thing." His facial expression was a question mark.

"Don't suppose you know what the rent is?"

"I don't," he said, "but a lady drops off a check on the first of every month, and a guy picks it up. Like clockwork."

B. J. had grabbed my belt. "Hey, Grandpa, what do you think about this knife?" He showed me a pocketknife with a painted horse on the handle. Probably worth a couple bucks, tops.

"You like it, B. J., it's yours." I turned to the kid, "How much?"

"Nine fifty," he said.

I swallowed my response and gave him a ten. "Keep the change." Hardworking kid deserved it. "Okay then, guess we'll be moving along. Thanks for your help."

"Don't mention it, and thanks for the tip."

As we started to leave, I thought of something else and went back. "Listen, kid, one more thing. When the lady drops off that check every month, you notice anything strange?"

He just smiled. "Seems strange to me, I suppose, but she always brings a pretty girl with her. Pretty girls, but don't talk much. They hang around until the guy picks up the envelope, and they leave with him. Different girls every month. Kinda weird, but you know, not really my business."

I processed that. "Anything else?"

"Nope, unless you consider it strange that when the lady drops off the check, the guy always gives her a present wrapped up in a bow. She ain't no beauty, but the guy might have the hots for her. Whole thing is strange enough, don't you think?"

I nodded in the affirmative.

Between the store and the highway, I was pretty quiet. B. J. was playing with his knife, and I was trying to process what that kid had said. The store was a loser. Crappy location, crappy presentation, crappy merchandise, and no customers. It screamed of a cover. Couldn't be money laundering because there wasn't any money, so throw in the piece about the girls and presents, and other possibilities came to mind.

But for now, all of that could wait. I needed to be a grandfather. "So tell me, B. J., have you got a girlfriend?"

"Jeez, Grandpa, no," he said with that look that says, "Are you nuts? Girls are dumb!" He looked out the window, not at me.

I'd have been disappointed with any other response from a fourteen-year-old boy. Plus, it answered my question. He had a girlfriend.

"Okay, so how about sports?" I asked and saw his eyes light up.

He proceeded to fill me in on all of his sports activities and the different jocks he liked. He talked. I nodded and listened.

"How about any classes or teachers that you like?"

"I don't like math so much, but I really like Mr. Jackson. He teaches English and history. He's not really happy about some of the changes that the school is making, though."

"Like what?"

"He says that we won't learn about our history now and the early presidents and things," he replied, looking confused. He didn't understand. He couldn't understand.

Truth be told, neither could I. After thinking about it, I decided it was not a topic to discuss with B. J. I slipped into a funk. Separation between church and state had been methodically debated but never removed. Now it was education. The new mantra seemed to be, "Don't learn from history. Ignore it." In Germany, they had burned the books. In America today, same thing. They just removed them from the curriculum. That topic was all-encompassing, and I couldn't afford to have it overwhelm me at this point.

"You know, B. J., all of us are born with what is called *free will*, the freedom to act and choose what you do and what you believe in. It's the highest human right, and it comes with great responsibility. Each of us deserves basic respect, but we earn that respect. In turn, we must give that respect to others who earn it. Do you know what I'm saying?"

"I think so, Grandpa."

"A good man is a man of honor, and he develops courage to stand up for those things he believes in. Know too that wisdom comes with age, but you've already been provided with the internal knowledge of right and wrong, so you will want to make good choices, those that relate to what you know is right and what you know is wrong. You make many, many choices every day, and the choices you make will define who you are and who you will become. Does that make sense?"

"Mom and Dad say those things too, Grandpa."

I smiled. Of course they did. "That's right, and your mom and dad do the things they teach you to do." I let that sink in. "So you will learn that you cannot always believe everything you hear on TV or in school as well. You will learn how important it is to verify the truth and come to your own conclusions. Too many people just believe what they hear, not knowing the reason why they want you to hear it. Oftentimes, it's the wrong reason, and it may not be the truth, and it may not be what you believe, so it's very important that you listen, but learn and form your own opinions in line with your own sense of right and wrong. I tell you these things because they're important life lessons, right?" I could tell that my grandson was absorbing what I was saying.

"Yes, and Mr. Jackson kinda said that too."

"Well, I would like to meet this Mr. Jackson."

We rode in silence for a time.

Eventually B. J. asked me, "Do you talk to Gramma, Grandpa?"

"You bet I do. We talk mostly about our wonderful grandkids. Gramma and I are friends."

He smiled.

We enjoyed the drive in a comfortable silence.

When we stopped for gas and a snack, B. J. pointed out a tree with a dozen or so crows cawing to each other. "Do you know what they call a bunch of crows, Grandpa?"

"Yup, a *murder*." I smiled.

My grandson looked surprised. "Doncha think that's pretty weird?"

"Supposedly, it came from a romantic time when groups of birds and animals were given colorful and poetic names, like a gaggle of geese, a pride of lions, and a school of fish. But from everything I've read, crows are amazing."

"Grandpa, you can't believe how smart they are. They're smarter than a lot of humans. I watched a YouTube thing where crows figured out puzzles before people could." B. J. was both excited and histrionic. "And they're really loyal and super-protective too."

I was familiar with what he was telling me. Crows have a rather complex communication system and possess a highly developed intuition. Sadly, most people consider them to be a nuisance, but only because they haven't taken the time or interest to study them.

"You never know, maybe we'll see a murder tomorrow." I gave him a scary face.

He didn't get it at first, then he gave me a knowing smile.

CHAPTER 16

When we were less than a half hour from Jekyll Island, it was close to suppertime.

I was tired and anxious to get home. "So what do you say we pick up some food to take home, B. J.?"

"Do you like tacos, Grandpa? I love Mexican." B. J. was excited.

"You got it, young man. I know just the place."

Although I hadn't been there, somebody had mentioned that Chile Peppers Island Cantina had the best Mexican food. When we got there, we grabbed a bagful of their specialties and got home just before seven. In that tomorrow was Thanksgiving, I wanted to see if the club had a shindig, so I called Curtis. We agreed to meet around five.

As we gobbled the food, B. J. and I watched a movie about a family and a dog that saved the day. B. J. teared up, and maybe I did a little too. We talked about our adventures tomorrow, and we both hit the sack and were sawin' logs in five minutes.

The next morning, we got rolling just after sunrise. As we drove to the historic sites, I gave B. J. a history lesson of the island. We did the parks and the beaches. It was a little chilly, so we skipped the swim. Around one, we ended up at the marina. The parking lot was relatively empty. There was plenty of open pavement, and B. J. had brought the Frisbee while I had my walking stick.

Several years ago, while on a walk, I had been attacked by a dog, a mongrel that, as it turned out, had been rabid. I had avoided being bitten, but thereafter, as a precaution, I had bought a walking stick just in case. This walking stick was both a disguise and a weapon.

There were boats moored in slips along the docks and several that were tethered to the quay. We toured the area, admiring the different sloops and ketches and several houseboats and pontoons.

As we drew near to a large powerboat near the end of the concrete wall, there was something familiar about the two men on board. They were big. I knew who they were. I signaled to B. J., and we turned back.

"Grandpa, can we play Frisbee?" B. J. said, running to the center of the lot.

I caught his first throw on the end of my stick. I still had some of my old athletic skills. B. J. cheered.

There was a van parked across the lot from the powerboat, and the big man was taking things to the van. As soon as I flipped the Frisbee back, the image appeared to me: one of disaster, like a slow-motion film.

Running to catch the disc, B. J. ran right into the back of the big man and tripped to the pavement. B. J. was slightly dazed, but he got up and turned to the man. "Sorry," he said in meek embarrassment.

The man looked at him with a frown and slapped him on the head.

"Hey!" I yelled, "what the hell do you think you're doing?"

B. J. ran over to me.

I gave him a reassuring nod and walked up to the man. He was a foot taller than me and a foot wider. His frown turned to a feral grin.

"Apologize to my grandson!" I screamed as I stared up at him. My look spoke of threat.

He laughed and turned to his partner and spoke in Arabic.

In English, it was essentially, "Hey, Kadir, old man thinks he can tell me what to do."

This time they both laughed.

I was as tight as a guitar string. I wanted to tell him, "*Ant ghabi*," Arabic for "You're an idiot," but my better sense told me not to let him know I understood Arabic. Instead, I took a half step closer, my eyes on fire. "I will only ask you one more time. Apologize."

He stuck his chin out and spit on my shoe. "What now, old man? You hit me with little stick?" He guffawed.

What happened next was only a flash. What looked like an ordinary walking stick was a Zap, a superpowerful stun gun with one million volts. What went through my mind was that if this dufus by some twist did have a girlfriend, she would not be happy with me. I pointed the Zap at his groin and pushed the switch. He dropped like a lead weight and writhed on the ground, holding his crotch. When he gave me a threatening look, I pointed the stick at his neck.

With a mask of fear, he looked at B. J. and said, "Sorry, sorry, sorry" over and over.

His sidekick, Kadir, was running toward me.

I walked toward him, and he stopped. "One step closer, and you end up like him."

I took another step toward him, and he put his hands in the air and backed up. I walked back to the big man to make sure he wasn't getting up. He crisscrossed his hands in surrender. Slowly, I grabbed hold of B. J., and we walked away. I did stop to memorize the license number of the boat before going to the car.

CHAPTER 17

The two girls were giddy. The older woman just smiled. They watched from the car parked in the upper lot overlooking the marina. They had been watching the powerboat for several days.

"It appears that the old man is not as fragile as he pretends to be," the older woman commented.

"No, he is not," replied the dark-haired girl. "I talk to him. He's a nice man, but I think he's a man to not fool with."

"Sometimes little presents come from unexpected places," the older woman said as she started the Prius.

CHAPTER 18

"Hey, little buddy, you okay?" I asked as I put my arm around my grandson.

He nodded up and down, but kept his eyes on the Zap.

"Don't worry. It's turned off." I laughed at that.

"Jeez, Grandpa, what is that thing?"

I explained what the Zap was, why I had it, and the conversation segued into a discussion about good and bad people in the world. My intent was to remove his naivete but to help him understand self-preservation, which to a child is a delicate undertaking. Make them aware but don't instill fear. In today's world, that can be a challenge. Knowing his parents to be somewhat naïve themselves, my guess was that B. J. hadn't heard that pitch at home.

It was Thanksgiving, and we were going to be eating turkey in the next couple of hours at the club with Curtis. I figured we wouldn't be seeing Ghulam and his two goombahs unless the big fella had a quick recovery system, but you never know. For B. J.'s sake, I hoped not. I told B. J. to perhaps not talk about the marina incident, as it would only get people worried.

I called my kids to wish them a happy Thanksgiving. After I talked to Winston, I handed the phone to B. J. and went to my bedroom. I had survived as long as I had because of my sentient radar and thus that nudge. I loaded five 22 mags into my derringer, which fit snugly into my ankle holster.

B. J. was all smiles when I returned. "Gramma said to give you a hug, Grandpa. She came for Thanksgiving, and I told her about all the things we've seen here and that we were going to your club for turkey." B. J. was on a roll. "I didn't say anything about the other thing, either."

I smiled and thought of the old Welsh proverb: *Perfect love sometimes does not come until the first grandchild.*

CHAPTER 19

I was relieved to see that there were not only no goons at the club, but the ever-present Hafeez was not there as well. To top it off, even the Prius was missing. I had told B. J. about Curtis on the drive over, and he didn't disappoint. He was dressed in what resembled Native ceremonial garb, though not ostentatious. The dining area was packed, and the savor was welcome and reminiscent of days gone by.

It didn't take Curtis long to captivate the fourteen-year-old with his personality and presentation. Curtis was a magnetic and romantic person by nature, but add doctor of psychology, and I don't imagine he has any problems with developing most relationships, no matter the age.

"I know the Indian names of the four winds, Curtis." B. J.'s face was filled with wonder. "And I read about the Pilgrims and the Indians having the first Thanksgiving."

"That's good, B. J. So, what are the four winds?"

"Well, there's Kabibonokka, the North Wind; Wabon, the East Wind; Shawondasee, the South Wind; and the king of winds, Mudjekeewis, the West Wind." B. J. smiled with pride.

"Excellent. So, you've read *The Song of Hiawatha*?"

"Yes, sir."

"Well then, sit back, and I'll tell you some interesting history about that poem and the author."

B. J. made an exaggerated point of sitting back in his chair. I couldn't help but grin.

Curtis began his lecture. "The backstory begins in Portland, Maine, home of Henry Wadsworth Longfellow, author of one of America's most idyllic, musical, and imaginative episodic poems, the one you've read, B. J.: *The Song of Hiawatha.* When you read the lines about Gitche Gumee and Shawondasee, it's difficult to believe the fact that old Henry had very little contact with the Native American environment or individual connections. His poem drew largely on letters and accounts of missionaries, manuscripts of George Catlin, stories of James Fenimore Cooper, and of particular interest and relevance to our discussion, Henry Rowe Schoolcraft. Henry Rowe Schoolcraft was an American geographer, geologist, and ethnologist, noted for his early studies of Native American cultures, as well as for his 1832 expedition to the source of the Mississippi River. If you haven't been there, you must go, B. J.

"Now the two Henrys were friends, and as interesting as Schoolcraft's biography is, our focus turns to his wife, Jane Johnston Schoolcraft. Jane was an Ojibwa from your Leech Lake area. Her Native name was Bamewawagezhikaquay, Woman of the Sound the Stars Make Rushing Through the Sky, and by the time she died, she had produced a large body of literary and other writings. Eclipsed from the historical record by her famous husband, Jane Johnston Schoolcraft was nevertheless among the first American Indian writers. She was also the first known American Indian literary writer, the first known Indian woman writer, the first known Indian poet, the first known poet to write poems in a Native American language, and the first known American Indian to write out traditional Indian stories, as opposed to transcribing and translating from someone else's oral delivery, which she did also. Her stories became a key source for The Song of Hiawatha. What do you think of that?"

"Wow, Curtis. You know so much about lots of stuff." After a brief pause, B. J. asked, "Can I go to the bathroom?"

Curtis pointed to the men's room. After B. J. stepped away, I told Curtis about the marina incident.

He absorbed that before replying. "You are one bad dude, Woody. We should have soldiered together. On the other hand, there is something most disturbing about these people. We'll meet them again soon, I'm sure."

Just before B. J. returned, I also told Curtis about my visit to the Arabian Knights store in Atlanta. His raised eyebrows told me his reaction.

The buffet was an extravagant feast. By the time I got to turkey and mashed potatoes, I was stuffed. For B. J., it was all turkey and spuds. Curtis was more refined. A trio played holiday music, and it felt like family. It was a fine day for me.

Curtis was an accomplished storyteller, responding to the tommy-gun queries of my inquisitive grandson. To me, the signs were clear. B. J., the product of good parents, would be a success if he made good choices. Five hundred years before Christ, Confucius had said that the strength of a nation derives from the integrity of the home, and that bit of philosophy hasn't changed. What has changed is the home. Single-parent homes, loss of discipline, and lack of parental awareness and control, entitlement and intrusion, and the inimical consequences of the yin and yang of technology. The character of humans has never changed, nor will it, So we debate whether the world is a better place today. A most subjective debate indeed. The pea-brained dinosaurs hung around for 65 million years. Will developed man, who so many now argue has been around for some 200,000 years, mired in his own self-destruction, be around for another 60 million? Fat chance.

B. J. interrupted my reverie. "Grandpa, Curtis says that problems are a good thing. How can that be?"

I had missed their discussion. "Well, first of all, know that Curtis is a doctor of psychology and has written books about such things, and yes, I do understand what Curtis means." I thought about my answer. "True success is almost always the result of a series of failures. Failure may be the greatest teaching tool. When you solve problems, do you feel good?"

B. J. looked at me, then at Curtis. "Yes, I do. I didn't think about it that way."

"It's healthy to not get discouraged by failure," Curtis stated. "Life is really a bottomless pit of problems. Solve one, another comes along. Welcome them, address them, find solutions, and you will achieve success." Curtis patted B. J. on the shoulder.

After dessert, the three of us looked at each other.

Curtis rubbed his belly and uncharacteristically said, "We kinda pigged out, huh, B. J.?"

We nodded with big smiles.

As we were leaving, B. J. gave Curtis a hug.

Curtis was moved by the gesture. "Don't stay away too long, young man," he said to the boy.

"Promise," B. J. said.

Whether from an itch to be scratched or from simple curiosity, I drove by the marina on the way home. There was a lot of activity, as the weather was beautiful, with a nice breeze perfect for sailing. The powerboat was not only there, but there was plenty of activity aboard. B. J. and I watched but said nothing.

As we pulled out, something caught my attention. It was the Prius, parked in the upper lot. The woman, Marylyn Ottesen, was alone. She had binoculars focused on the powerboat. Whatever was going on with this woman and the young girls was certainly a mystery, but it was most apparent to me that at some point I would need to have a discussion with her.

When we got home, B. J. found a movie, some animated story, and I sent an email to Tommy with the powerboat registration number. I answered other correspondence and cleaned up a bit before B. J. and I played cribbage. He loved the game and kicked my butt. We didn't have to leave for Atlanta until eleven tomorrow morning, so we agreed we would find some pancakes for breakfast.

CHAPTER 20

We left at ten, and forty miles later, pulled off the road for an IHOP breakfast. The parking lot was full, with parents and kids running in and running out.

My grandson was one. B. J. was a resilient kid. The marina incident was in his rearview mirror as he talked about Jekyll Island, what he had seen, what he had learned, and he had obviously been enchanted by Curtis.

America wouldn't exist were it not for resilience. Character is formed by resilience. And what is character but the willingness to accept responsibility for one's own life. Whether it's sports, business, or war, I want resilient people by my side. The profile of a resilient person is grounded in a positive and realistic attitude, accepting what they cannot change while putting their energy into that which they can. They seek meaningful opportunity in difficult situations. They have a strong moral compass, they're altruistic, and they believe in something greater than themselves. One can usually identify these people. I am one, and it makes me proud to recognize the trait in my kids and grandkids.

"Grandpa, when we talked about that problems are good, Curtis told me I should rely on my intooishun. He said yours was really high. What does that mean?" B. J. looked befuddled. Pretty heavy for a fourteen-year-old.

I formed an answer. "Well, have you ever heard someone say, 'Listen to your guts' or 'I'm going with my hunch'? What they mean is, 'Listen to your intuition.' You see, everyone has the same sense of feel, hearing, smell, taste, and sight, but that which is called a sixth sense, intuition, is different for everyone. Your intuition will provide you with insight and knowledge when you make decisions and choices. Your intuition can assist you in reaching accurate conclusions based upon inadequate information. Does that make sense?"

"I think so, Grandpa. Like, if I don't know something for sure, but I just feel something strongly. Like that?"

"You got it. You see, most people are out of touch with their intuition. They may ignore it and don't recognize it when it comes. And it also works with your other senses. For example—and I don't expect you to remember the words, though you might want to look them up—but there are some people who are what's called *clairvoyant*. These people receive intuition visually, through images they see in their mind's eye. Like maybe you have a vision of someone, or something that later happens. Has that ever happened to you?"

"I think it might have, Grandpa. Last year, I had this picture in my head of our baseball team celebrating, and when we later won the tournament, I told my friends about that." B. J. spoke with excitement.

We watched as the landscape rolled past.

I continued with the thought. "There are also those who are called *clairaudient*, and these people receive intuition through sounds, like a beating heart maybe, or even external sounds. And the third type is called a *clairsentient*— and I'll write these down for you, B. J.—but this is someone who receives intuitive messages through sensations in their own bodies. As an example, let's just say you were talking to someone on the phone and you could sense there was something wrong with them. Suddenly, your arm hurts or begins to feel numb, and you ask them if they're feeling okay. Then they tell you that their arm has been bothering them. You've already felt their pain and identified it. Do you see what I mean?"

"Holy smoke, Grandpa, I've seen that kind of thing in a TV show." He pondered that for a couple of minutes.

"So you can see how amazing someone's intuition can be. The real message is that people should be aware of it and how it can influence their decisions and choices and not ignore it. Make sense?"

B. J. nodded, thought about our discussion, and kept nodding.

CHAPTER 21

Wе pulled into Carol's place at 3:50. After a nice conversation with John, Carol's husband, an advertising executive, we loaded up and headed for the airport. We hugged and promised to stay in touch. B. J. was sad and made me promise to do this again. As I've said, I have always liked beginnings better than endings.

After two great days with my grandson, I felt a letdown on the drive home. Turns out, listening to talk radio is not a remedy, in theory or reality. Both the form and the substance of the bickering between the two polar opposite journalists were indicative of jerkwater reporting. Journalism had gravitated to an embarrassing level.

The iconic Hunter S. Thompson stated that "journalism is not a profession or trade. It is a cheap catch-all for fuck-offs and misfits." He also said that "there is no such thing as objective journalism. The phrase itself is a pompous contradiction in terms." In a softer criticism, Norman Mailer claimed that "if a person is not talented enough to be a novelist, not smart enough to be a lawyer, and his hands are too shaky to perform operations, he becomes a journalist." On the other hand, as in most professions, there are talented and admirable journalists, several that I know personally. Strangely, seems it's always the idiots who get the spotlight. I turned off the radio, but the theme of growing incompetence played on.

Take the country's infrastructure. Without the technology or the sophisticated equipment of today, our predecessors built a transcontinental railroad in six years. In contrast,

Californians have tried to build a high-speed rail line. At this point, they have all but given up after more than a dozen years of government incompetence, lawsuits, cost overruns, and incessant bureaucratic bickering, still without one foot of track laid. The same story for roads, airports, major bridge repairs, dams, and water projects. Our ancestors were builders who strapped their boots on, went to work, and finished the job. Today, we experience idleness, whining, and delay from regulators, bureaucrats, auditors, critics, plaintiffs, defendants, adjudicators, media rebels, and of course, politicians. Sadly, on scale, our distant generations were, on a relative measure, arithmetically more competent than today.

Once again, the drive was comfortable. The sun set and the colors of magenta and blue segued into a dark gray before settling into a thick black shroud. My thoughts turned to the cast of characters of Jekyll Island. Suspicions aside, there was something going on that just didn't pass the smell test. What I had to do was provide definition. I was sure that the woman, Marylyn, could provide insight, but she would have no reason to talk to me without some incentive . . . or leverage. Ghulam was off that list as well, and Hafeez was complicit.

Eventually, I arrived at a plan. With the cooperation of certain people and the right circumstance, it could work.

Ten hours of driving had taken its toll. When I got home, I wanted only one thing, so I went to the bedroom, stripped, jumped in bed, and was asleep in minutes.

CHAPTER 22

The next day was a lazy one. Free to be, so to speak. I slept late and got caught up on my pile of reading. Curtis and I agreed to cocktails at five thirty.

The tension was palpable as I walked to the table. The usual affable expression was replaced with concern as Curtis nodded toward the center of the dining room.

Hafeez and Ghulam were sitting at the window table. Two tables over sat the two bodyguards. The big man noticed me and started to get up, but his partner grabbed him by the sleeve and pulled him back down. Our eyes met. I gave him a pleasant smile and raised my walking stick in mock salute. I now took the Zap with me at all times. He couldn't hide his hatred, and I took pleasure in that.

"You look uncomfortable, my friend," I said to Curtis.

"Don't think that big boy is going to let it go, Woody."

"Not to worry, I can handle that tub-o-lard. My real concern is that we keep a low profile with Ghulam and Hafeez."

"You know, I don't see a phone booth, Clark Kent."

We shared a grin.

"Don't need it, Laddie, not with me magic shillelagh," I said with a passing Irish accent, lifting my walking stick.

He just shook his head.

"Anyway, forget them. I want to bounce something off of you."

"Why not? In for a penny . . . You're not the only senior citizen who can throw caution to the wind."

I shared my conclusions about the players before presenting

my plan. "Our next step is to find out what's in those books that Hafeez is always working on. Think I've got a quasi-legal way of doing that." My impish smile didn't make the sale.

"Quasi-legal?" he asked.

"Okay. So what I'm hoping is that such a likable celebrity as yourself might have a personal relationship with one of the cops on the island." I let that dangle before his suspicious look.

"Well, it so happens that I do. Why?"

"Good, so tell me about the relationship," I said. "Can you trust him?"

"He was a student at one of the colleges I consulted for. On top of that, his mother is Seneca. Yes, I trust him. I wouldn't want to jeopardize his position in any way, however."

"Not a problem, and know that I would never ask you to. He just has to do his job and be discreet about his source."

"Well then, what are you thinking, Sherlock?"

"Hafeez is always here for hours, drinking wine. She seems to pace herself well, but let's say one night she has one too many, gets stopped on the way home, and is over the limit. She would be taken to the station, and her car would be towed. So let's say that from the time she was taken to the station and when the tow truck showed up was around twenty minutes. Seems to me a phone camera could get some pictures of those books, huh? And from the cop's standpoint, all on the up-and-up, right?"

Curtis thought about that, then formed a conspiratorial smile. "She *would* be breaking the law."

CHAPTER 23

After a late afternoon call the following day, Curtis and I met for coffee at a place called *Cup-A-Joe* with a reputation for homemade pastry, just like Granny made. It had rained most of the night, and we both had umbrellas.

"I met with Patrolman Monroe," Curtis said. "He doesn't see any kind of conflict in tagging any driver who is under the influence. Frankly, for what sounds like personal reasons, he has a low tolerance level for drunken drivers. He said he would follow the usual protocol, which included the car being locked when the tow truck arrived. He didn't want to know anything about why I was interested in doing this. He's by the book, Woody. I suggested that this woman could be involved with some kind of illegal activity. He was most reticent to go beyond his duty. He did say that sometimes he's pushed the wrong button on those keyless remote fobs, however." Curtis was appropriately protective of his friend.

"Perhaps that part of the plan can work. Hopefully, the car is unlocked when we get there. We'll lock it when done, and nothing will ever be tied to what's inside." I hoped my assurance quelled his apprehension.

"Yes, indeed. This is, of course, far more your bailiwick than mine, but let me know where I can assist. I recall Sherlock claiming, 'Never trust to general impressions, my boy, but concentrate yourself upon details.' Something like that anyway."

"Yes, Watson, our next goal may require assistance from your friend, the bartender. And so, Mr. Holmes also said, 'It is a capital mistake to theorize before one has data. Insensibly one begins to twist facts to suit theories, instead of theories to suit facts.' Together we shall advance the cause by accumulating data."

I couldn't help but laugh when he raised his hand for a high five.

Five days later, the ideal circumstance arose at the club. There were very few people, and Hafeez was alone and seemingly frustrated. She was working her books and the computer and was on the cell phone from time to time. Curtis and I gabbed while keeping watch. She had had several glasses of wine. Curtis had paid his friend Thomas, the bartender, for a bottle of expensive wine and said to send it to Hafeez, compliments of the management for her loyalty and ongoing patronage. She had initially resisted, but then poured a half glass. When she followed that after a while, filling the glass, it seemed as though it would be enough to do the trick.

Curtis stepped out and called Patrolman Monroe to alert him to the status of things, and he confirmed he was on patrol. When she poured another half glass, nearly chugged it, and started packing her stuff, apparently emotional, we were prepared to follow. I knew her route home, so we were most discreet. After a little more than a mile from the club, the patrol car passed us with its flashers on, and we pulled over, well behind the two cars. We watched as Hafeez got out of the car and apparently "walked the line." We saw her arguing with Monroe, who eventually put her in the back of the patrol car and drove off. Once they were out of sight, we drove behind Hafeez's car, hoping it was unlocked. It was.

I ignored her computer. There were two sets of books, the first much like a bookkeeper's ledger with financials: income statements, balance sheets, schedules, the kind that could be audited. The second was more cryptic, with numbers and letters, maybe initials. The book was simply titled *2018*. Because of time restrictions, I did the second book first. There were eleven months, January to November, and to include the many notes, forty-four pages. In a flyleaf were tucked away what appeared to be contracts. The ledger was quite redundant on the other hand, so I just took pictures of the most recent pages. When finished, I replaced the books exactly as I had found them, wiped off any prints, locked the car door, and went to Curtis's car. Luckily, there were no cameras that we could find that would have recorded the scene.

Curtis had access to equipment that would print out the pictures in legible form. Once that was done, we each took a copy and agreed to meet at my place the following day. There's no way I was going to be able to sleep, so when I got home, I fixed a pot of coffee and started to absorb.

There was nothing about the ledger that raised an eyebrow, but then, I was not a CPA, nor a bookkeeper, nor a guy who balanced his checkbook. Still, I wanted to double-check and so made a note to see if Curtis might have a qualified accountant friend. The other book, in contrast, was a puzzle. If I had been into sudoku, it might have helped. As it was, I accepted the challenge.

This book, too, was a ledger of sorts. As I stared at the pages, I couldn't help recalling Churchill's definition of Russia: "a riddle wrapped in a mystery inside an enigma." It was arranged by month. There were multiple headings under which were letters, maybe abbreviations, maybe initials, or some kind of crypto IDs. One thing I had gotten from the ledger was the locations of the Arabian Knights stores, and I was able to pair the initials up with the Sanskrit location identifiers. Alphabetically, the company had twelve stores located in Atlanta, Atlantic City, Baltimore, Boston, Daytona, Miami, Myrtle Beach, New York City, Philadelphia, Richmond, Virginia Beach, and Washington, DC. Hafeez used first initials except for *AC* for Atlantic City, and *MI* for Miami, and *MB* for Myrtle Beach. Geographically they appeared to be almost evenly spaced between New York and Miami.

The more I looked at these pages, the more I began to see that I may have overrated the sophistication of the encryption. I didn't believe that Hafeez was using cipher codes that would require Alan Turing or "Wild Bill" Donovan, who broke the German Enigma Code, but rather it was her own rather simplistic way of hiding business transactions from amateur scrutiny. Whatever this business was that was going on, it was obviously illicit on some level. The interpretation of the headings would tell a story.

Each month had ten headings, ten columns, and no notes. Backup pages were the notes. The headings consisted of *L*, which I figured was location, then *C*, *R%*, *PH*, a series of ten numbers which were likely phone numbers, *HK*, *HKSTAT*, *HKMEDST*, *REVOLVDES*, *DEL/PU*. On the surface, it seemed a hodgepodge, but after I read the accompanying notes, things began to make sense.

After a pot of coffee and two more hours of concentrated study, the puzzle began to unfold and form structure to an operation that was clandestine at best, but more likely nefarious and illegal. Reality would say it was conjecture, but my intuition and experience told me it was something else.

When I checked my watch, it was 2:30 a.m., and I needed sleep. Curtis was coming by for lunch, and we would coordinate our thoughts and analyses. I fell into a deep sleep and dreamed. This time it was a good one.

CHAPTER 24

Curtis said he was bringing some submarine sandwiches. I saw him drive up front just before noon and walked out to greet him. My awareness radar was always turned on, and so I noticed a white van parked down the street. It was familiar. I had seen the same kind of van at the marina.

As I shook hands with Curtis, the van started up and drove past us. Ghulam's bodyguards stared at us. The big guy was driving.

"Did you notice if you were followed?" I asked Curtis, nodding at the disappearing van.

"Sorry, Woody, guess I was paying too much attention to the directions. What are you thinking?"

"Ghulam's goons," I said.

"Probably not dropping off a housewarming present, huh?"

"More like a scout patrol, I figure," I said, opening the screen door.

"Need I say, watch your back?"

"Always do, *mi amigo*," I replied, noodling the implications. Since I was convinced that Ghulam was a pretty smart guy who would avoid controversy, I figured these two mental midgets were off of the compound in search of revenge. I shook my head. I wasn't surprised. With an aggregate IQ of under fifty, this breed was usually visceral in their actions. I would have to deal with it . . . later.

We sat out back on the patio, enjoying the thick submarine sandwiches with Sam Adams.

"So," I said between bites, "you reach any conclusions, reading those papers?"

"Well, first of all, I must admit that my review was a cursory one, as it was late and I was beat. Also, contrary to some opinions, I do know my own limitations. This kind of decoding is certainly better analyzed by a black ops intelligence geek than by me, but that said, I do have several generic opinions. For one thing, Mr. Ghulam certainly doesn't need bodyguard protection because he sells trinkets. He must feel threatened on some level. Secondly, from what I read, this operation is far too complex for several retail import shops. There are way too many people involved. Finally, this elaborate exchange of presents every month gives me suspicious pause. That off the top of my head."

"I think you would have fit in quite well with my unit, Doctor. You undervalue yourself, and I endorse your conclusions. That being said, let's go through these crypto sheets. Before that, if you happen to know a CPA, I would like to know if he finds any "red flags" in the income statements and balance sheet book. I think it's prepared for an external auditor, so I don't expect any surprises.

"The other book is a bit more cryptic, though after cross-referencing with the notes, not so much. It tells an interesting tale, but I'll save my conclusions for the end, so let's start back with the first four pages: January and the three pages of notes. I'll tell you that these abbreviations are meant to be just a simplistic disguise to confuse a cursory review. I drew my interpretations reading the notes and the contracts. Even considering my background, it wasn't that difficult. If I'm correct, we can reach certain conclusions about what's happening here.

"In regard to the headings, *L* is clearly the location of the stores. Per the contracts, the *C* is either *customer* or *client*. *R%* is interesting, and I believe it stands for *percentage of risk*, maybe assigned to the client. *PH* is simply a phone number, although disguised by reversing each sequence of numbers, amateur stuff.

"Now, here's where it gets a bit interesting. You remember the consulting company we found under Hafeez named Zeefa? Well, the contracts are between Zeefa and 'the client' and separately between Zeefa and 'the housekeeper' and a third one between 'the client' and 'the housekeeper.' If my guess is right, Ghulam is a major shareholder, if not a majority shareholder in Zeefa. The reported assets of Zeefa are around a million dollars. My guess is that they're more, but put that on hold for the moment. The *HK* heading is for *housekeeper*, a person yet to be defined. *HKSTAT* would follow as *status* or *statistics* of the housekeeper. *HKMEDST* would perhaps imply the *medical status*. You tracking with me?"

Curtis simply nodded.

"Okay, so *REVOLVDES* remains a mystery, though I have my suspicions, and *DEL/PU* would logically be *delivery and pickup*. Since the locations of the stores are the entries under *REVOLVDES*, and they change every sixty days, I surmise that it stands for *revolving destination*. If you process this in light of my conclusions, what do you see?"

Curtis was quiet for a long time. Eventually he shook his head and said, "Woody, I'm genuinely hesitant to give you my impression. It's disturbing."

"There's more, starting with *Sources* as referenced on page three of her notes. She lists five countries with five names. Pakistan-Dalir, Russia-Nikki, Iraq-Zamir, Syria-Nabil, and Lebanon-Immad. She underscores *Requirement/Mission: complete and total satisfaction of client* in several notations, including the contracts. In another note, she refers to three incentives: citizenship, Rm/Bd, and $1K/mo. Another note of interest is *Shipping-$300/hd-Dalir*. Perhaps the parts seem disjointed, but when you look at the composite, it tells a story. I believe we're looking at a pretty sophisticated human trafficking operation."

We looked at each other for a while, not speaking.

Finally, Curtis said, "If that's the case, it's a whole lot bigger than you and I."

"I agree with you, but with the caveat that we need to gather a lot more evidence before we take it to the feds. They can fuck up a wet dream and will blow this out of the water. What I want to do next is to bring Tommy down here for a day. You'll both like and appreciate him."

"From everything you've told me about him, I have no doubt," Curtis said with an emphatic nod.

I poured Curtis a glass of high-test sherry that I had picked up, and we switched gears and talked about unrelated things.

"You know, Woody, I watched a passionate debate on TV this morning and realized that I'm becoming less and less tolerant of reporting, or maybe it's just reporters. Whatever has happened to the wise men?"

"Somebody once said that people will stand for anything, and what they won't stand for, they'll fall for. Like you, it's been difficult for me to have to continually lower my expectations, but necessary for my mental health. The masses aren't only willing to accept, but even applaud, untruths, distortions, fabrications, and worse . . . ineptitude, and so it will continue to flourish until there is proper resistance. At that point, however, those opinions have become widely held, usually with great passion."

"Just because opinions are widely held is by no means evidence that they aren't utterly absurd," Curtis replied. "In fact, quite the opposite. A wise man might conclude that opinions held with passion are those for which no good ground exists and may be the holder's lack of rational conviction, as often seen in religion and politics."

"So let's not forget what Bertrand Russell said: 'A stupid man's report of what a clever man says can never be accurate, because he unconsciously translates what he hears into something he can understand.' As history has shown, wise men may argue causes, but fools decide them."

"Indeed, the wise man will process," Curtis said. "He will hear and heed his inner voice with a sound mind and purehearted critical thought process, immune to the cries of the self-righteous, resistant to the mentality of the herd, external manipulation, and internal self-delusion, so is the persistent challenge to the wise." Curtis was lost, peering at a distant cloud. "It seems that the great and the wise are misunderstood."

"If I'm not mistaken," I chimed in, "it was John Dryden who wrote a pertinent couplet: 'Great wits are sure to madness near allied, and thin partitions do their bounds divide.'"

As we smiled at each other, Curtis suddenly chuckled before he spoke. "Several weeks ago, I read an anecdote about when Albert Einstein first met Charlie Chaplin. I paraphrase, but Einstein said to Chaplin, 'What I admire most about your art is its universality. You do not say a word, and yet the world understands you.' And Chaplin replied, 'It's true, but your fame is even greater! The world admires you, when nobody understands you.'"

We laughed and nodded agreement.

CHAPTER 25

After Curtis left, what had been weighing on my mind returned. Bruce Lee claimed that the superior warrior is just an ordinary man . . . with laser focus. The word *laser* was now my focus.

I had been to this rodeo before. The two low-intelligence musclemen had been humiliated by an old man, and they sought revenge. Forrest Gump said, "Stupid is as stupid does," and these two fit that profile. I would have to slam this door shut if they did what I suspected they would do.

I found a building-materials store several miles away that carried what I needed: laser sensors like those that signal garage doors. The place I was renting had access to the backyard from both sides of the house. The access was narrow, however, as thick arborvitae hedges separated the properties. I picked up two sets of sensors, one for each side of the house, a buzzer connection, and a 12-volt battery. On the drive home, I stopped at a sporting goods store and bought a Louisville Slugger.

Setting up the lasers took about an hour. The plan took another hour. I would leave the front light on, forcing them to the backyard. I would leave a low-wattage bulb on in the back bedroom, with the shade only partially closed. Over the years, I had seen various shows about prison breaks. In the 1930s and '40s, a bank robber named Willie "the Actor" Sutton escaped from the penitentiary by shaping his body asleep in bed. I borrowed his idea. These two gorillas would wait until I was asleep and arrive after midnight. I had everything in place in time for a late dinner of mac-and-cheese, tested the buzzer, strapped on my ankle holster, and then dozed for an hour. I was back up by eleven, made coffee, and settled in to wait.

Turned out, I didn't need the lasers after all. Ah well, better safe than dead. Sometime after midnight, I heard the intruders before seeing their shadows pass on the left side. When I knew they were around in back, I grabbed the hickory bat and quietly went out the front door, following their path. What came next was quick and pernicious.

When I peered around the corner of the house, the big man was about twenty feet away, peeking in the bedroom window. The hefty one was about eight feet away with his back to me. When I got within about three feet of him, I did a John Henry overhead, pile-driving swing of the slugger, and the sound told me that his right clavicle was shattered. He screamed and fell to the ground. The big man turned, went for his knife, and charged me. When he was within four feet, I went to the ground, starting my homerun swing about two feet off the ground. I could feel the pain when the wood met the kneecap, followed by a screeching moan. When I got to my feet, I saw that there was no threat. To cover my ass for any investigation, I kicked my door in before calling 911, suggesting two ambulances.

Interestingly, though he didn't know who I was, I recognized the patrolman who arrived just before the ambulances. It was Curtis's contact, Monroe.

"This certainly appears to be a robbery gone bad, Mr. Woodward," he said while writing in his notebook. "Did you play for the Yankees?"

My phony guffaw was almost embarrassing. "Guess it's lucky I woke up when I did. That's a mean-looking knife," I said, pointing.

"Just curious, Mr. Woodward, but how old are you?"

"Seventy-four," I replied.

"So what did you do before you retired?"

"Government work," I said.

He gave a questioning nod and wrote in his book. "Seems you can take care of yourself. Actually, I would have to think twice before getting into a scrap with you." He did a version of a stare down.

I gave a friendly smile.

"You missing anything?" he asked.

"Nope, caught 'em just as they were breaking in," I said, still smiling.

There was a long pause.

"Okay, then. I might have some more questions later. You going anywhere?"

"Nope, just trying to get back to enjoying my retirement."

He gave me an apprehensive nod and left after handing me his card.

CHAPTER 26

After brewing a pot of coffee the next morning, I called Curtis to tell him about the late-night activities.

"What the hell, Woody, are you some kind of ninja warrior? Are you aware of your age?"

"'Let your plans be dark and impenetrable as night, and when you move, fall like a thunderbolt.' So said the iconic Sun Tzu. Preparation, not magic. In any event, a minor irritation eliminated. By the way, your buddy, Monroe, was the investigating patrolman. Cautious fellow. I'm going to try to get Tommy to come for a visit, but let's you and I plan dinner tomorrow night, say five thirty or so. I've got some repairs today."

"I'll book it, my friend." Curtis signed off.

I spent the rest of the day repairing the back door after taking a picture, should I need it. I had some other chores as well and did do some planning for the holidays. Christmas was coming. I figured I owed myself a treat as well, so I grabbed a dozen crab legs, a bottle of wine, and found an interesting program to take me away from current events.

The program was a documentary about EI, *emotional intelligence*. I was sure it was now incorporated into the intelligence community curriculum.

It seems that a high number of psychologists and many business recruiters today feel that EI is the key to both personal and professional success. Measuring EI, or technically, EQ, *emotional quotient*, is relatively new in the field of psychology, only first being explored in the 1980s. Both groups claim that it is the linchpin of mental toughness, that being defined as the ability to process strong negative emotions and turn them into something productive.

Unlike IQ, *intelligence quotient,* which is fixed, one's EQ is actually a flexible skill, one that can improve with effort and understanding. Data shows that close to 90 percent of top performers have high Eqs. Noted psychologist Daniel Goleman developed a model that shows that there are five key areas that comprise one's emotional intelligence: *self-awareness,* knowing one's feelings; *self-management,* the ability to control one's feelings; *motivation,* not just monetary and material, but the personal rewards of being productive; *empathy,* the skill to read and appropriately respond to the emotions of others; and *social skills,* such as negotiation and persuasion. In a study of one million people, the conclusion was that only about a third of them were able to accurately identify their emotions as they happen. One of the things I learned that was most insightful was the view that emotions are biological suggestions, not commandments. In other words, a choice. Difficult, but still a choice.

As Aristotle put it, "Anybody can become angry—that is easy, but to be angry with the right person and to the right degree and at the right time and for the right purpose, and in the right way—that is not within everybody's power and is not easy."

As with everything, I knew that for every yin in life, there's a corresponding yang. Like the high number of lottery winners who reach a point where they wish they'd never bought a ticket. For many of those, it wasn't, however, that they couldn't handle the money. They just couldn't handle themselves. In regard to EQ, I assumed there was an alternative view. I did my Google thing and found several opposing arguments.

There's one school of thought that concludes that high EQ people will be great managers and followers, but may not be visionary leaders and agents of change. They see a negative correlation between EQ and many of the traits, such as artistic moodiness, that predispose individuals toward creativity and innovation. They have trouble both giving and receiving negative feedback and will have a reluctance to ruffle feathers when it's needed. They, too, have a tendency to overuse their social skills to manipulate. In addition, by nature, they will be averse to risk, without which change cannot take place.

I found the topic to be impactful and grabbed a notepad, taking notes and forming questions to ask my psychologist guru, Curtis. I felt confident that after a cursory self-analysis, I was a mix, a mongrel, if you will. What I questioned was how much had been developed in the Darwinian world in which I'd lived, and how much was innate.

CHAPTER 27

When I awoke the next morning, I once again felt a strong sense of gratitude. It seemed the magnificent sunrise was an unearned gratuity from the higher power. I may have been feeling a touch of guilt from my severe response two nights ago, but rationalized that I had been pushed to remove the threat. A-plus on the self-awareness, a checkmark on self-management. That said, it was a quiet serenity.

Feeling the need to put some structure in my plan, I drove to the marina. The powerboat was moored to the levee, and there was no activity. I then drove by Marta's apartment. Again nothing, and the same at Marylyn's home. I saw what I had expected: nothing. I assumed I would see Hafeez at the club.

After that, I went to the small mall to look for ideas for Christmas presents for my family. I don't like shopping, but in this case, it was fun. I decided to spend a lazy couple of hours on Driftwood Beach before heading to the club to meet Curtis.

CHAPTER 28

When I sat down with Curtis, I noticed that both Hafeez and Ghulam were at their window table. At the table where Ghulam's former bodyguards used to be, sat a short, thin, pointy-nosed man with sleepy eyes and an overdose of Brylcreem in his slicked-down hair. The two previous goombahs who were currently either behind bars or still in the hospital, I can tell you from fifty years of experience, were benign compared to this guy. I could see that he was packing. He was lethal, and a professional.

I studied him for several minutes before turning to Curtis. "Something I gotta do, Curtis. Give me ten minutes."

I got up and walked to the table where Hafeez and Ghulam were talking. There was an empty chair. Without saying anything, I sat down and just stared at Ghulam.

His face expressed his anger. "Can I help you?" he asked.

I noticed that his new bodyguard had stood up. "It would be very much in your best interest to tell short-crotch over there to sit back down," I said, nodding toward his guy.

He paused and gave me a challenging stare, but something in my eyes made him turn to the man and gesture with his arm to sit, which the man did. He turned back, and for a long time, glared at me. "What's your business?" he finally asked.

I took my time before slowly and quietly saying, "I don't know who you are, nor do I give a damn. What I do know is that two oversized idiots who apparently work for you came to my house. Two weeks ago, my fourteen-year-old grandson came to visit me, and we were playing Frisbee down at the marina.

My fourteen-year-old grandson accidently ran into one of your boys, and he slapped my grandson. I asked him to apologize. He refused, so after warning him, I put him on his ass. Seems he wanted revenge, so two nights ago your boys came to my house in the middle of the night with designs on doing me great bodily harm. Didn't happen. They're both in the hospital with major injuries. Now, I don't know if you sent them or not. What I do know is this: should that oily little slick . . ." I nodded toward his table. ". . . ever come on my property, he will leave in a body bag, after which I will come looking for you." I breathed a big sigh. "I'm a simple retiree who is not aware of any conflict you would have with me, so if that's true, we can agree that there will be no repeat episodes. Do you agree?"

He processed what I had said before speaking. "I wasn't aware of their behavior, nor would I ever condone such behavior, and I can assure you that I did not send them to do you harm. Yes, I agree." He watched me with a quizzical look and finally asked, "What is your name?"

I stood up before answering. "Good to hear," I said. "Bruce Wayne."

He showed no reaction, but Hafeez muffled a snicker. I walked back to Curtis's table, noting that Hafeez was familiar with Batman.

"Was that wise?" asked Curtis as I sat.

"It was necessary. After the other night, I didn't want any more late-night visitors. Now he's been warned. And as I suspected, he knew nothing about the attack. Keep in mind that he has no idea that I'm looking into his affairs. What he does know now is not to fuck with an innocent old retired guy. More importantly, I got that message to Hafeez. The time will come when I'll want her to know that."

I watched as his new hire stared back at me until Hafeez whispered something to Ghulam. He glanced at me, then at his henchman, and with a stern look, gave him a hand signal to turn around. He did. I smiled. Successful dog training . . .

at least for now.

"So, my friend, that done," I said, "let's catch up on things. I talked to Tommy, and he'll be here on Thursday for a nice dinner." I gave Curtis the happy look.

"Bruce Wayne, really?" is all he said, shaking his head.

"Caught that, didja? Bit more subtle than Clark Kent, don-cha think?"

He just gave me a funny look. After he stared out the window for a bit, he turned to me. "'Mysteries abound where most we seek for answers.' So said the writer Ray Bradbury. I feel like we're in the middle of a Bradbury novel. We have suspicions, we conject based on a lot of circumstantial material, but we lack evidence and proof. So where do we go from here, Woody?"

"Well, it may have been Tolstoy who said that 'we're penetrating the unknown and fashioning our actions in accord with the new knowledge thus acquired,' and so we keep digging. I sent the Hafeez material to Tommy and his team for their analysis. I'm hopeful I'll have a convincing enough argument to get Marylyn's attention and perhaps the proof we need to bring the authorities in."

"But not too soon, huh?" Curtis gave me a questioning look.

"When they do come aboard, it has to be a shock-and-awe approach. Hafeez has done a good job at disguise. Without undebatable proof, they'll skate. At this point, we just don't know if their operation is illegal. If it is what I suspect, I show 'no quarter,' going along with the view of General Antonio Lopez de Santa Anna."

"Well, in line with recent events, I wouldn't want to be in their shoes," said Curtis.

"Come on, Curtis, I'm really just a teddy bear."

"Teddy? More like grizzly."

It wasn't long until Hafeez and Ghulam got up together and left, followed by Little Slicky. We watched them go, but not before Ghulam turned his head toward me and gave a rather obsequious nod.

"Hope I made them uncomfortable," I said, smiling. We were quiet until I asked, "Speaking of Santa Anna, you ever been to the Alamo?"

"I *am* from Texas. Duh."

"Well, of course. I did read an interesting book, Curtis, and since I think lots of Texans are crazy, present company excluded, wondered if you're aware. The book is titled *The Immortal 32*, written by a Texas gal, cheerleader type. You familiar with it?" I could detect the knowing smile on Curtis's face.

"Go on," was all he said.

"Well, you'd know better than I, but in 1836, many of the residents of south Texas were called Texians, kind of a hybrid Texan and Mexican. About a hundred Texians had taken refuge in the Alamo mission. With all the skirmishes going on with Mexico, Colonel William Travis and Jim Bowie took command of the mission, and the number grew to about a hundred fifty, including old Davy Crockett. Travis sent out a scout, who came back and reported that hundreds of Mexican soldiers, under Santa Anna, were headed their way. Travis read the tea leaves and knew he needed lots of help, so he wrote letters to General Sam Houston and anyone else who would listen, pounding the patriot drum. Nobody came, and on February twenty-third, the siege began.

"Here's the interesting piece. Seventy miles to the east of San Antonio is the small town of Gonzales. One of the town residents was a doctor who had passed by the Alamo mission and passed on to the residents that Travis needed help. Thirty-two men ranging from fifteen to sixty-three years decided that it would be Texas and freedom, or death. In the dead of the night of March first, they finessed their way past hundreds, if not thousands, of Mexican troops and into the Alamo. The Alamo defenders now numbered just shy of a hundred ninety. The Mexican troops were several thousand. For five days, they took potshots at each other until the morning of the sixth, when Santa Anna's troops stormed the mission, and within ninety minutes, all but three or four of the defenders were dead, as well as around fifteen hundred Mexican soldiers, and the last man standing was Crockett himself, according to one survivor.

"So in the overall scheme of things, the thirty-two patriots from Gonzales were only a footnote—until this year, when they were celebrated at the Alamo as the 'Immortal Thirty-Two.' My kind of guys. My kind of story. What say you, Dr. Red Crow?"

"Woody, you're a great storyteller," Curtis said. "Interesting, passionate, involved, and even though I was aware of the thirty-two Texians from Gonzales, I wanted to hear you tell the story. And yes, they were patriots, the kind that are disappearing from our country's landscape. That, however, segues into another discussion, one we might enjoy with your friend, Tommy." Curtis's look begged response.

"I appreciate your compliment, my friend. My passions are sometimes walking ahead of me. Tommy would jump right into the patriot game. We'll enjoy tomorrow's dinner."

CHAPTER 29

Tommy was idiosyncratic. One such example was his passion for waffles, so we met at a local spot that was only open from 7:00 a.m. to 1:00 p.m. and only served breakfast. The proprietor was in his sixties. He had been the cook at one of the biggest fraternity houses on the campus of Georgia Tech, where he was beloved and famous for his personality, his size, and mostly, his scrumptious belly-timber. He was a three-hundred-pound ganglion of effervescence and cholesterol, who was known as Biggie. No one seemed to know his last name. His shop was called *Biggie's Breakfasts* . . . what else? I had only been there once, but he remembered my name.

"Woody, my man, welcome back. Eggs Benedict, if my memory serves." He slapped me on the back and took me to a table by a big picture window.

"Your cognitive powers are most impressive, Biggie. I'm meeting an old friend who lives for a good waffle. I want to impress him."

"He will never forget Biggie's, Mr. Woody." Even his smile was a caricature.

Tommy walked in twenty minutes later. My first reaction was anything but selfless. He didn't look a day older than he had twenty years ago. Standing next to him, I might have been his dad. We didn't say anything at first, just looked at each other, grinned, and hugged.

"What the hell, Tommy, you find Ponce de Leon's map, or what?"

"Just genetics, old friend, not a workout regimen or some

oriental root stalks. My father died at ninety-five, and my mother is going strong at ninety-three." He took inventory of me. "You look pretty fit to me, Woody."

We shared a look of agreement, mine more like resignation.

Tommy continued. "Truth is, I needed a diversion. I was getting a little schizo with all the political crap that we were investigating, so a couple days on the road and a tourist center was what the doctor ordered. I have some updates and opinions on the stuff you sent me, but don't want to repeat myself, so let's wait until dinner. In the meantime, how about we take a tour of this place after we eat and drop my stuff at your place? Right now, I'm starved. You think they serve waffles at this joint?"

I smiled and nodded my head in the affirmative.

When we finished breakfast, Tommy sat back, patted his stomach, smiled, and said, "I've had waffles all over the world, but never better than these. Might be the almond extract, or something. Think the chef will tell me?"

I hunched my shoulders with an "I don't know" expression. I motioned Biggie over. "Well, Biggie," I said, "seems you exceeded my friend's expectations. He wants to know the secret sauce."

Biggie just smiled before replying, "Well, Mr. Woody's friend, I have a policy. I never tell the secret recipe until you come back a second time." He stood there, arms folded over his massive body, grinning in silence.

"Fair enough, Mr. Biggie. Like MacArthur said, 'I shall return.'"

When we walked to our cars, I told Tommy, "Not to worry, my friend. I'll get the ingredients to you, maybe as payment for your work."

We laughed. After we dropped off Tommy's stuff, he jumped in with me.

Since he was familiar with some of the players, I filled him in on the others, like Marta and the two goons I had put in the hospital. "Seems the more things change, the more a leopard doesn't change his spots. If you can't tell, I really love to mix my metaphors."

Tommy just grinned.

I drove past Marta's apartment, Marylyn's home, the marina, Hafeez's place, and then out to the driveway to Ghulam's home. After that, to change the pace, I drove him to the DuBignon ruins and historical site. I gave him my history lesson on the island and hinted at the longtime treasure hunt for the gold bricks.

The discussions and tour were most rewarding, reconnecting with someone who had been so integral and vital to my life. All those special moments. It might have been Dr. Seuss who said, "Sometimes you will never know the value of a moment until it becomes a memory." So why did I feel alone in this moment? A million feelings, a thousand thoughts, a hundred memories . . . but one person.

I had an uncle named Eli who was a curmudgeon, an antagonistic old goat. He accumulated wealth by self-serving and mercenary methods. He was, essentially, miserable. I visited him two days before he died. He had seemingly received some sort of divine intervention. He said to me, "Lance, for decades I took all the good moments and memories, never recognizing what they were, and I stuffed them in a bag—I should say a metaphorical bag—and I put that bag in the back of my closet behind my material goods. Yesterday, I went to find that bag. I've been going through it piece by piece. You were in there too. They were a salve upon my hardened, brittle heart. I know it's too late, but for at least one day, I've found a peace, one that I can share with someone." The man cried.

I was most uncomfortable, but I nodded as we drank a beer. I think I was about thirty at the time. I think of him now and then. He'd lost so much, for so long. I swore that I would never have that kind of bag in my closet.

Tommy broke the silence. "Woody, this is planet Earth. Can you read me?"

"Sorry, old friend. I was musing, in the clouds, I guess." I smiled at him. "So, how 'bout we grab a six-pack and relax before going to meet Curtis?"

He gave me a thumbs-up.

CHAPTER 30

There is certain reward in connecting people that you know and like. You already feel that they will like each other based on your own relationship with each. Still, they're people and thus hard to predict. As Yogi Berra said, "It's tough to make predictions, especially about the future." In the case of Tommy and Curtis, it was a successful matchmaking.

"Seems you've been in the intelligence game since Nam, Tommy," Curtis said.

"That's true, Curtis. The country had been a dormant volcano in the mid-1960s, just starting to boil. Then in 1968, the assassination of MLK, Bobby Kennedy, civil rights and Vietnam protests, the Cold War, and the fires burned and the cauldrons bubbled. Still, maybe a watered-down version of what's happening today. But there were lots of threats, lots of spooks, and in my business, lots of customers. I started as a consultant, and the government provided lots of clients. The intelligence departments within the government were disjointed and competitive. It didn't take long to realize that I didn't have the bandwidth to service the demand. I raided a couple of the 'initials,' CIA, NSA, ex-army and naval intel men and women, and even unsolicited contact from college grads with high credentials in the burgeoning field of computer science. Woke up one day with twenty-five people counting on me for a paycheck. I still fly under the radar, however. Don't need to advertise, and my clients like it that way." Tommy had always had a smooth and anodyne delivery. "I kind of miss those early days, Curtis."

"Don't we all?" Curtis said with a nostalgic smile. "Don't we all?" After a short pause, he continued. "And that segues into the topic of where you feel the country is headed. Tommy, I would consider you to be a bipartisan insider with access to some pretty interesting information." Curtis raised his eyebrows.

"Well, please consider this pure speculation, but as Sir Winston would say, there is a gathering storm. No doubt there are cracks forming in the very foundation of democracy as we've known it. If you're familiar with Lord Woodhouselee, Alexander Fraser Tytler, his most prescient claim was made over two centuries ago and has proven to be disturbingly accurate. He said that a democracy cannot exist as a permanent form of government and that the average age of the world's greatest civilizations has been around two hundred years. These nations progressed through this sequence: from bondage to spiritual faith, from spiritual faith to great courage, from courage to liberty, from liberty to abundance, from abundance to selfishness, from selfishness to apathy, from apathy to dependence, and from dependence, back to bondage. America has completed that cycle, Curtis."

"Aristotle claimed that republics decline into democracies and democracies degenerate into despotisms," Curtis said. "So what now, Tommy, back to bondage?"

"Well, we're talking interpretive definition for sure, but there are strong and influential forces within the government that are moving toward socialism, which, of course, has many forms." Tommy looked to the ceiling, forming his thoughts. "In 1963, Nikita Khrushchev spoke to the United Nations. Over time, he's been severely misquoted, but the essence of his message is relative. Call it extended paraphrase, but his claim was that America's children's children would live under Communism. I don't have his exact words, but it was something along the lines of, 'You Americans are so gullible. No, you won't accept Communism outright, but we will keep feeding you small doses of socialism until you will one day wake up to find you already have Communism. We will not have to fight you. We will so weaken your economy until you will fall like ripe fruit into our hands.'"

I had begun to feel like I was eavesdropping on a tete-a-tete, but was into the discussion. I kept my silence.

"You know, Curtis, much like the Tytler cycle, there's a template for the creation of a socialist state. It follows nine levels of control. One, control the media. Control the people's thoughts, control the people. Two, health care. Control health care, control the people. Three, poverty. Increase the poverty level and then provide for them. They won't fight back. Four, debt. Increase debt to an unsustainable level, then increase taxes, which will produce more poverty. Five, gun control. Remove the ability for the people to defend themselves, and you have a police state. Six, welfare. Take control of all aspects of people's lives, like food, housing, income, and the people become dependent upon the government, the last step in Tytler's cycle. Seven, education. Control what people read and listen to and control what children learn in school. Eight, religion. Remove the belief in God from the government and schools so that the people need only to believe the government knows what is best for them. And nine, class warfare. Divide the people into wealthy and poor, causing even more discontent so it's even easier to tax the wealthy with the support of the poor." Tommy spoke with resignation. "Sadly, America can put checkmarks after all of them."

I intervened. "So why do recent polls show that a majority of American millennials have such a favorable view of socialism, Tommy?"

We had been sitting at Curtis's table for some time, chatting and sipping cocktails. The room was about half-full. Hafeez sat alone at her table. I noticed that she occasionally glanced my way but gave no hint of recognition.

After the server had refreshed our drinks, Tommy

continued. "No easy way to answer that, Woody, so you'll have to settle for my opinion, which starts with socialism hasn't worked, and it won't work. The closest form of quasi success will be heard from the soft-socialist European Union countries, but they're stagnant and dependent upon other countries, mostly the US, for military protection. Russia and China still struggle with the legacy of genocidal Communism. Eastern Europe still suffers after decades of Soviet-imposed socialist chaos. The pan-Arabic socialism ruined the postwar Middle East. And how about Cuba, Nicaragua, North Korea, and Venezuela? Poor, unfree, and failed states. So why the attraction, or at least the growing trend? For one thing, massive immigration has changed the demography of the US. Almost thirty percent of Californians were born outside of the United States, in mostly poor, socialist countries, and these people are very naïve. Many have no marketable skills and don't speak English. They not only believe, but take for granted that the government will provide them social services, so they naturally support progressive socialism.

"Almost as a paradox, you have another perfect storm. The rich grieve because of their affluence while the poor suffer because of their lack. The very wealthy from Hollywood, Silicon Valley, corporate America, and Wall Street feel guilty about their unprecedented wealth, so they champion redistribution, subliminal penance that alleviates their guilt. The result is that the higher taxes don't really affect them too much, yet the middle class suffers.

"And then there are the universities, which manipulate the government to guarantee student loans, which in turn allows them to jack up college costs with no accountability. They aren't concerned whether their graduates can market their expensive degrees, while the grads become embittered that their high-priced degrees don't earn them competitive and commensurate salaries, and they now want some entity to pay their debts.

"Add to that, asleep-at-the-wheel Republicans who advocate free rather than fair trade that left so many unemployed, and you have a whole generation of broke college grads, impoverished immigrants, wealthy advocates of boutique socialism, and suddenly . . . the Cobra Effect." Tommy just stared at me.

"Remind me again," I said.

"It's simply where the solution is worse than the problem." Tommy raised his upside-down hands in the air. "As the story goes, there were once so many cobras in Delhi that there was a bounty placed on each dead one delivered to the government. At first, it worked. But then, entrepreneurs began breeding cobras for the income, and the authorities had to cancel the program. The breeders then released their snakes, and the cobra population exploded worse than ever." Tommy looked at both of us with that look that says, "Do any of these bureaucrats have an IQ over thirteen?"

Tommy paused while we each placed our dinner orders.

After ordering dinner, Tommy took several papers from his carrying case. "Okay, boys, sit back while I give you the whole megillah: fact, fiction and opinion." Tommy was in instructor mode. "There's a matrix here, so I'll start with the facts. There was nothing clever about the phone numbers. Hell, even you figured that out, Woody." Tommy giggled. "What my team was able to do was to convert those numbers to names and addresses. Further investigation revealed the profiles of those people, so now, if my analysis of this operation is correct, it should be no surprise that these are very wealthy, middle-to-older-age guys.

"So leave that for a moment, and let's move to other things." Tommy shuffled his papers before continuing. "Oh, and an interesting anecdote is that the Atlanta phone number is registered to a Ryan DuBruss, former husband of Marylyn DuBruss, now Marylyn Ottesen. And last year, the housekeeper at that location had the initial *M*. Perhaps *M* stands for

Mickey Mouse, but then it could stand for *Marta.*" Tommy gave me a smug smile. "In any event, we verified that Ms. Hafeez owns fifty-five percent of Zeefa, while Ghulam owns forty-five percent. Hafeez's travels are interesting, which I will get to, but know that Ghulam travels to Galveston and San Diego in the first week of every month."

"What's that about, Tommy?" I asked.

"Just conjecture, but hold that thought." Tommy grabbed another slip of paper. "Hafeez travels to the Middle East, but it appears to be random, probably a supply-and-demand response. She'll go to Pakistan, Syria, Russia, Lebanon, wherever, but always ends up in Sevastopol, on the Black Sea. From there she flies to Amsterdam and back to Atlanta, or sometimes, New York. In Sevastopol, a transport ship leaves and ends up in Galveston. If it does stop, it's outside the twelve-mile radius. So what's the cargo?

"We know the Zeefa operation has twelve locations. The twelve phone numbers belong to what I will call clients, each in proximity to the twelve Arabian Knights locations. The contracts are between Zeefa and these clients and between the clients and the so-called housekeepers. For argument's sake, let's say Zeefa is providing these housekeepers to the clients. Those Hafeez papers show that these HKs are clearly vetted relative to certain 'risks' to include contractual, medical, and contacts. Also, from the papers, the *Revol-Dest*, it could be revolving destination which implies that the housekeepers revolve between clients.

"And then you have that list of *Incent,* seemingly incentives, under which we see *Citshp*, guessing citizenship, room and board, cash allowance, and *Conseq*, again assuming consequences, of which some would be deportation, IRS, and physical threat. Keep in mind, the single requirement is client satisfaction." Tommy let those things sink in as he looked at Curtis and me. "My conjecture is simple logic. I believe this could be a rather sophisticated human trafficking operation, and the Arabian Knights business is the cover. I think it's been structured in a way that provides the perpetrators an escape route, should they be caught. And this may be a stretch. I think that the Arabian Knights/Zeefa operation may be one of three similar operations . . . maybe more.

"Whatever my thoughts, what I can tell you is that at this point, there is no case. It's all circumstantial. At best, probably illegal immigration violations, with limited consequences." Tommy sipped his drink and let it rest.

"Well, first let me thank you for confirmation that I'm not a conspiracy theorist," I said. "On the whole, we're humming the same melody." I spoke to Curtis as well as Tommy. "From my perch, the only thing that will legitimize an indictment would be eyewitnesses, and I intuit that we may have a couple of those. Also, the only way to pin them down is through the former Marylyn DuBruss, so my next connection is clear." I nodded to Tommy, looking for confirmation.

They both nodded in agreement.

"So what's next for you, Tommy?" Curtis asked.

Tommy formed a thoughtful expression before looking at me. "Woody, do you remember Jack O'Brien, the Irish capo?"

"Of course. Plucky SOB. Got a Bronze Star, as I recall."

"You got it. Well, Jack joined the FBI after Nam. Looked like he was a rising star until he hit the skids on a drug raid. Self-control issue, as I understand. Most didn't disagree with what he did, but you know how it goes. The brass said he showed a lack of self-restraint, and so they black-marked his file and he got demoted. After that, anger issues, he hit the bottle pretty hard, a divorce, usual stuff. Then an angel appeared. He met a gal who, as I hear, kicked his ass with some tough love, and he rehabbed. Sadly, his star had fallen, and he was stigmatized. In spite of that, he found a senior position in the Bureau's Civil Rights Office of Victim Assistance. He was quite a bit younger than us, and I know he's about to retire, but I think there could be a mutually beneficial relationship there."

"Great idea, Tommy. Once we put this package together, that's exactly the resource we'll need. Any more little jewels, Mr. Hoover?"

"Just one. I have an insider down in the Caymans. If these guys are hiding assets in an offshore account, we might be able to wrap this thing in a pretty bow to hand off to the big boys." Tommy seemingly couldn't help his prideful smile.

"Remind me to never get on your bad side, Tommy." Curtis grinned, shaking his head. Things turned quiet before Curtis whispered, "Frail human nature."

A wistful inclination infringed our otherwise upbeat mood.

"Slavery encompasses more than race," Curtis added. "Follow the money, follow the power." He looked over at Hafeez.

"You seem surprised, Doctor," I offered.

"There are no more surprises, Woody, just sad realities, maybe."

"And so it is with injustice," I replied. "Justice and the law are oxymoronic. The gap between the two is wide and getting wider. Injustice is simply the world's largest whack-a-mole game. Justice is more of an ideal than a reality. If you let injustice get you down, you'll forever be on a downward spiral, my friend." I spoke with a sympathetic expression.

"Indeed, Woody. As far as I'm concerned, you can practice psychology all day without a license." After another pause, Curtis continued. "If it weren't such a heavy topic at this time, I would speak about more of the most egregious injustices in American history, but for the sake of collective attitude, I have to put that on hold for the moment."

Tommy took us in a new direction. "What are your plans for Christmas?" he asked us.

I had been thinking about my plans for Christmas for a while, until Mary Beth called and told me, not asked me, that she was coming to see me. Still, that seemed to fit this year. I'd bought my presents and sent them in the mail.

I needed to call my boys. "You know, Tommy," I said, "Christmas has become paradoxical, it seems. Probably happened when the commercial took over the spiritual. I remember the 1950s, even the '60s. And yes, I know that Christmas is a very different thing for a child than it is for an adult, many who feel great pressure that results in stress, and often, depression. But as a kid, it was a season of visions and wonderfully delusional. I went to Mass because if I didn't, I would burn in hell for eternity, but at Christmas, it was an enchanting adventure: the music, the outfits, the decorations and the shared joy. The whole story, really.

"And then there was Santa Claus. No one had told me yet that he was a fictional fellow. I found that out all on my own. Against my brother's attempt to stop me, I snuck downstairs to catch a glimpse of jolly old Saint Nick sliding down the chimney, but then I was a rebel, not a genius who would have noticed that a squirrel would have been challenged to do that. In any event, there was Dad, wrench in hand, putting my Schwinn together. And my mom, drink in hand, telling my dad, 'Don't forget to take a bite out of the cookie,' the one I'd left for Santa. Probably the most iconoclastic moment of my life, at least my young life. My brother was standing at the top of the stairs. He asked me what I saw. I remember thinking about that. Finally, I responded, 'Nothing. Must be too early.' It took a long time for me to fall asleep. After that, I just pretended." I looked at Tommy and Curtis with a nostalgic smile. "And so, I picture my grandkids. I'm sure B. J. doesn't believe in Santa, but the twin girls are as naïve as their parents, who I wouldn't be surprised still believe. In any event, my daughter has given me my instructions, and she'll arrive Christmas Eve morning."

"Seems she's no shrinking violet," Curtis said with a grin.

"Well, you'll find out," I said, "if you'll be around."

"Unfortunately, Woody, I won't be. I'm actually pretty excited about Christmas. An Oglala Sioux spiritual leader and former colleague has invited me to come to the Pine Ridge Reservation. There will be ceremonial dances. Most people don't understand that there has been a multi-century amalgamation of Native American pantheism and Christianity, in some cases going back four hundred years. One will experience many representations and perceptions. In American Indian tradition, Christ was a star person, an avatar. He was a Red Man, and a Hebrew, taught from the wilderness by great teachers like John the Baptist and Moses, and Jesus provided the foundation of the holistic method.

"The spirit of Christmas is pervasive in Native America. At every meal, a small portion of the food is offered to the spirit world on behalf of the four-legged and the winged, as well as the two-legged. We offer thanks to the grandfathers, the Great Spirit, and the guardian angel. The Indian culture is actually grounded in the traditions of a roving angel, as the lifeways of roving angels are the way Indian people live.

"Indians believe they have abundance. The Great Spirit has provided everything: water, the air we breathe, Mother Earth and the energy source, our heart. Indians pray before sunrise, to the morning star and the evening star. Indian people don't believe in taking without asking. Herbs are prayed over before being gathered by asking the plant for permission to take some cuttings, and an offer of tobacco is made to the plant for gratitude. The herbs aren't pulled out by the roots, but are cut with the surface of the earth so that another generation will be born in its place.

"In regard to gifts, the children are taught that to receive a gift is to enjoy it, and when the enjoyment is gone, they are to pass it on to another child so that they too can enjoy it. So daily living is centered around the spirit of giving and walking the Red Road. Walking the Red Road means making everything you do a spiritual act. The more one gives, the more spiritual one becomes. Indians will call it a Christ Consciousness."

When Curtis paused, I could feel his level of sensitivity.

"Know, too, that Native Americans have their own ten commandments, not in contrast but perhaps a simpler set of guidelines than what Moses found. They are as follows:

"'Treat the earth and all that dwell thereon with respect.
Remain close to the Great Spirit.
Show great respect for your fellow beings.
Work together for the betterment of all humankind.
Give assistance and kindness wherever needed.
Be truthful and honest at all times.
Do what you know to be right.
Look after the well-being of mind and body.
Take full responsibility for your actions.
Dedicate a share of your efforts to the greater good.'

"The ceremonies at Pine Ridge will incorporate all of these customs, traditions, and teachings. And they will open with a prayer credited to the great chief White Cloud of the Iowa Tribe. Like your Confederate soldier prayer, Woody, it's a personal favorite.

"'Oh, Great Spirit, whose voice I hear in the winds and whose breath gives life to all the world, hear me. I stand before you, one of your many children. I am small and weak. I need your strength and wisdom. Let me walk in beauty and make my eyes ever behold the red-and-purple sunsets. Make my hands respect the things you have made, my ears sharp to hear your voice. Make me wise so that I may know the things you have taught us, the lessons you have hidden in every leaf and rock. I seek strength, oh Creator, not to be superior to my brothers, but to be able to fight my greatest enemy, myself. Make me ever ready to come to you with clean hands and straight eye, so that when life fades, at the setting sunset, my spirit may come to you without shame.'"

We were quiet for some time, sipping drinks and absorbing what Curtis had said.

"That's truly beautiful, Curtis . . . and moving," Tommy said. "Can you send me a copy?"

"I'd be honored." Curtis made a note. "And both of you will be interested to know that as I leave Pine Ridge, I'll spend a day with a friend who has done much volunteer work for NAVA, Native American Veterans Assistance. He and his co-workers are vets who provide special assistance to older vets who need food, clothing, and shelter. You would hang your head at the abject conditions that so many honored vets must endure. They deserve better."

Tommy and I looked at each other. We were both aware of the injustice to the Native American veterans. No ethnic group had ever had a higher percentage of volunteers for military service. These were real warriors, twenty-four Medal of Honor recipients, patriots, and the government had left them out to dry when they left the service. We had both been honored to serve with them. We shared more than empathy, closer to anger and resentment.

"Well, I'm excited for your trip, Curtis. You're a genuine inspiration. I will say that you and Mary Beth would have been a real pair to draw to, but that event will happen at some point. In the meantime, what are your Christmas plans, Tommy?"

"As you know, I'm a traditionalist, maybe even retro. Christmas will always be as you described, visions of sugar plums and all that jazz. No frustration or depression for me. I love buying presents for the grandkids and some special gifts for kids and friends. A real tree that smells of pine with a thousand ornaments and a thousand presents underneath. It takes hours to open them all, plenty of photos and snacks, and a twenty-pound turkey with homemade cranberries. We love the church service and giving to the Salvation Army bell ringers and plenty of Bing and Nat and Elvis. I'll probably lose it when Celine does her version of 'O Holy Night.' We're anachronisms . . . dinosaurs, old friend. Accept it and move along down the road."

When he finished, he had what we used to call a shit-eating grin, which prompted the three of us to laugh out loud.

On the drive back to my place, Tommy said to me, "You know, I don't make a practice of disparaging my clients, but before we turn this thing over to the FBI, we need to have all of our ducks in a row. There have just been far too many shootings and deaths where it has come out later that the Bureau had been informed about the shooter, had them on their radar, profiled, and yet, not stopped. I know that most agents are solid, but my confidence level isn't high."

"You're singing to the choir, my man. Top of that pyramid is corrupt and incompetent, but I think we both know that our Irish capo won't put up with any bullshit when the time comes."

"Amen," Tommy said.

CHAPTER 31

M uch of my life has been mired in conspiracies. They were the bad kind, with bad people and bad intent, but not to-day. It was Tuesday. Christmas was Thursday. Tomorrow was Christmas Eve day, and my daughter was coming. I recalled another time, and another conspiracy, the one a man named Mabie referred to: "Blessed is the season which engages the whole world in a conspiracy of love."

I knew that I would relive some childhood memories as well and could understand what Laura from *Little House on the Prairie* meant. "We are better throughout the year for hav-ing, in spirit, become a child again at Christmastime." Was I really just a softy at heart? Did others see it? Did I care?

I thought about my Psych I class from over fifty years ago and the discussion about Johari's Window. Back in the mid-1950s, two psychologists whose first names were Joe and Harry, developed a technique for people to better under-stand their relationship with themselves and others. Self-help was a buzz phrase as the Minnesota Multiphasic Personality Inventory was developed and a mother-daughter team created the Myers-Briggs personality test. Johari's Window was used in settings primarily as a heuristic exercise. So, in layman's terms, life is like a window with four panes. The first pane is who you really are, known by yourself and others. The sec-ond pane represents who you believe you really are, known to you but not to others. The third pane is who others think you are, known to them but blind to you, while the fourth pane is the mystery of who you think others think you are. It's here that such things as self-delusion come into play. To me, this creation plays an interesting role in self-evaluation and our problem-solving and decision-making process.

People tend to complicate life. Me, on the other hand, I prefer to simplify. I see life as a simple balance sheet with math on one side and people/relationships on the other. Math is easy. People are difficult. Math is a controlled environment, often with black-and-white solutions or at least, options. "How am I going to pay my bills?" we ask.

The vast majority of our hundreds of daily decisions relate to this form of math, but people, with their feelings, their agendas, their brittle psyches—indeed, this is an art form. So I surmise that we make decisions from four parts of our bodies, each with different success records. Decisions I've made from my brain maybe have a success ratio of 70-75 percent. Decisions from my heart, oh, maybe about the same. From my groin, 10 percent at best. But my guts, I figure I have been right about 90 percent of the time. My instincts, my intuition, my learned experiences. Yup, I listen to my guts. As a betting man, that's where I put my money. Pretty simple, huh? And I know the hoards that want to argue those points with me, but I don't care. Come up with your own philosophy. If you don't like mine, go tell your priest, minister, or rabbi.

Tommy had left at the break of day. I jogged for two miles, showered, ate some PB and J toast, all the while giving my cognitive powers a workout. It was strange to me that in the center of this rather complex, potentially criminal structure was a rather, at least seemingly, benign woman who flew well below the radar. My visit with her would be delicate, and I would have to plan accordingly. I would need to think it through and provide a scenario that gave her little choice but to level with me. In line with that, I had a basic plan.

I had told Mary Beth that I would pick her up in Atlanta.

She told me that she was "a big girl" now and could actually rent a car "all on her own." "Two trips instead of four, Dad, and you should see these nifty gadgets called a GPS that can get me right to your doorstep." She did excel in the numbers business. Why not the sarcasm business?

So I went to a Walmart and bought her a Christmas present, a Fitbit, on the assumption that she worked out. If not, I'd get another zinger.

CHAPTER 32

Around noon the next day, a sporty little red car drove into the driveway. I walked out to the front stoop and watched as Mary Beth got out.

She cocked her head and looked at me with a questioning look on her face before she spoke. "Sir, I'm looking for a Mr. Woodward." She drew closer, and with an exaggerated surprised expression, said, "Dad?"

I stared back until she broke into a spasm of laughter, followed by a big hug.

"Just givin' you shit, Pops. Haven't seen you for a while."

I thought of the words to the song "Turn Around," sung by Belafonte. *Turn around and you're tiny, turn around and you're grown.*

She was quite stunning. She wore long brunette hair in a ponytail under a yellow ball cap with some weird logo on it. Her perfect teeth centered a magnetic smile. When she removed her Ray-Bans, her dark eyes glittered with the message that there was wonder and excitement everywhere.

She surveyed the neighborhood and assessed the house. "This place is you, Dad! You like it?"

"Surprisingly so, TeeBee. Comfortable house in a place I'd never heard of before." TeeBee came from *TB*, which stood for *tomboy*, the nickname she got when she was ten after she knocked Richie Goldberg on his ass for calling her a sissy. "I should probably be embarrassed to tell you how I wound up here, but you know me too well and won't be surprised." And so I did.

"Thanks for the confirmation of where my own whimsy comes from." She looked at her hand. "Wonder if my pointy finger has the same magic when I pick my stocks." Another laugh.

I grabbed her overnight bag while she grabbed a package with a big bow and a bag with handles, and we went inside.

She took a quick look around and peeked out the back window. "So let's have a glass of wine and sit out on your veranda," she said, with special emphasis on *ver-on-da*. "I picked up bottles of red and white just outside of Atlanta." She handed me the bag, from which I took out the wine. As I stared at the bottles, she again giggled. "Especially for you."

On the labels were two pictures of old geezers with bold letters: *OLD FART*.

"Salesman told me they had delicate aroma, body, and a necromantic taste . . . his term, not mine."

"Yeah . . . I'm sure that's why you bought it," I said in a grumpy voice, encouraging another giggle.

Contrary to what I wanted to say about the Old Fart, it was pretty good, but then I'm no wine connoisseur. Still, the day was a beauty. As we talked and I rediscovered my daughter, I was struck by her intelligence, her presence, and that certain guileless pulchritude that is the essence of so few. My furtive glances were unintentional, merely confirmation of my biased assessment. At one point, while washing my hands in the bathroom and absorbing my well-worn reflection in the mirror, it crossed my mind that perhaps I should have a DNA test to double-check that I really was her father.

"Enough about my job and the mad illusions of the financial markets," she said. "Have you done any painting?"

"Funny you should bring that up, as I picked up some art materials a few weeks ago, but they're still in the bag."

"Waiting for inspiration?"

"More so, that illusory respite of solitude that occasionally comes along."

"Good one. You and solitude are contrasting terms, or at least, strange bedfellows, Dad." She paused for a brief moment. "This may surprise you, but I've dipped my toes into the world of art . . . well, more in the philosophical-psychological end of it, I guess. I needed a deflection, so I bought a book titled *Great Art-Great Artists*. As I went through the book, I discovered something. I found it impactful as it related to my feelings. I had physiological responses to different paintings. A seascape or children playing on the beach would bring a smile, a gentle calm. Then, to study *The Scream*, the famous work by Edvard Munch, I found myself wrestling with anxiety.

"So I did the same with music, listening to 'The Sound of Silence,' by Simon and Garfunkel, then listening to the version by Disturbed. I could feel a change in blood pressure. So, paintings and music, why not poetry? Serenity came from Robert Frost, a walk on a snowy evening with miles to go before I sleep. In contrast, I found a poem that created the same anxiety as *The Scream*. An American educator and poet wrote it 120 years ago, titled 'Antagonish.'

"'Yesterday upon the stair,
I met a man who wasn't there!
He wasn't there again today,
Oh how I wish he'd go away!'

"Paranoia? Whatever. In any case, it seems I greatly underappreciated the power in art, and the exercise uncovered what I've taken for granted, and that I've been dismissive about its titanic significance."

We stared at the horizon and sipped our wine while processing her disclosure.

When she spoke again, she had shifted gears. "I know you can't keep your sticky fingers out of places they maybe shouldn't be. What intrigue is entertaining you these days?"

Most parents, I suspect, practice the primal instinct of

protection—or in many cases, overprotection, and in some ways, perhaps self-protection—when it comes to their kids. I was forthright with my kids, but here I chose to be selective. Nothing fun about human trafficking, so I told her about Curtis, and as I suspected, she was enchanted and regretted having missed him. I told her about my self-education of Jekyll Island history.

She was amused, with a hint of suspicion. "So nothing nefarious, huh?"

"Nothing I could talk about without having to dismember you," I replied and laughed, okay with my pale shade of cover-up.

CHAPTER 33

'Twas the night before Christmas,
and all through my pad,
My daughter was cooking a dinner for Dad.
'Twas spaghetti and meatballs instead of a roast,
And with butter and garlic,
she made my favorite toast.

What the hell, it was Christmas Eve, and the Old Fart had done its job. Still, I could probably apologize for the zany shit that comes out every so often, but then you already knew that.

"You remember that Christmas Eve when Aunt Bea had one too many Manhattans and fell asleep in the bathroom?" TeeBee asked me as she stirred the sauce.

"What I remember is that she was still sitting on the pot when your genteel brother, Winston, found her. I'll bet he still hasn't gotten over it." I chuckled as I sipped my Sam Adams, having finally abandoned the Old Fart.

"He went to his room and stayed there, as I recall. We'll call him after dinner. Maybe shouldn't bring it up, huh?" Her expression was a question.

"It would be fun for you and me, but yeah, probably not."

After dinner and cleanup, we got on the phone. As usual, Winston and Sam were staid, steady, and conventional, but always warm and comfortable.

B. J. was a dust devil of excitement. He fired questions at me like a Gatling gun. "How's Curtis? Have you seen those big guys again? How's your magic stick? Don't worry, Grandpa, I haven't told anyone. When can I come see you?"

We signed off with cheers and phone hugs.

Sonny and Barbara were in a different zone. If they had been imbibing, you could never tell. They were always flighty, as were the twins. Genetics can be a challenging study.

I poured two cognacs, and we sat down to open presents. I was pleasantly surprised that TeeBee was excited with her Fitbit. I too was excited with the *Victory at Sea* complete series CD set, which she knew I had loved. But also, there was a framed picture of the two of us on a ski hill from decades ago. I was genuinely moved. We toasted each other and sat back to a period of quietude.

Eventually, she spoke. "Gotta tell you, Dad, I've become disenchanted. Not with my job, so much, just life in general. What am I doing? Where am I going? Some sort of self-evaluation, I guess. Any advice?"

I thought about her dilemma and formed an incidental smile.

"What's so funny?" she asked defensively.

"Sorry, just recollecting. I'm familiar with your concern, so can I assume that among other things, you're feeling a loss of excitement, motivation, purpose, and even gratitude? A subliminal dissatisfaction with life, maybe, to quote Peggy Lee in 'Is That All There Is?' And, if I assume that to be the case, the common phrase is *midlife crisis*. The perception is that this is only a male regression. You know, sports cars and young women, but that's false.

"What if I told you that you're right on schedule for this phenomenon? There have been studies that go back decades, but the subject has again resurfaced with our new changing world. Technology, accelerated social change, and increased pressures all contribute. Understand that for most people, life satisfaction declines with age for the first couple of decades of adulthood and bottoms out, let's say somewhere in the forties to early fifties, and from there, will rise until one's final years, often reaching levels higher than young adulthood. This pattern has come to be known as the happiness U-curve, easy to visualize as a *U*. Those same studies found that the use of antidepressants peaked in people's midforties."

Mary Beth was nodding her understanding.

"What happens is the expectation gap closes as we get older. Gratitude returns as life grows shorter and people live more in the present, evaluating priorities to what is most meaningful. People become more comfortable with uncertainty and ambiguity, and several important traits take on greater significance, like wisdom and gratitude. The essence of life is now more than just the sum of its parts, so in the end, my dear, you're just part of the script. Acceptance, managing expectations, no guilt, few regrets, and consider yourself as part of the rule and not the exception. Make sense?"

My daughter took her time. Eventually she simply smiled.

"Few people have said it better than Mark Twain: 'When I was a boy of fourteen, my father was so ignorant I could hardly stand to have the old man around. But when I got to be twenty-one, I was astonished at how much the old man had learned in seven years.'"

We laughed together.

"Need I say more, Pops, other than thanks."

Since Santa had already been there and we could sleep in tomorrow, we did something trite after fixing a nightcap. We watched *It's a Wonderful Life*.

CHAPTER 34

I fried bacon, and Mary Beth and I had some of those little waffles you put in the toaster for breakfast. We got in my car and headed out for our adventure. I followed the same itinerary that Tommy and I had done. It was that poetic trip down memory lane with father and daughter laughing, pointing, and tossing barbs at each other, ending up on Driftwood Beach. There was a strong wind, and the rollers were crashing the shore. That's a sound that cannot be duplicated, an antediluvian echo from the eighth day of creation.

We got lost in our own worlds, wading, picking up shells, and watching children flying multicolored kites while applauding an athletic border collie that would leap a metaphoric mile and catch Frisbees in the surf. It was a milieu made for putting priorities in their right order.

Life is such a beautiful trip, but if I had the choice—not yet, of course—this would be a good place to die. A thought from da Vinci came to mind as I stared at a cruise ship moving across the horizon. All these years, while I thought I had been learning how to live, I have been learning how to die. When and where and how? I will put a twenty on thirty-six red, and in the final analysis, me and Marcus Aurelius agree: "Death smiles at us all; all we can do is smile back."

CHAPTER 35

We arrived at the club around six. I was relieved to see no Prius, no Ghulam, and no Hafeez. I was looking forward to a fun, quiet dinner with my daughter. She was leaving in the morning. It had been a great several days, and now, knowing TeeBee was a great fish lover, I could show off with the sea bass I. She ordered the drinks, two whiskey sours, delivered by William. I was sitting in Curtis's usual seat at our usual table. I wondered how Curtis was doing.

After a toast and a visual inventory of the dining room, TeeBee spoke. "You know, Dad, after mulling over our conversation yesterday, several things occurred to me. First, I really need to thank you for a discussion we had over twenty years ago, as I left for college. You lectured me about choices. You were emphatic about how critical our choices are in forming character and setting the stage for one's future. I specifically remember you saying that 'one bad choice could hurt you for the rest of your life.' Of course, I thought you were blowing that out of proportion, but it stuck with me. And now, every day I see or read about someone who has destroyed their life, their family, their financial future, their health, and their reputation, a consequence of one bad choice. And that topic is integral to and segues to our whole decision-making process."

"And here I thought I was just beating my gums. Still, if you didn't hear much, I'm glad you heard that."

"The second thing," she said, "is something I know will interest you. My firm is initiating a new marketing program based upon recent research about decision-making. I'm sure you've seen some of those ads on TV that discourage kids from using drugs and starting smoking. A fried egg representing a drug user's brain or the ugly, scorched lung of a smoker. Scare tactics. In a similar vein, our pitch will be to promote people's choices to make good financial decisions for their future. I'll tell you how in a minute.

"A British philosopher, Derek Parfit, reached a conclusion after years of study that humans are not a consistent identity moving through time, but a chain of successive selves, each tangentially linked to, and yet distinct from, the previous and subsequent ones. So that boy who decides to smoke, though aware of future consequences, does so because he really doesn't identify with his future self. Many psychologists now believe that this plays an essential part in human decision-making. Though we inevitably share their fates, the people we will become decades from now are essentially unknown to us. We consider that future self as if it's another person.

"Conclusion? This disconnect between our present and our future self has significant implications for how we make decisions. One might choose to procrastinate and let another version of our self deal with the problem. The boy who chooses to smoke will go with that pleasure-seeking version and just ignore the one who will pay the price. So we believe that by strengthening this connection between present self and future self, people will be more responsible in decision-making and choices."

TeeBee was right: I was most enchanted with her presentation. I held my thoughts as she continued, thinking this was right up Curtis's alley.

"Back to the question of how do we do that in financial planning. Well, it seems that when two groups of people were put into a virtual reality setting, one group watching images of their current self and the other seeing digitally aged images of themselves decades into the future, the latter group was far more inclined to increase their pension allocations and 401(k)

contributions. So, as a start, providing people with the opportunity to see these future images should create the motivation for future financial planning. We think providing access
to that option over the internet will initiate a beneficial result
in our marketing program. What do you think, Dad?"

"I get it. Interesting. In some ways, it's like the eraser on
the end of the pencil. Why didn't we think of that before? It
just makes sense. So the insurance and health care industries
will adapt to promoting weight loss. 'Do it now or you're gonna look like this old fatso.'" I spoke with enthusiasm.

"Indeed. I knew you would find it of interest," my daughter
said with palpable pride.

And I did the same when the sea bass arrived. She loved it.
Better than last time, and it was the dollop of whipped cream
on this metaphorical sundae of a Christmas holiday with Mary
Beth.

CHAPTER 36

Damn endings. I like beginnings. Mary Beth's little red sports car left my driveway at 6:30 a.m.

My funks don't ever last too long. A new year was coming, and I had things to do. I didn't have a "bucket list," as I avoided the phrase. Sort of sounded like a "kick-the-bucket list." Me, I just had a lot of shit to do, sans the reminder tag line of a droopy old fart editing his obituary. At this point, top of the list was a conversation with Marylyn.

The week between Christmas and New Year was always unpredictable. If Marylyn was around, it might be opportune. I did have a bit more planning to do, but decided to drive by her place. I did that and noticed the Prius was in the driveway. Since she hadn't left town, I figured that tomorrow morning would be as good a time as any for this intervention, which could either set the plan in motion or blow it up. *C'est la vie.*

CHAPTER 37

It was a brisk morning, but the sun was shining. Wispy strands of cirrus clouds moved slowly from west to east in a squad of Casper-like ghosts, watching, curious. I could almost hear Judy Collins singing, "Rows and flows of angel hair . . ."

I rang the doorbell. In my peripheral vision, I saw the curtain draw back. It was a long time before the door opened, but only the inside door, not the screen door.

"Yes?" she said, in a defensive pose.

I'm not sure why I was surprised that she was quite attractive. In her fifties. I suppose I saw her as adversarial, and the enemy is never attractive. My bad.

"Good morning, Marylyn," I said, letting it linger.

"I'm sorry, have we met?" She cocked her head with that questioning expression.

"Not yet, but I thought it was time." Again, I left that hanging.

Our eyes were locked for a bit.

"Really?"

More hang time.

"And just why did you think it was time?" She wasn't intimidated, and something about her body language gave me the impression that she knew who I was.

"My name is Woodward, and to relieve any concern of my presence here, I'll tell you that I'm only well-intentioned."

"Again, really? And pardon my redundant response, but I'm quite confused. So what might be those good intentions?"

"Well, would you consider inviting me in? I'm not a threat."

It took her a while to process the situation, but eventually she opened the screen, and in a voice that seemed to accept the inevitable, she dropped her bomb. "I suppose I would feel a bit more threatened if you had brought your walking stick."

We shared a knowing smile as I entered. I followed her to a curve-around leather couch and love seat setting. "You were at the marina, I take it?" I said.

"I have great admiration for grandpas who protect their grandkids, though the outcome of that encounter was quite the surprise. Not your first rodeo, I take it?" She gave me a genuine smile. "Please have a seat, Mr. Woodward. I have some fresh coffee if you're so inclined."

"I would appreciate that. Just black, please. And do call me Woody."

I watched her walk to the kitchen. Nice. When she returned, she set the cup down. "I was enjoying the view on that fine day from my car, Woody, in the upper lot of the marina." She smiled.

"The gray Prius," I said.

Her smile disappeared.

"The same one that often occupies the back lot at the club."

She absorbed that. She apparently felt no pressure to respond, so I continued.

"And you're Marylyn Ottesen, formerly Marylyn DuBruss. And now that you're trying to figure out this puzzle, let me say that my good intentions begin with a concern for Marta, if that's her name."

I kept my silence as she formulated a response. She was quite composed. "Well then, seeing as you know so much about me and the only thing I know about you is that you're some kind of well-seasoned ninja warrior slash knight in shining armor out to rescue the pretty maiden, it begs many questions. How about we start with you telling me who you really are?"

I couldn't help but smile at her description. And then I gave her a truncated but edited description of myself.

"So, a military man who morphed into a secret agent man who is now a retired grandpa living out his years in a vain attempt at solitude. So where does Marta fit?" she asked, I told her about the hitchhiker incident.

"Tender and sweet, Woody, but still doesn't add up. What's to be concerned about?"

"Okay, Marylyn, first let me say that both you and Marta were not only ancillary to my initial concern, but were late arrivals to the party. It was only after some investigation that you appeared on the radar and, seemingly, provided a critical piece to the puzzle." I thought about the next step and decided on full disclosure. "The beginning was pure coincidence prompted by an innate curiosity, a high-level intuition, and years of training." I proceeded to tell her about my relationship with Curtis and my initial suspicions about Hafeez, and later, Ghulam. I told her about my friend Tommy, but didn't name him. I told her that I had uncovered information that brought me to certain conclusions, to include her former husband and their former live-in employee, Marta.

"There's a great deal more that we could discuss, but I would need assurance that I can trust you." I let that dangle for a minute, with a certain intensity in our eye contact. "Bottom line, Marylyn, I believe there's a human trafficking organization that could be large-scale, headed by Ghulam and Hafeez."

She stared at me for some time. A knowing smile formed. "You just don't seem to be the politically correct type, Woody. Why not call a spade a spade? Call it what it is: sex trafficking." Her visage had turned hard.

"Well, I generally eschew the delicate boundaries of vulgarity when speaking to a lady, a term I deem even more elegant than *woman*."

"And a sweet-talking bullshitter to boot." She grinned.

"So does that mean I can call a spade a fucking shovel?" I grinned back.

Then we both broke into genuine laughter.

In the midst of all of this, something else was happening. A certain excitement, a certain attraction.

"And so, I wonder, Marylyn, how do you and Marta fit at this juncture? Oh, and the other girl?"

"My, my, you *have* done your homework." She paused. "And so, 'the time has come,' the walrus said, 'to speak of many things. Of shoes—and ships—and ceiling wax—Of cabbages and kings.' Shall we enter the rabbit hole, Woody?"

"Why not, my dear? And to follow your theme, 'Ding dong bell, Pussy's in the well. Who put her in? Little Hafeez Flynn?'" In my mind, I started to wonder, *Who pulled her out, little Marylyn Stout?*

"Indeed. Seems great minds run in the same . . . gutter? At the risk of boring you with my earlier life, before Mr. DuBruss and I moved to Atlanta, I'll tell you that life was pretty good at that point. Ryan, my ex, won a contract to build a movie studio, which expanded, and money became a nonissue. Along with his bank account came similar growth in his hubris and power grab. Usual pattern, actually, with the usual consequences of corruption that power brings.

"I was teaching kids at a local grade school. We had bought a house that could have housed the Green Bay Packers and their families, too much for me to handle, so he magnanimously offered to hire a live-in housekeeper. Turns out she was learning English and looked like a *Playboy* centerfold. It smelled funny right away. Well, it didn't take long to discover the hanky-panky. In the end, I was more offended that he thought I was an idiot than I was angry with his brash infidelity. By that time, I really didn't like him anyway. I basically threatened him with exposure, told him I was leaving, gave him a settlement figure—which, by the way, was a steal for him—and told him to send the paperwork and good funds to my parents' address within ten days, or I'd be back with an attorney and a meeting with the tabloids.

"The funds arrived, along with what I'll call a guilt tip. I did some traveling and some writing and was living in a condo on the Jersey shore. Life was hunky-dory until my mom called to tell me she had given my address to my friend. I didn't have many friends at that time, so when I asked my mom which friend, I was blown away when she said, 'Marta. Sounded like she was foreign.'"

She had been talking nonstop, like most making cathartic confessions, I suppose. We stopped to refresh our coffee, and she brought some coffee cake.

"That's when the fun started, so to speak. When Marta showed up at my door, I was impressed with how well she spoke English. I was also surprised at how she had let herself go, physically. No longer centerfold material. She was very apologetic to me for the part she had played in destroying my marriage and said that she had admired me and that I was one of only a few people she felt she could trust. I told her she had actually done me a great favor by accelerating the end of that unhappy and dysfunctional union.

"When I'd left, I thought she was a gold digger, or worse, but I didn't blame her, nor did I care. I really hadn't thought about her until my mother's call. Well, it turns out that she's far more of a victim than I." Marylyn spoke analytically but with genuine empathy. She continued. "You've done quite the job in reaching some pretty accurate conclusions based upon sketchy and circumstantial information, Woody. Little bit of Sam Spade and Columbo. Oh, and I shouldn't forget, Chuck Norris." She grinned. "The fact is, she came to me seeking help, but she and her Russian friend were committed to vigilante justice. They still are." She didn't equivocate.

"I have to ask you, what's your take on that, Marylyn?"

"Up to this point, I've been a deterrent. Although I can assure you that my own moral compass will prevail, I have to tell you that I have mixed feelings. Within our legal and judicial system today, I wouldn't wager much on an outcome of justice. In addition, I have very little faith in the FBI, and be most assured that I'm not the only one who questions their competence. There have been multiple instances in the past several years where the FBI has been alerted to the circumstances, personalities, histories, and the threats of what ended in mass killings, and they failed to prevent them. Hasn't changed, but what has happened to these girls is horrific, and I empathize with their vengefulness."

I agreed, but kept that to myself. I formed my pitch. "As with most transgressions, you want the punishment to fit the crime. That's justice at its best. So, first of all, I believe death is an inadequate punishment for these people when compared to years in prison and the loss of their everything. Could you convince your girls to hear me out? All of us, including these victims, need to understand that eliminating but one or two of these perpetrators from what appears to be a much larger and quite complex organization will only provide warning to close it down, most likely only temporarily. A number of these 'johns,' if I can use that term, will skate. Many of the other girls, the victims, may not be rescued. What happens to them? And Marta and her friend will spend the rest of their lives in prison. Is that justice?"

"Of course not, Woody, and it's not like I haven't provided argument. It's just that these two have been willing to take that risk, and they don't seem to care what happens to themselves. If there is a difference now, they've been identified, and any chance of escape is lost." Marylyn sighed. "They really do care about the other girls." She left that thought unfinished. Her frustration was evident.

"What you need to know, Marylyn, is that with or without your intervention, there is enough evidence to bring these girls in now, and my guess is that they don't have green cards as well, and that means deportation, or worse. However, you and I both know that for their own good, and certainly for their mental well-being, a cooperative effort is the best result. Let's not forget that the authorities will need both of them as critical witnesses in order to get convictions."

Marylyn slowly nodded agreement.

I continued. "There's still a lot of work to be done. We need proof that a similar operation exists in Galveston and perhaps other places. Your girls will be needed with that. It's my belief that Marta was one of about two dozen girls who met with the recruiter and Hafeez in Sevastopol, where they received their instructions, the promises, the threats, and where they signed contracts. They left there on a ship that stopped somewhere outside of Atlanta, in international waters. Marta and some of the others disembarked and boarded a speedboat, the one you saw in the marina, and were brought here before they were transported to the various locations. Marta's friend, Ilana, went on to Galveston." I stopped to read her face. It seemed that, at least for now, our discussion had run its course.

Marylyn got up and opened the blinds on the rear windows that overlooked the water. "How about I mix a couple of Bloody Marys? We can move out to the patio, and I can have a smoke. I pace myself. I've been cutting back for two years. Impressive, huh?" She snickered.

"We have something in common, except that I've been cutting back for fifteen years."

She enjoyed that.

It was a nice setting. Marylyn was grounded and secure. We watched fishing boats as they trolled to the deep water while we smoked her long menthol Virginia Slims, not the Marlboro image of my youth.

"Well then, Mr. Woodward, if my deductive powers are still intact, you have a grandson. Thus you have kids, and so you're married. Am I close?"

I told her about my personal life and history, sharing nods and laughter. She did the same. It was natural, easy, and comfortable, much like old friends do. It was strange territory for me, like coming home after years of absence, never the same as having never left, but perhaps more endearing, a chance to see how all the dots in your life are connected. Is it so with romantic notions? Was I sensing a certain vulnerability? Marlboro men don't smoke Virginia Slims.

"Whether it was fate or serendipity, I'm both pleased and relieved that you came today. For me, the course has now been set . . . without options. I've become cautious, but there's something about you, Woody, that makes me trust you and your judgment. I want these girls protected, so you will come back to meet with us. Sooner the better. Sound good?" She spoke with conviction.

The die was cast. Now it would be on me.

"Sounds good."

We talked a bit about Jekyll Island.

When I left, I gave her my cell number. We said the nice things. I thanked her. She thanked me. All was good except for that certain thing. That thing, like the wind that you can't see, but you feel it. That accidental thing that sneaks into your life, uninvited, which is different from unwelcome. Maybe the Zen masters were fucking with me again. What the hell? I'm seventy-four, my destiny carved in stone, so, thing, leave me alone.

CHAPTER 38

As I drove home, I realized that there may now be enough evidence to convict Hafeez of certain serious crimes. If that were true, a "come to Jesus" meeting just might turn her. The art of the deal is one thing, but leverage is more effective.

I called Tommy that evening.

"Just thinking about you, old timer. I was having a Macallan on the rocks." Tommy gloated.

"If you think you're a spring chicken, you're delusional."

"Oh, but Woody, I love delusion. Makes me happy."

We giggled. I knew he was mocking me.

"Tommy, I'm beginning to make some headway. I could use some advice at this juncture." I filled him in on my meeting with Marylyn. "I think these two witnesses may provide enough evidence to scare the hell out of Hafeez. I might be able to push her to turn on Ghulam, as well as expose the whole organization. However, should she turn tail and go to Ghulam, we have to be in a position to pounce immediately. We want the whole enchilada, but it still might be too soon to bring in the FBI. What say you?"

Tommy took his time before responding. "You know, I actually think it might be time to bring in our Irish capo, Woody. Here's why. First thing is to swear him to confidentiality until the three of us—and add Curtis to that—all agree to take it to a higher level. I trust Jack, but not his superiors. When Jack sees that this could bring him great personal benefit, like hero status, medals, whatever, he'll jump on board."

I could hear the tinkling of ice cubes and Tommy sipping his scotch.

"Why don't you get yourself a drink, old friend, and plant your ass in a comfortable chair. And don't worry about taking notes. I'll put my thoughts in an email and send them to you tomorrow."

Silence.

"Go on. I'll wait." Tommy was a bit giddy. It may have been his second drink.

I was just fine following his instructions. Tequila and ice and my comfy Lay-Z-Boy. "Okay, hit it, maestro," I said.

"Understand that, especially with your latest disclosure, I'm shooting from the hip to some degree. My notes will be more organized, but I agree with you that this thing is taking form. Where do we want to go, and how do we get there?" Tommy set the stage. "This will have to be a highly coordinated raid if we're going to net this whole operation. Who and what that is, we don't really know at this point. In order to do that, we do need to bring Jack in soon. But before we do that, we need more. Timing will be critical. If these people are to be convicted, we need solid evidence. We have some, but it's not tight. We need witnesses. We have three, if we include Marylyn. Now, what we really need is to find the money. Tomorrow, first thing, I'll put my Cayman boy in fast-forward mode. My take is that Hafeez is the key. She knows the players, she's the recruiter, and she knows where the money is. She cannot be trusted, however, so any intervention will be very delicate."

I could hear Tommy sipping.

"It would seem that you have adequate leverage, Woody, but if she sees that she can squirm through a hole, she'll do it. The sentence and penalties are pretty substantial: up to fifteen years in prison and a million and a half in fines. I think you need to surprise her. Give her no wiggle room in your threats, but keep the ace up your sleeve, if we have one. Again, that's the dough. And don't forget, if we find it, remember what it was that sent one of the country's most notorious murderers, Mr. Al Capone, to prison? The IRS. Also, if we should find it, you do not want her to know that."

More silence. I didn't interfere.

"We know we can't get a legal phone tap on Hafeez, so when you go to see her, you need to plant a listening device. We have to know if she spills the beans and be ready for it. We have some things to do before that meeting and need to be prepared to move immediately if she tries to cut and run, but let her think she's got a couple weeks before there's a strike. I'll connect with Jack and have him come to Jekyll Island. I'll come down and meet you guys. How does all that sound?"

"Let me say that you have something in common with Wyatt Earp," I said. "You both shoot well from the hip. I cannot disagree with you on your analysis, strategy, or tactics. And you're right about Jack. We need him in at this point. Timing will make or break it." I tinkled my cubes and took a sip. "So let me know how it sets up with Jack and any progress you make in the Caymans. I'll look for an email. One more thing, Mr. Bond. When you come down, bring along one of your listening devices, please."

"You got it, Ace. And like you weirdos from Minnesota say, skol!"

I pictured him hoisting the Macallan.

After hanging up, I considered Tommy's evaluation. I could see that finding the money could be the crucial component that would close down this operation, the blade that would cut the horsehair of the Damocles sword, but were the Caymans the location? There were a number of options where one could hide funds. I wondered, mixing metaphors, were we putting all our eggs in one fire?

My cell buzzed.

"Hello."

"I just confirmed that brisket is tonight's special. Does five thirty work for you?" It was Curtis.

"Kind of presumptive, don't you think?" I retorted. "I might have a date with some hot tomato."

I heard a giggle.

"Like I said, five thirty work? You should be done with your gardening by that time."

This time, I heard a snort.

"If I can get past the disesteem, I'll be there. And welcome back."

CHAPTER 39

No Prius, no Hafeez, and a tired-looking Curtis.

"You know, Woody, these so-called golden years kind of suck. That's not a reflection of my normally cheery attitude, just that I've been around a lot of energetic youth lately. They run and they dance like I used to do, but not anymore. Tell me, Woody, if you could go back and relive one year of your life, what age would you pick?" Curtis smiled a cherubic smile.

It's not like I hadn't thought about it. Everybody thinks about it. My guess is that today, people would make a different choice than me. You see, I loved my teen years. In truth, I've really liked them all, but my teen years, as opposed to those of kids today, were not filled with stress and depression, maybe because life was so much simpler then. No cell phones, no internet, no Facebook, no school shootings. Teens didn't get too involved in politics. It goes on and on, but it was fun. Still, to pick just one year?

"I'll go with twenty-one. Like the song says, 'It was a very good year. It was a very good year for city girls, who lived up the stair, with all that perfumed hair, and it came undone, when I was twenty-one.' I was dumb and stupid. I threw away my fake ID. Ignorance was blissful. I forget what my dreams were, but I can assure you they were big. 'Dreams and schemes and circus crowds.' Bruce called them 'glory days,' but they were more than that. Life was one infatuation after the next, and love was just a synonym. We didn't have time to absorb the deep meaning of that word. At some point the world forced us to grow up, but for that precious period of time, it was simply a calliope of dreams and adventures." Mine was a wistful stare through the big windows, soft blue backdrop, cumulus puff balls, capricious, mutating, and I saw an alligator cloud lose its tail from some kind of gust. Behind it, a Delta 747 left a long white funnel as it headed . . . somewhere.

"Hello. Woody. Breaker one nine, do you read me?" Curtis broke my reverie.

I turned to see his empathetic smile. "Sorry, my friend," I said. "I went away. I think it was your fault. But thanks. I like going away."

"Funny, Woody, it seems that time is a redundant topic for us, as it probably is for most older folks. Along that line, I tore out an article from some periodical on the plane, mea culpa, where a theoretical physicist named Rovelli contends that time doesn't really even exist, except in our heads. He claims that time is just a story we're telling ourselves in the present tense, a collective act of introspection and narrative, record-keeping, and based on a relationship to prior events and the expectation of continuation. He states that from our perspective, we see the world flowing in time, whereas at the quantum level, durations are so short they can't be divided, so there's no such thing as time. He goes on to say that because of our perspective, the world seems ordered, flowing from past to present, linking cause and effect. And so, we simply superimpose order upon it, fixing events to a particular linear series. We then link events to outcomes, which gives us our sense of time. His example of our 'now' being fallacy is that when we see the light from the planet Proxima B through a telescope, it's conveying what existed four years ago. He describes time as a multilayered, complex concept with multiple distinct properties deriving from various different approximations. Does that sound like gibberish to you?"

"At first blush, maybe. Then again, once you factor in that the average person cannot process the enormity of time and space, it begins to make sense."

After minutes of trying to reconcile this theory, Curtis stated in a frustrated voice, "Enough. It seems it's not just children who get easily distracted. Let's get caught up with each other."

I went first, talking about Mary Beth's visit, noting her regret at not getting to know him. I spoke about my time with Marylyn, omitting certain things, but alluding to my upcoming meeting with Marta and Ilana. I spoke about my planning session with Tommy and that we would be meeting with Jack as soon as Tommy could arrange it. "I expect to get Tommy's email tomorrow, and we should have our timeline."

"Well, you've certainly been a busy boy," Curtis said. "And with good results. When do you plan to talk to Hafeez?"

"Not until we've met with Tommy and Jack, and I hope that's soon."

"Things certainly have happened to our quiet little island since you rode into town, Mr. Wayne. That could be either John or Bruce." Curtis chortled.

"Seems them beans had to be stirred, pilgrim." I could just hear Mary Beth suggesting I work on my "Duke" impression. "So tell me about your adventure, Dr. Red Crow."

"My trip was a mix of philosophical, nostalgic, and certainly paradoxical. My friend introduced me to people I liked and admired, yet, to them, even I was in subtle ways an outlander.

"The Pine Ridge Reservation is made up of eleven thousand square miles or two-point-seven million acres. In most ways, it's a desolate place, Woody, a forgotten land, one of America's red-headed stepchildren. The unemployment rate is eighty to ninety percent. The annual per capita income is around four thousand dollars. The rate of diabetes is eight times the national average, the rate of cervical cancer is five times the national average, the rate of heart disease is twice the national average, and the rate of tuberculosis is eight times the national average. The alcoholism rate is as high as eighty percent. The suicide rate is double the national average, with teen suicide four times that number. The US government doesn't seem to care and hasn't for a hundred years, yet with the help of a prejudicial and self-serving media, they flaunt their magnanimous gestures of sending the nation's tax dollars to countries that don't even like the United States. Am I bitter? What do you think? Still, the Native American spirit is, and always has been, one of resilience. Contrary to the downward spiral of dependency that America is in, the nadir of the nation's self-destruction, Native America will survive. That was my takeaway from this past week.

"I went to the Red Cloud school. The dedication of those teachers and volunteers is most uplifting. The spirit of those young students is a ray of hope. The ceremonies and traditional dances exemplify the need for tradition, something that America hasn't simply lost, but is intentionally eliminating under the government efforts to foist a fallacy.

"I also spent a day with volunteers who bring food and clothing to the Native American veterans. They're funded by donations, Woody, but sadly, they only scratch the surface. In retrospect, it's with effort that I search for hope and encouragement for that almost sacred place. I'm glad I went, but I've been hardened by the trip."

An aura of melancholy came over us, lingered, and tiptoed away.

I felt the urge to provide some positivity. "You know something, Curtis. I have this certain gift, which on rare occasions, just shows up. It's a kind of prescience that gives me visions of something good to come. I've made it quite clear that bad visions are unwelcome, so they stay away. Your Native Dream catchers. What I see is a great celebratory powwow with thousands of Native dancers, traditional food and music, and many drums beating. Believe, my friend. Believe that good things happen to good people."

Curtis gave me one of those looks that say many things, like, *Even though I find it difficult to give much credence to such clairvoyance, as a friend, I do appreciate your effort to create the sunlight of hope.*

We had some excellent brisket and wine. We talked about the upcoming Super Bowl and other trivial things. We were both tired and left early.

At home, I watched the news, but it was the usual garbage. Several politicians and lobbyists were promoting issues that served their own interests but were clearly unrelated to the greater good. In America, they label it lobbying. Everywhere else in the world, they call it bribery and corruption.

I recalled a quip by Robin Williams: "Politicians should wear sponsor jackets like NASCAR drivers. Then we know who owns them."

I fell into a restless sleep.

CHAPTER 40

The next day, surprisingly, I was invigorated. Instead of a run, I drove to a sporting goods store where I bought a one-man kayak, paddle, a car rack, and headed to the marina. Tomorrow was New Year's Eve day, and the boat enthusiasts were out in numbers, some putting decorations and flags on their crafts, apparently preparing for a boat parade. I got an upper-body workout I hadn't done for some time. I checked out the Ghulam-Hafeez speedboat, but there was no sign of activity. I sat on the dock, watching, while listening to a backdrop of noise: people conversing, children's happy screams, and the distinguishing rumbles of outboard and inboard motors. Just as I began to doze, my cell phone sounded . . . reveille.

"Hello."

"Woody?"

"Yes."

"It's Marylyn. Is it a bad time to talk?"

"Not at all. Nice to hear from you." And it was.

A pause.

"Is that a horn blowing?" she asked.

I laughed. "Indeed it is, a boat horn. I'm at the marina." I proceeded to tell her about the kayak, my workout, and the surrounding activity.

"I see. Important to be ready for that next encounter with some bad guys, huh?"

"I really hope that stuff is over, also, far less dramatic." If she knew about that encounter at my house, she would think

I was a raving maniac, or worse. "At this point, I just want to make it to the next decade."

"I have no doubt you will." After a moment of silence, she continued. "Reason I called was, I met with Marta and Ilana last evening. They agreed to meet in three days, so if it works for you, how about Tuesday, the second, my place, at noon? I'll have sandwiches."

"It's a date," I said. I heard her giggle. I stumbled. "What I meant to say was, it's a meeting. You know what I meant."

"Yes, Woody. Certainly not my idea of a date." She giggled again.

"Agree, slip of the tongue," I replied with a nervous laugh.

After a moment she asked, "So, you have big plans for New Year's?"

"Only if you consider a bottle of cheap wine and a corny TV movie to be *big plans*. How about you?"

Hmm, was I fishing? Was she? Was this that weird prelude game that people play as they scout out the lay of the land, evaluating risks, measuring intent, imply, infer, who's it?

"Something like that. I'd prefer a game of Scrabble, but I quit playing against myself a while ago. It felt like cheating, and I got tired walking to the other side of the table after every word."

"Did Nurse Ratched refuse to play with you? Just kidding, my dear." After a pause, I cast the lure near the lily pads. "Could it be I'm hearing a challenge, or is that my delusion?"

"Aha, a Kesey fan. One of my favorite books and a decent job with the film. Anyway, maybe it's me being coy, calling that spade a spade instead of a fucking shovel. But since I'm already this deep, if you bring the steaks and champagne, I have a grill and all the fixins."

"Now that's what I would call a date."

CHAPTER 41

So now I was the one walking around the table after every word. Uncomfortable? Not sure. With what? My discomfort? When I'd said, "Leave me alone," was I just throwing down the gauntlet to see if the boogeyman would pick it up? I'm good at controlling the game with others . . . not so much myself. Beware the wilderness of feelings.

Early that evening, I got Tommy's email. His plan was laid out like a military op. Also, Tommy had never been one for procrastination, and somehow, he had gotten Jack to commit to coming to Jekyll Island on Thursday. Tommy could dangle that string and tease a kitten. I called Curtis and told him that we would meet at my place at three. I emailed Tommy and suggested that he escort Jack to my house. Seemed as though the fog was beginning to lift.

When you're nearly seventy-five, you take lazy walks on the beach with your grandkids. You join a bridge club or take a cooking class. What you don't do is get involved with an international crime syndication. And you sure as hell don't get fucked up with a romantic tryst, especially when the two are integrated. No sir, you check the obits and get your senior discounts at Denny's by 5:00 p.m. Unless, of course, you're of a different breed. Unless you jump on board with a certain theory by a fellow named Rovelli, who claims there's no such thing as time, only a series of events, all squished together until they're not.

I picked up two New York strips, a recognizable bottle of champagne, two cheap New Year's Eve hats, two cardboard horns that I tested in the store, and a new shirt—red-and-white gingham. As an afterthought, I grabbed a small bottle of that green Mennen aftershave. I arrived at six.

Marylyn's attempt to look casual had failed. She was stunning. "I like your new shirt, Woody," she said with a pleasant smile.

"And what makes you think it's new?" I asked.

"Just a guess," she said as she peeled off a white price sticker thing from my sleeve. "So let's watch the sunset from the patio. There's vodka and scotch on the cart. I'll put the steaks in the fridge." From the kitchen she said, "Hope you like jazz. I'm intrigued by, should I say, atypical musicians, like Art Pepper."

"Atypical, as in jailbird?" I replied.

"Back to the fucking shovel, it seems." She shook her head, smiling, as we went outside.

"What would you like?" I asked.

"Scotch and soda."

I made two. The grill was already stacked with charcoal, and from the speakers came Art's version of "Nature Boy." I glanced to the western horizon. It would be a radiant sunset. Oranges and purples. No stress.

"He was a man of great passion . . . Mr. Pepper," Marylyn said as I handed her the scotch. "Salut!"

We both took a generous gulp.

"That would be plural," I replied. "Most of his passions he couldn't control, as I recall."

"But he was resilient. More comebacks than Pelé."

"And more addictions than Elizabeth Taylor," I added.

"Yet he let it all come out the end of that alto sax, like no one else ever did," she mused. "So how about you, Woody? What's your passion?"

I watched as a trimaran scooted along, the bulging, rainbow-colored spinnaker pulling the boat, like huskies on a dogsled. The question called for introspection.

"Well, I'll start with the old statement, there are two kinds of people in the world, those who have passion and those who don't. I'm one of the passionate, and what I choose to do, I do with passion, which in this case is really an attitude. My self-concept passion is a commitment to providing justice in all its forms. Unfortunately, achieving justice in any form is a task designed for Sisyphus and his quest to find meaning in a task that can never be completed."

Marylyn seemed to be processing my thoughts. She spoke. "I too feel that passion. I've personally seen and experienced it. Politics, prejudice, money, and power have rendered our legal and judicial system as having only a passing interest in true justice. And the ones who do care are overrun. As for the real culprit, these days, my mental and emotional balance nearly requires me to avoid the unbridled lies and corruption of an inept media that no one holds accountable. As a result, I've pulled in the boundaries of my life into a much smaller circle than I ever wanted or intended to."

I showed no outward sign, but I found her frustration somewhat amusing. There was nothing surprising to me about the confederacy of power mongers, criminals, and idiots who worked the system. I've been managing my expectations quite well for decades. Still, I smile inside when people say, "Can you believe it? How can they get away with that? That's just plain hypocrisy!" Really?

I took Marylyn's glass, refreshed our drinks though they were still half-full, and started the charcoal before returning to my chair. "There's a lot of emotion in that topic, so I shall return to the more benign question of passions. And let me preface by saying that there are some credible arguments that hold back the applause for those who claim a passion to be the end-all. Before that discussion, however, from the generic to the specific, I would have to say that my life passion probably falls under the general category of metaphysics, specifically, *ontology*, the philosophical study of being, and *epistemology*, the theories of knowledge. I don't intend to sound pedantic, so forgive that if you will." I looked at her.

She cocked her head. Her smile was warm and accepting. I felt certain relief.

Her tone was mellow. "My goodness, Woody, but you're filled with surprises. Nice surprises. Please go on."

"I have this need to learn something new every day. I try to understand the world's great thinkers and often find it so arduous I have to set it aside. My own limitations, I suppose, so now I have my fictional library filled with shelves of things I've set aside. At least, unlike Art Pepper, there's nothing self-destructive about my passion. But it does raise the question: Is finding your passion a good thing? Some espouse the Latin term, *caveat emptor*, promoting caution before jumping headfirst into what our educators preach when they say, 'You need to find your passion.'"

"Really?" she said. "I've never heard a criticism of passion."

"The criticisms aren't of the concept or the goal. The warnings are more specific, like speed bumps on a road where children play."

"I'm intrigued."

"It relates to definition. The self-help sections of bookstores are filled with books that portray passion in some über-positive light. Finding your passion is what the teachers and motivational speakers are selling, and there are companies that even consider it a prerequisite to hiring. Thing is, most people have a superficial understanding of what passion really is. As a result, people expect to magically find their passions, but that's rare. Almost seventy-five percent of people adopt what's called a *fit mind-set*, an almost instant passion for a job or activity that seems intuitively right from the get-go. Many of these enthusiasts, however, soon become disappointed, and they give up and move on, not unlike what happens in new relationships when the infatuation fades."

I noticed that Marylyn blinked, looked away, and took a healthy sip of scotch.

"Studies have shown that there's a much higher success ratio for long-term passions with a *development mind-set*, recognizing and discovering one's passion and then cultivating and nurturing it over time. The other thing is recognizing the distinction between *harmonious passion* and *obsessive passion*. With harmonious passion, one will pursue the activity because they love the activity. With obsessive passion, one will pursue it because what they love is the external result and the recognition it brings. Harmonious is associated with well-being and self-satisfaction, whereas obsessive is associated with burnout, anxiety, and depression. Like most things in life, I guess, *know thyself*." I made that gesture with my hands that says, "So, what do you think?" I waited.

"Well, Woody, my first thought is that I could get my butt kicked in a Scrabble game. You could have been an Ivy League professor."

We both enjoyed a big grin.

"But seriously, your lesson gives strong argument as to processing before you make choices. What you've said makes so much sense, yet it never occurred to me, and I can see where it actually happened to me . . . with chess." She looked away, absorbed in thought. "How about we put that on hold while you get the steaks going and I make the salad?"

Okay, so I can't fry an egg. What I can do is grill a steak, which I did. The food was tasty; the milieu was relaxing, comfortable, and fun; the company was interesting; and the subtle magnetism was palpable.

"In Jersey, there were some holes in my life that I thought needed to be filled," she said as we were finishing up. "For whatever reason, I took a class on chess at the local technical college. I knew nothing about the game, but was immediately intrigued. I read everything I could find, including a history of past champions. I fell in with a group of women who were fanatical and competitive. Pretty soon, I was falling into the trap. It lost its sizzle, Woody. Lots of anxiety. I dropped out. In truth, the whole Jersey experience had gotten to that point, and so, with my new empathy for Marta's plight, I packed up and came here. This place fit me much better."

We shared the feeling.

"So I don't know if that's a great example of your obsessive passion, but it seems so to me."

"In some ways we're into the *tuh-may-to, tuh-mah-to* thing, semantics. I don't know anyone who hasn't shared your experience. I certainly have, but it does prove the point and the challenges of managing our own expectations."

She nodded.

We let that simmer for a while.

The sunset exceeded its billing, and with it, Marylyn brought out the Grand Marnier. It was probably the ambient comfort, but we let the Scrabble game quietly disappear from the evening's agenda. Nat King Cole and Dean Martin provided the holiday sounds, and we talked about easy things and avoided stressful topics. I had a tough time recalling the last time I had been in such a place. Before my kids were born, I suppose.

As midnight drew near, we turned on the TV to catch the flavor. I got the cheap hats and horns, and a small but noticeable vexation showed up in my gut, but not as much as it would have had it not been for New Year's Eve . . . the excuse for a kiss. I could pretend it was simply ritual, like a kiss for Mom. Close to the vest. No risk for me. Happy New Year. Gotta go.

The drive home was not without confusion. That ganglion of irreconcilable antagonisms again. "Hey, Zen masters, what part of *leave me alone* don't you understand?"

I had turned off my phone. There were a number of calls, including my kids. Voice messages. I would call them tomorrow.

That night I had my flying dream. I loved my flying dream, but I woke up to take a leak. I couldn't get back into the dream. I hate that.

CHAPTER 42

New Year's Day, a time for cognitive relief. Never-ending football can provide that. My kids, the twins, B. J. were all hugs and giggles. So was Mary Beth, except for her über-intuition.

I answered her question. "I had a steak and a couple drinks with a friend. Pretty quiet, TeeBee. How about you?"

"Nice deflection, Pops. Tell that to your two naïve kids. I know better. Who was she?" She heard my phony laugh.

"Jeez, women are all romantics. Thought you were the exception. Nice try." I knew it didn't work, so I doubled down my deflection. "I talked to Curtis, and he's pushing me to get you back here."

"You just confirmed my suspicion. Whatever. I'll find out. Men are dumb. In any event, I really enjoyed our time, and tell Curtis I'll see him."

We said, "Talk soon."

In between bowl games, I put together my thoughts for tomorrow's meeting with Marta and Ilana. I wondered how that would go, in more ways than one.

CHAPTER 43

Turns out, I didn't need a great performance. Marylyn had more than greased the skids.

Not for me, but for Marta, our reunion was a bit uncomfortable. Ilana was somewhat of a Marta clone except that she was a redhead and took more pride in her appearance. The profiling of these girls was disturbing. I felt a slight shudder. Ghulam and Hafeez were evil, and I was making the metaphorical adjustments to the windage and elevation on my rifle scope.

It became clear that the girls had handed the baton to Marylyn and by de facto, to me. I gave them a general description of the plan going forward, providing assurance that they were an integral part of the solution, not the problem. Their biggest concern was that all of the girls could be rescued and provided a safe path forward. I gave them my best promise, with appropriate equivocation.

I was pleased that there was no discomfort or hidden agenda between Marylyn and me. She filled her role perfectly: advocate and protector for the girls, and mediator and supporter for my position. With formality and respect, I left the three of them to their own discussion.

I called Curtis but had to leave a voice message. I then drove by Hafeez's house. Her car was gone. It hit me as I drove into my driveway. I was sure that she was the woman who delivered the envelope to the Arabian Knights store in Atlanta on the first of every month, periodically with a girl, while picking up a so-called present. Today was the second, but that would make sense since the first was New Year's Day. Although still just conjecture, it did seem to fit.

That begged the question of what was in the present. In the scenario that Curtis, Tommy, and I envisioned, it was payment for the "housekeeper." Suppose that payment was something other than cash, like diamonds or precious metals? It might have to be converted, but still would need to be delivered or transferred to an offshore account, wherever that may be, so in the big picture, all of the in-betweeners were ancillary to the evidence that would convict the perpetrators, which was tying that account to Ghulam and Hafeez for money laundering and tax evasion. Without that, they could get off with a slap on the wrist, and with a competent defense, not even that. If ifs and buts were soup and nuts, what a fine world this would be.

Curtis returned my call, and we set dinner for six. I then got back in my car and drove to a music store, where I picked up an Art Pepper CD. Some kind of weird subliminal urge. Wonder where that came from?

CHAPTER 44

There were only a handful of patrons in the club dining room.

"Happy New Year, my friend," I said to Curtis. "Any New Year's resolutions?"

"I'm not a poster child for resolutions, Woody. Last year I resolved to lose ten pounds over the year, and after all my hard work, I can proudly say I only have fifteen pounds to go." He chortled.

Me too.

"How about you?"

I tried to think of a clever response. It was rather lame. "Well, once again I resolved to give up smoking for good, so I tried those nicotine patches. They aren't working so well, and they're a nightmare to light."

He gave me a corny grin. "You probably don't want to quit your day job. I won't be doing any stand-up comedy myself, but at least we try. Any kind of levity will work these days. You look energized."

"I have to say, it's been an enjoyable few days." I proceeded to tell him about my kayak, which segued into how well my discussion went with Marylyn. I kept the date to myself. "Those two girls have been bent on revenge. I understand and share their emotions. Hell, they're just kids looking for a better life. They believed and stepped into a snake pit. Marylyn has been filling the role of counselor, keeping them grounded for several months. Once I got past her initial suspicions, she was not only receptive, but most welcome to my plan. And relieved, I might add. It's been a heavy load for her.

"When I met with the girls, Marylyn had set the stage. My pitch was easy, and textbook. *Ethos*, my credentials and trust; *pathos*, my empathy, understanding, and connectivity; and *logos*, the sheer force and logic of the plan and how we collectively achieve the overall goal of closing down this operation, saving the other girls, arrests, convictions, and consequences. All three of them are essential to that end."

"What about Hafeez?"

"We'll discuss that with Tommy and Jack on Thursday, but in many ways, my intervention with her could be what makes or breaks it. She's a cool customer, but you can be sure that she'll be like a cornered bobcat. Also, totally unpredictable and untrustworthy, no matter what her outward reaction is to my leverage. I've thought about that encounter from every angle, and the intel I need to squeeze out of her is the who, what, where, and when of any extended operations that we suspect exist in Galveston, and maybe other places. I believe I can get that."

"I'm confident you can too, Woody. You've been spot-on up to this point. Do you think she'll turn on Ghulam?"

I thought for a minute. "Can't answer that. It would be a smart move on her part, but we just don't know much about that relationship. I can say we'll know in a hurry if Tommy brings the right technical equipment. She'll warn him or she won't."

We were relaxed, drinking Arnold Palmers. We both ordered the special: lasagna with salad.

Curtis opened a new door. "Switching gears, Woody, you'll be interested to know that along the lines of our recent discussion about Rovelli's theory that time doesn't exist, I'm speaking to a small group of psychologists tomorrow about the latest theories on *solipsism*, that being the claim that the external world, outside of one's own mind, also does not exist."

"It seems that nothing exists anymore, Curtis."

"The silver lining being that Armageddon should be a very quiet happening."

We shared a giggle.

"It certainly isn't prevalent, is it?" I asked.

"It's becoming more so in its extended definition. As an epistemological position, solipsism holds that knowledge of anything outside of one's own mind is invalid and that the self can know nothing but its own modifications. But the extended definition relates to extreme egocentricity, and I don't have to tell you that in today's world, many parts of our lives are affected by narcissists, megalomaniacs, power, and control. The psychologists are studying how this relates to division, and the country has become more divided in the past decade than it was in the sixties. Solipsism is on the rise, Woody."

"Well, I hope that you brainiacs can come up with some answers."

I meant it. The country needed to undergo a fearless moral inventory.

CHAPTER 45

The following day I spent kayaking and getting ready for Thursday.

On Thursday, Curtis got to my place early.

"How was your talk, Dr. Red Crow?"

"Most engaging. I thought of you when we discussed whether solutions even existed at all. Since solutions are dependent upon changes in human behavior, I can't say I have a great deal of confidence in that happening."

"You're not creating a warm and fuzzy optimism, my friend."

"And you're not Walter Mitty, who lives in a bubble," Curtis replied. "I know you don't like reality, but you don't deny it."

"Guilty as charged. On a lighter note, how about helping me with the snacks and drinks?"

Tommy and Jack arrived just before three.

CHAPTER 46

I wouldn't have recognized Jack if I had passed him on the street. It wasn't the sparse head of silver hair or even the slow gait with which he walked. It was the eyes, those eyes of age, shadowed in dark skin tones, wrinkled and baggy.

But then, that signature voice of bona fide enthusiasm recaptured the old rapport. "Woody, you old rascal. Damned if you don't look like you're about to re-up. Good to see you, old friend." With a big smile, he went right for the hug.

"Howdy, Irish. Didn't know I would ever see you again. Think it's been since the reunion thirty years ago."

I introduced him to Curtis, and we went inside. Curtis had reserved two rooms for Jack and Tommy at the club and made dinner reservations for seven.

"I have snacks, beer, wine, and soda, so help yourself. If you prefer coffee, got that too."

Tommy and I had beer, Curtis had wine, and Jack had coffee. We spent the next half hour catching up.

Jack was totally transparent in talking about the troubles he had undergone and his "little miracle" in finding Jenny. "You remember Master Sergeant Ricci?" Jack looked at Tommy and me. "Talk about a pit bull. Well, Jenny makes him look like an altar boy. She kicked my ass into shape in a matter of months, dragged me to the altar, and we've been lovebirds for twenty years."

We all laughed at that.

"The Bureau took me back for my final years, and I've been busy as a bee with the number of immigration issues, so when

Tommy told me about this conspiracy you guys have become involved in, I got my ticket. I'm anxious to hear the story."

It was almost an hour before I had brought Jack up-to-date. He had a number of questions, which Tommy and I answered while Curtis listened.

"I need to tell you, Jack, I do have some trust issues with the FBI." I was prepared to tell him why, but he had already put his hands in the air.

"You don't have to explain," Jack said. "We're on the same page, Woody. I have my own trust issues, but we do seem to all agree that without the Bureau, this operation will not be shut down. At what point do you see bringing them on board?"

When Jack said bring "them" on board, as opposed to "us" on board, I knew he was on the right team.

"So, are you guys familiar with the artillery tactic known as TOT, or Time on Target?" I posed.

"Tell us," Tommy said.

"A TOT is the military coordination of artillery fire by many weapons so that all the munitions arrive at the target at roughly the same time. The military standard for coordinating a TOT strike is plus or minus three seconds from the prescribed time of impact. An old E-7 who had been in Korea described one he had observed as a forward observer.

"In a nutshell, there are three parts to the artillery: the forward observer, or FO, provides the eyes; the FDC, or fire direction center, the brain; and the guns are the muscle. When the FO identifies a target, he sends the coordinates of the target to the FDC, which calculates the direction and necessary elevation for the guns. Now, depending on the size of the target, the number of guns and munitions are brought into play. The five-inch guns of a naval vessel may be fifteen miles away and the time from 'fire' to impact may be, from high-angle arc, let's say five minutes. The 155-millimeter guns may be two minutes away, while the 105s might be a minute away. The countdown begins from the farthest guns with appropriate 'fire' times for the closer ones, so that they all arrive at the same time. The results are devastating. I'm using this as an analogy because once we've identified our targets in this operation, we'll need to coordinate the raids just like a TOT."

The other three absorbed this until Jack spoke. "So if I'm reading you right, it sounds like you believe you can get the information about any other locations from this Hafeez, especially if we can find the money."

"And this is where we get into the timing issues, Jack. There's certainly a sense of urgency to have that confrontation, and it would be more powerful to have an offshore account in my pocket when I did. On the other hand, I don't want her to know that we've located the account. If she knows that we know, and she chooses to skip, she won't go there, and we could lose her for good. If she doesn't, and skips, that's where we nab her.

"Just as important, I'll tell her that we don't plan on making any move for at least a week, but we must be prepared to move on everybody the next day in the event that she decides to blow the deal and vamoose. If we don't find the money, I still need to confront her, and we go with what we've got. I'll need to polish up my bluffing skills in that case.

"What that means for you, Jack, is that once we set the time for my meet, you'll begin coordinating the raids on all the Ghulam-Hafeez locations, and if I do get the intel on the other locations, you'll have to work double time with the Bureau assets in those places for the simultaneous raids. You hear what I'm saying?"

"This is playing some old tapes, Woody. Any updates on this fictional account, Tommy?" Jack sounded a wee bit stressed.

"I did talk to my guy last night, but nothing yet," Tommy replied. I detected a touch of pessimism.

"Jack, if you do have a couple of people you trust," I said, "I would encourage you to get the ball rolling when you get back to your office. You'll need help."

"Already going through names in my head, Woody."

"Tommy, tutor me on the device you brought. I'm no techy."

Tommy showed me the listening device. Two, actually. They were simplistic, tiny but powerful. We processed what we knew and what we were facing, absorbing the many complications.

"Okay then, why don't you guys follow Curtis back to the club, get your rooms, relax a bit, and we'll meet at seven."

They nodded.

CHAPTER 47

I n the old days, military operations similar to this had code names, like Operation Housekeeper or some such moniker. It was the perpetrators and operators who presented the danger. The "johns" were just arrogant idiots who believed they were untouchable, men like Ryan DuBruss. The thought of that dickhead prompted a reaction. I picked up my cell.

"Hello!"

"Hi, Marylyn. It's Woody."

"What a pleasure. Are you calling from the kayak?" She giggled.

"You kidding? Afraid I'd tip over and lose my phone."

Another giggle.

"I really called to let you know that my FBI contact is here, and we're putting our plans in place."

"Good to hear, Woody." She paused. "I was thinking you just wanted to hear my voice . . . only kidding."

"Well, there was that too." How pathetic, an old fart flirting. "I'll keep you in the loop."

"And I'll look forward to that."

High School 101. Life is a hoot. It was true. Mankind really is a melody, and everyone in your life is a note you have to mix into it in the right order, and from time to time we need to be reminded that the most important thing in life is knowing the most important things in life. It's so easy to forget. I like to muse. I protect my own little corner of delusion with poppies and rainbows. No one bothers me there.

CHAPTER 48

For some time, I had felt that Hafeez was the epicenter of this operation. Ghulam had the contacts and provided the muscle. He appeared to be the overlord of the organization, but Hafeez was the brains and the puppet master. She knew where all the bodies were, including the ones that were buried. If there was an exit strategy in place, she would have put it together, and five will get you ten, unbeknownst to Ghulam, she had her own. My guess was that her loyalty to Ghulam was thin, at best, and that if they did have plane tickets out of the country, hers was a day earlier than his.

In the end, however, slaying this dragon was dependent upon finding the money, and that was in the hands of Tommy's guy, who was only in the Caymans. Still, there were a number of other havens, like Switzerland, the Channel Islands, and the Middle East. True, Tommy's argument about the Caymans did make the most sense, but it was still low percentage. Welcome, Lady Luck. There was little doubt in my mind that after my confrontation with Hafeez, she would skedaddle ASAP. My other question was, What made Tommy think that his guy could pierce the confidentiality vail of the Cayman bankers?

I arrived at the club a little before seven. Tommy and Jack were at the bar, smiling and telling stories. Tommy had a scotch, while Jack was drinking iced tea. Curtis hadn't arrived yet. It was interesting to see that Hafeez and Ghulam were at the usual table, while the bodyguard sat alone. He was glancing at me. I ignored him. It did occur to me that if this job didn't work out for him, he might try a screen test audition for Brylcreem ads.

When Curtis arrived, we went to his usual spot, and when we were seated, I pointed out the "bad guys" to Jack and Tommy. Though our table was forty feet away, we tempered our volume accordingly. It seemed the fun had carried over from the bar when Tommy asked Jack about his future vacation plans.

"Well, since you asked, I'm planning a surprise trip for Jenny and me to the Canary Islands in the Mediterranean," Jack said with a certain pride.

It was Curtis who responded. "Then you should know, Jack, that there is not one canary on the Canary Islands." He paused. "And on the Virgin Islands? Same thing." He paused again. "Not one canary."

Yuck-yucks all around.

"So," I said, "you two should know that Curtis and I are thinking about becoming a comedy team, and this would be my follow-up. So my chubby friend went in for his physical last week. After stepping on the scale, the doctor said, 'Well, well, it seems your weight is perfect. You just happen to be nine feet too short.'"

This was greeted with boos and a thumbs-down.

After another drink, we got down to business. I asked Tommy why he thought he could get the bankers in the Caymans to spill their guts.

"It's really a combination of the official and the not so official, Woody. Officially, in 1984, Great Britain and the US signed an agreement, a response to the Escobar-Colombian drug wars, that accounts suspected to be protecting drug money could be penetrated by law enforcement. It was relatively loose-knit, but opened the door, not just to law enforcement, but to bribery. That said, don't ask me any more questions or I'll have to kill ya."

We all nodded at Tommy's smile.

"I'm most confident in stating that there are drugs involved in this operation," I said with a wink, nodding toward Hafeez.

"What a coincidence," Tommy said with a grim. "So does my guy down there."

"I have my fingers crossed that this mythical account is not on Guernsey," I added.

"Amen," said Tommy.

"So let's go through a hypothetical meeting with Hafeez. Depending on her response, we'll want to have things in place. The best scenario is to have found the account before my meeting, but the alternative is to have our people in place to follow her if she does scoot. In that case, we would probably not be able to keep her from getting the dough, but we could arrest her on several counts when she leaves the bank. Depending on the country, we may or may not be able to bring her back, at least immediately or without lots of red tape. It occurs to me, Jack, you could end up being that guy. Has she seen your face yet?"

"Don't think so," Jack said. "Her back has been to us since we came down. I'll keep a low profile while we're here." He nodded toward her table. "Do they always argue like that?"

"Looks one-sided to me. I think that Ghulam is a dominating asshole, and that, my friend, is actually a good thing."

"How so?"

"Don't think she cares for him, which makes things more predictable," I commented. "What I will guess is that with those 'housekeeper' contracts and other things, these two have covered their tracks pretty well. The two witnesses and Marylyn will mitigate that to a degree, but without a money trace, it sure isn't airtight. Still, the sense of urgency is that the pain and damage to these victims goes on every day." I thought about that for a minute. "I think I should schedule this Hafeez meeting for next Thursday, whether we've found the money or not."

"I'm hesitant, but I have to agree," Tommy said, with a certain resignation. "Can your end be ready, Jack?"

"I believe so," Jack replied.

We watched as Hafeez and Ghulam got up and left together, with the grease monkey following like Fido. They never glanced our way. The rest of our meal was relaxing as we joked, reminisced, and finished up our planning. Tommy and Jack were heading home tomorrow. For the next few days, we would all be on alert.

CHAPTER 49

Monday came with a heavy rain. I had been on statins for a few years, since my surgery. An ad for some weird-sounding drug had reminded me that my prescription had run out. By the time I had jumped through a dozen hoops and made another dozen phone calls, I was green-lighted at the pharmacy. Those drug ads were a definite deterrent to being on pills, no matter what they did for you. By the time they finished telling you that "you may experience diarrhea for the next ninety days and lose feeling in your gonads for up to two years" and other stuff, you might conclude that you'd rather head to the happy hunting ground instead. Then, when you pick up your pills, the pharmacist hands you your bottle and says, "You may experience irritability and pain in the hands and wrist . . . and that's just from trying to get the cap off."

That evening, my thoughts were cycling and recycling. Eventually, I quit trying to guess how this deal was going to go down. I grabbed a Bud and turned on PBS. That was a mistake. A cleric was talking about predestination. Talk about cognitive cycle-recycle! No wonder shame, guilt, and fear has worked so well. The concept, I thought, was simple if grounded in interpretive convolution.

The simple definition of *predestination* is that fate has predetermined all events. The Christian doctrine, however, sometimes called *theological determinism*, relates more to the ultimate fate of the individual soul, as willed by God. The age-old arguments center around the paradox of free will and the implied incompatibility therein. God's sovereignty versus man's free will.

But then, according to this guy, here's where it gets dicey. Whereas the doctrine of predestination is based on the positive aspect that God chooses some for salvation, the opposing doctrine of *preterition* emphasizes the negative, that some are *not* chosen. They are simply "passed over." So now, behind door number three, we have *double predestination,* which teaches that God proactively elects some to heaven and proactively elects some to hell. More irreconcilable antagonisms, more confusion.

I decided I liked the one that says, "If I'm not chosen for heaven, then just leave me to my own devices." I should have just watched *Everybody Loves Raymond.*

I remembered what Stephen Hawking said. "I have noticed that even people who claim everything is predestined, and that we can do nothing to change it, look before they cross the road."

CHAPTER 50

On Wednesday, right after lunch, my cell buzzed. It was Tommy.

"We got 'em, pardner. Bank is Financiera Internacional, Grand Cayman. Account is H&G Enterprises, two-point-four-three million dollars." Tommy didn't hide his excitement.

"Should I call you M or Double O Eight?" I fawned.

"How about just Double O Twenty-Five-Year-Old Macallan?" Tommy sang.

"We'll talk about your reward when we bag these birds. So tell me the story."

"Turns out it was like one of those B-movie scripts. Once my guy flashed his credentials and told the bank president about the illegal monies from drugs and human trafficking, with maybe a touch of hyperbole, the president was all smiles and most cooperative. Enthusiastic even. He did make it clear that he would need all required documents and paperwork, and said, 'Oh, by the way, it will require a good deal of work, so there will be several fees involved.' These, my guy said, consisted of normal bank fees, and what we'll call ancillary fees, both of which will come from the account. Bit of a win-win, wouldn't you say?"

"Indeed, old friend. For now, they'll freeze the account?"

"You got it. Now I need to reach Jack and tell him to bring in the big dogs and begin preparations for potential raids. He'll also have to clear his deck in case he has to travel." He paused. "I want to see if we can arrange a private jet if one is needed."

"That would solve the extraction," I said. "Once again, you're the hub of this wheel, Tommy. I have some work to do before tomorrow. Keep your cell phone charged. And by the way, can you find out if Hafeez and Ghulam own or lease their properties?"

CHAPTER 51

It was Thursday morning. I showered and shaved and did the best with what I had to work with, even dabbed on a touch of the Mennen. One can only do so much with a three-quarter-century-old carcass.

The day seemed appropriately overcast. There was little activity on the street as I pulled in front of the house. There were two cars parked down the way, one with tinted glass. The shades were drawn. I rang the bell and waited. I could hear movement. I rang again. She must have concluded that I wasn't going anywhere, so she opened the big wooden door and just looked at me.

I broke the silence. "Hello, Hafeez."

She covered her surprise quickly with a quizzical stare. She was processing. Finally, she responded. "Hello, Bruce." She let that hang.

I smiled.

"Fadi never did catch on, but then he's not as worldly as I." Another pause. "So how do you know my name?"

"It's required on property leases." I let *that* hang.

"I'm suddenly uncomfortable with this conversation, Mr. Wayne, and I'm sorry that you drove over from whatever part of Gotham City you reside in, but I will ask you to leave and I'm shutting my door. You pose a threat. Don't make me call the police."

"Before you do that, you should hear me out. First of all, I'm no threat, at least not a physical threat. You see, I'm one of the good guys, which I guess depends on point of view. Secondly, I doubt you want the police to get involved, as they'll only complicate matters. Thirdly, if you shut the door and refuse to talk to me, you'll eliminate your options, force me to call the FBI, and make me wait in my car until they arrive, which could take a while. How about you invite me in and we have a nice, friendly chat?"

Tommy had called me back. He had been able to confirm that Ghulam owned his house, mortgage-free. That told me he hadn't planned a quick exit strategy. The million or so of equity wasn't liquid. Hafeez, on the other hand, was leasing and thus had no ties. The name on that lease was Hafeez Saeed.

Hafeez had weighed her options. I sensed her resignation.

She opened her door. "I have two initial questions, Batman, but first show me some identification."

I gave her my driver's license. She sat in a comfortable chair and looked it over. I sat on a divan.

I spoke first. "Call me Woody."

"Okay, Woody, now tell me who you really are and why you're investigating me." Her look was stern, somewhat unpleasant. "But first, I need my coffee, and I'm not rude, so would you like a cup?"

"That would be nice. Just black, please." As she walked to her kitchen, I did a quick survey of the house. I needed to find two strategic locations for the bugs.

"So . . . Woody, please answer my questions," she said as she handed me the cup.

I took a long sip. "Actually, the answers run together. I was military intelligence for a few years, which segued into working for a government agency for several decades. At some point, I met a woman who told me a most interesting story about the illegal import of young girls. She introduced me to one of those girls, who confirmed the story. After several more coincidental events, the link traced to two people named Hafeez and Ghulam."

We locked in a rather intense stare for an uncomfortable time.

"Well," she said, "let's go with two more questions. Who is it that you represent, and are you here to arrest me on some fabricated hearsay and circumstantial window dressing?"

"As we speak, I represent myself. I'm prepared to make several calls to contacts who will take the necessary steps to make arrests. However, before I do that, I wanted to offer you the option to become part of the solution. If you can provide the names and locations of the guilty parties, I can provide an element of assurance that your part in this operation will receive appropriate recognition." I let her absorb that.

"Are you familiar with the word *casuistry*?" she asked me. She followed up quickly. "Webster's definition would be something like 'specious talk, intended to confuse or mislead.' My definition is 'bullshit.'"

"Okay, Hafeez. Since you're being a bit cavalier about the egregious nature of the crime I refer to, let me clarify, starting with the fact that convicted sex traffickers will spend up to fifteen years in prison and pay fines up to one-point-five million dollars. Now let me tell you what I know about Hafeez, Ghulam, Arabian Knights, Zeefa, so-called housekeepers, and 'johns.'" And that's what I did, being selective in not disclosing everything, especially any reference to bank accounts.

Hafeez digested my disclosures for a long time before going to the kitchen again. "More coffee?" she asked.

"Please," I said. This time I removed one of the transmitters from my pocket, peeled off the plastic sticker cover, and attached the transmitter to the underside of the coffee table. I also noticed that she left her cell phone on the kitchen counter, a logical place for the second bug.

"So, right now, you haven't shared all of this with others, right?" she asked.

My sentient radar told me that this was a question with certain nefarious implications. "Not much." I left it at that.

"All right, that then leads to two more questions: What are you offering me, and what is your plan of action?"

"First, by your cooperating, your sentence can be substantially reduced. I can only promise that I'll use the extent of my influence to accomplish that. As for the plan, it'll take at least two weeks to put all of the pieces in place. For that to happen, I'll need from you a list of all of the parties involved, including names and addresses. And that will include the operation in Galveston, which we know exists, and any others. This information will provide the credibility you'll need to protect your cooperative position."

"So then, Woody, how much time do I have to get you that information?"

I knew she had accepted her fate. Her response also told me that she was a person devoid of loyalty. If she was going down, so was everyone else. She didn't care.

"Before I leave," I answered. There was no equivocation in my quick reply.

"I need some time for that," she responded.

"In that case, I'll give you a half hour while I drink coffee and enjoy your nice view of the ocean. I know you have the information here." I gave her that *don't fuck with me* smile.

She didn't. She went to what I figured was her office. This gave me the chance to place the second surveillance bug under the kitchen counter. I returned to my seat and could hear a copying machine. Twenty minutes later, she came out, exuding a rather cooperative spirit. A bit phony, I thought.

"Here you go, Woody. Know that this will be a difficult time for me over the next couple of weeks, so I do expect you to be there if I should need your protection." She handed me a stack of papers.

I could sense the manipulation. I spent five minutes going through the paperwork. It had what I needed, including names of another operation in San Diego. We would now be able to close it down. The only question that remained was whether Hafeez was tooling me. I would know that in the next twelve hours.

"Just operate with Ghulam as you normally would," I warned her. "I'll keep in contact."

She simply nodded.

Once I got in my car, I turned on the small receiver. I was relieved to hear movement and the shuffling of papers. No phone calls, at least not before I got home. She had surrendered too easily. I saw a rabbit.

The man who sat in the black SUV with dark, tinted windows looked at his watch. He had been there for almost four hours. He ran his fingers through his greasy hair and hit the call button on his cell. "I need to see you. Something very interesting. Be there in about half an hour." He signed off, started the car, and glanced at the house as he drove by.

CHAPTER 52

About an hour after I got home, Hafeez made a phone call. I was monitoring the receiver constantly. It seemed to me that it was an overseas call, which I couldn't know without a tap. The call was answered in Spanish. Luckily, Hafeez had the phone set on hands-free.

Hafeez responded in English. "When can you get to Grand Cayman?"

"What do you mean?" the man replied with a strong Spanish accent. "What is the urgency?"

"You have to trust me, Mateo. I have the required passport and the signed power of attorney. You need to tell me how soon you can be there so I can get my flight booked. I'll fill you in when I get there, but please, Mateo, put this as a top priority. I'll be going back with you." Hafeez's voice sounded almost pleading.

"I will call you back," he said before hanging up.

No surprise, she was flyin' the coop. But who the hell was Mateo, and where was he coming from? Time to call Tommy.

I filled him in on my meeting with Hafeez.

"Can you send me those papers? I need to get them to Jack ASAP."

"Tommy . . . you know I'm a technical dinosaur, but I do have a fax machine."

"What the hell is a fax machine?" Pause, then a giggle. "That'll work. Monitor that receiver closely and call me when you know more."

"Gotcha."

LINES THROUGH A PRISM

Within the hour, the receiver sounded. Mateo was calling back. "I can be there by Saturday afternoon. You get a room at the Coronado, on Seven Mile Drive. What name?"

"Elizabeth Hepburn."

"Where did that come from?"

"Just a couple of old Hollywood celebs. Never mind." I heard anxiety in Hafeez's tone. "I'll fill you in on everything when I see you," she said, "but know we need to be at the bank when they open on Monday morning."

"All right. See you then . . . Elizabeth." Mateo laughed.

Hafeez didn't.

Her next call was to Atlanta, Delta Airlines. She booked a Saturday morning flight to Georgetown under the name of E. Hepburn. I emailed that to Tommy. Twenty minutes after that, her phone rang again.

"Hello."

"When were you going to tell me?" It was Ghulam.

She remained silent, then seemed to recover. "I just got back, damn it. What is it I'm supposed to tell you?" She was on the offensive.

"A little birdie told me you had a visitor this morning."

"It so happens that I did, which I want to talk to you about, but first, about this birdie. Are you watching me?" She sounded angry.

I knew it was an act.

"Of course not. Silva was going to drop off a pie. I picked up an extra last evening and thought you might enjoy." He paused. "So where have you been?"

"I've been tracking the guy who came by. His real name is Woodward, not Wayne. Found out where he lives. Not really sure why he came by, but he did ask me about you. I didn't tell him anything, but it does raise a red flag."

"What did he want to know about me and why?"

"He asked what you did for a living. What concerned me was when he asked if you did business with Ryan DuBruss. I said I had never heard the name. If he's not just a nosey old coot, he just might pose a threat. You maybe want to follow up on that, Fadi."

There was a long pause.

"By the way, I'm going down to Atlanta this weekend to meet a girl I worked with in New York. A show, some shopping. I'll see you at the club on Monday, usual time."

"Yeah, okay." Ghulam hung up.

He may have hung up, but I suspected he was deep in thought. I felt a chill. There was trouble in paradise with these two. Silva, the little henchman, was watching Hafeez for Ghulam. They were lying to each other, had big trust issues. Hafeez was not only leavin' town and ditching Ghulam, but she just threw me under the bus. Curiouser and curiouser, messy and messier.

I called Tommy back and brought him up to speed. He told me he would give an update to his guy in the Caymans and that Jack was getting his network in place. All three of these operations and all the john locations would require a small army of agents.

Next, I got my derringer and loaded it with five hollow points. Let the games begin.

CHAPTER 53

A round seven thirty that evening, the doorbell rang. I was wearing my dark hoodie and the baseball hat Mary Beth had given me years ago. It said, *DON'T DO IT!* She had called me impetuous, and that was her subtle message.

I peeked out of the side window. I could envision the old SNL church lady saying, "Well, isn't that special?" It was a delivery service man, short, with greasy hair, his hat pulled down over his eyes.

If one is to survive in today's world, one best develop a hardened shell against being incessantly offended. I did that decades ago, with one exception: when people assume I'm stupid.

I opened the door with my left hand. My right stayed in the hoodie pocket. He had a small package in his right hand and a clipboard in his left. Vulnerable. I waited for him to speak.

"I have a package for a Mr. Woodward." His head stayed down.

"Really?" I said.

"Yup, just need a signature."

"I see." I let that hang.

His head stayed down.

"Well, before I sign anything, you need to listen very, very carefully. I have a gun filled with five hollow point shells, with the hammer cocked, pointed somewhere between your stomach and your balls. Now this is only conjecture, but I would guess that you too have a gun, tucked in your belt, behind your back. Let's move to our next topic of physics. Your right hand is holding a package while your left is holding a clipboard, so even if you were Doc Holliday, which you're not, it would take you at least four seconds to drop those things, reach around to your back, grab the gun, bring it around, and pull the trigger. In the meantime, most unfortunate for you, there would already be one hole in your lower abdomen and a second hole through your left occipital orb, which for mentally challenged people like you, is your left eye. Let's move on to the third of four topics to be discussed."

His head remained down, but his body language showed an intensity. Still, he hadn't moved.

"The next thing you will do will be to extend your arms out toward me, keeping hold of the package and the clipboard. Place them together while I wrap a piece of rope around your wrists. Any quick movement will initiate a loud bang. And now, number four, the grand finale, and the most critical one for you, which falls under the category of intuition, is for you to decide whether I'm bluffing or not."

At that point, he raised his head to look me in the eyes, same as I would have done. His eyes went to my right-hand pocket and back to my eyes.

"Decision time, Mr. Silva. I suggest you consider the message on my favorite hat."

He looked up. After another five seconds, he slowly extended his arms. When I did bring the gun from my pocket, I saw that look that gamblers make when they walk away from a bet before going all-in on a losing hand.

I had prepared. I pulled the three-foot length of clothesline from my back pocket with my left hand and wrapped his wrists, at which point I put the gun in my pocket and secured a knot. I turned him around and removed the Beretta from his back. As I figured, it had a silencer.

I called Curtis and told him what just happened. I asked him to get hold of his pal, Officer Monroe, the local cop, and come to my place as soon as possible. I had fully secured Silva and set him on the couch. His acquiescence was palpable, and he looked like he was going to take a nap.

"I'm sure you've heard this pitch before, Mr. Silva, but if you choose to cooperate with the government, it really will make your future a bit brighter. Got any interest?" Might as well give it a shot. "Hell, Silva, you're just a gun for hire. You'll get no loyalty from Ghulam. He doesn't give a shit about you. You're not getting another dime from him, and now he's better off if you're dead. Fifteen years minimum for attempted murder!"

Silence.

Then a response. "I didn't even pull a gun. I'll be out in twenty-four hours."

"Not what the witnesses saw, Mr. Silva."

"That's a good one. There weren't any witnesses." Silva sneered.

"Oh my gosh." I exaggerated my words, hitting my forehead with the heel of my hand. "I must have forgot. So then, it's your word against mine, a highly decorated government agent, essential to bringing down an international sex trafficking ring, against a hit man with a gun, with a suppressor, with fingerprints all over it, wearing a disguise, working for a felon, who pulled his gun on me and would have killed me if I hadn't been better, smarter, and faster, *and* exercised great restraint by not putting a bullet through his tiny brain. Good luck on that defense."

"Then you'd be lying," he stated.

I couldn't help my spasm of laughter. "You really are a slow learner, Silva." I just grinned at him. "Yup, supermax in Colorado for at least fifteen, assuming you make it that long, cute little fella like you. Might even get some use from that grease."

CHAPTER 54

A police car pulled into my driveway. Curtis and Patrolman Monroe got out.

Monroe spoke first. "What a surprise, Mr. Woodward. More people trying to kill you. Just a guess, but I'd bet you weren't labeled *BEST LIKED* in your high school yearbook."

"Not to be argumentative, sir, but I actually had a lot of friends in high school." I smiled.

"Seems that took a turn for the worse somewhere along the line. In any event, this time you're going to tell me the real story, or I might have to book you for . . . oh, I don't know . . . anarchy, civil disobedience, jaywalking? I'll come up with something." He shook his head.

My smile was genuine. "You do deserve to hear everything I'm allowed to tell you, Officer Monroe, and I do thank you in advance.

"Although retired, as a former government agent for over three decades, I'm currently an integral part of an ongoing FBI investigation that involves multiple locations, some here in Georgia. Highly confidential. When this operation is completed, I'll take you, along with Curtis, out for a nice meal and tell you all about it. In the meantime, you'll receive a call in the morning from a Mr. Jack O'Brien of the FBI, and he'll confirm my position in this investigation. For now, though, on the charge of attempted murder, you have the right to hold this man for seventy-two hours, with absolutely no calls until the specific charges can be brought. It's imperative that this remain confidential: no press, no outsiders. You understand?"

Monroe looked at Curtis, who nodded. We went inside to get the prisoner.

As Silva got into the patrol car, I said to him, "Think about what I said."

He gave me a dead kind of look.

I turned to Monroe. "I'll give Curtis a ride home, Officer, and again, thank you."

Curtis and I cracked a beer and sat on the back patio while I gave him an accounting of what happened. "Here's what I see for the next couple of days. I want Ghulam to be in the dark until Saturday, which is when the FBI will arrest him, after I've had my alone time with him. I'll need your help with that. Until then, he won't know what happened to me, or Silva, and will be getting very nervous. As I see it, Jack will be making that arrest, and then head to Grand Cayman. There, he'll meet with Tommy's guy, and the two of them will be there on Monday morning when Hafeez and her significant other show up at the bank. I'm hoping Tommy, or Jack, can arrange a private jet to bring her back. Neither Hafeez nor Ghulam will have opportunity or incentive to give a heads-up to the other players, which means Jack should have plenty of time to schedule the raids on the perps in all of the operations: this one, Galveston, and San Diego." I let that sink in. "Any thoughts?"

Curtis ruminated. From my angle, there was a resemblance to the most famous Native American profile in history, that on the Buffalo nickel. I could see that strength, resilience, and magnetism that history has so capriciously discounted, and in so doing, weakened the fabric of our country since its formation.

"You're a good man, Woody Woodward. No moral crime is more egregious than the abuse of children, and here were such people operating next to me for several years, and I did nothing. Had no idea. Then you come along. Now these wicked miscreants will pay, and all good people everywhere thank you, Woody."

"I do appreciate your commendation, Curtis, but please don't take on any guilt. My empathy for abused children is no bigger than yours. This is simply what I do, my training and experience, and remember, we got to this point together. Your input has been invaluable."

I've never been comfortable with compliments. Most contain hidden agendas. Even a genuine compliment will make me shuffle, figuratively, but from Curtis, it was meaningful.

"Regardless, your strategy and tactics have been right on, Woody. There's nothing of substance that I could add, other than you need to get hold of Tommy and Jack."

Curtis was right. I had hooked up the Bluetooth in my car, and we talked to Tommy as I drove Curtis home.

CHAPTER 55

For the rest of the night, I drew the shades and kept the lights off. I had taken Silva's cell phone. Eventually, a call came from Ghulam. I let it go to voice mail.

The message was short and sweet. "Call me."

I knew he would be getting more anxious with each passing hour. He could only wait. He had no one else to call. If he did drive by my house at some point, he would only see a dark silhouette. Three more calls came in the next twelve hours, all to voice mail. His anger increased with each call and brought a bigger smile to my face each time.

Friday would be much the same. I kept a sliver of curtain open to watch for passing cars. At nine thirty, a black Cadillac SUV with tinted windows drove up the street, turned around, and disappeared. I figured it was him.

Outside of that, I spent the day refining the plan and talking to Tommy and Curtis. Jack was on his way. Curtis had him booked into the club. We agreed to have dinner at a barbecue joint west of town. They would pick me up a block from my house wearing a quasi disguise. I needed to be sure Ghulam didn't see me and wasn't surveilling my place.

The car was a gray sedan. I didn't recognize the driver. Jack sat in the front and Curtis in the back. They introduced me to Billy James, FBI agent out of Atlanta, who had driven up that morning. He would be assisting Jack in the arrest and taking both Ghulam and Jack back to Atlanta, where Jack would fly to Grand Cayman and Ghulam would be incarcerated until things were straightened out.

We got a corner booth, private enough so that if we had to get Tommy on the phone or Jack had to call his office, we could do that. Jack was on a roll. The hierarchy in his office was on board and committed. Seems they saw this as a real positive promotion of the public's perception of the Bureau. He agreed that since neither Hafeez nor Ghulam would be able to forewarn the operators in Galveston or San Diego, or any of the so-called johns, there was adequate time to coordinate the raids.

We got into a discussion of the various offenses, charges, and penalties for each of the perpetrators. Ghulam and Hafeez were guilty of multiple crimes as we saw it. Same was probably true for those running the operations in Galveston and San Diego. For the johns, it was certainly less, except for their reputations and consequences from that. Buying sex is prostitution, and these guys would all be charged with a misdemeanor, with zero to thirty days of jail time. It might certainly be more if it was determined to be commercial slavery or some such. But assuming they hadn't physically harmed any of the girls, that wasn't the real punishment for these guys. It was the publicity, and I had just the person to do a major story: my daughter-in-law, Sam's sister, Carol.

I set it up so that Jack and Billy would arrive near Ghulam's house around ten tomorrow morning. I would text Jack when I was ready for their arrival. Curtis and I would arrive around nine. I would attempt to get what I wanted from Ghulam in that hour. Tommy didn't need to be there, but he was available for contact at all times.

After our meal, they dropped me off near my place. I checked to be sure there was no one watching my place and then went in through the back door.

Before I hit the hay, I reviewed what I wanted to get from Fadi Ghulam. I doubted I would be successful. I would meet Curtis at eight thirty in the club parking lot. He would drive to Ghulam's.

CHAPTER 56

Curtis, Jack, and Billy were just finishing breakfast when I arrived. We reconfirmed that Jack and Billy would be close by and come to Ghulam's house after my text. Then Curtis and I got into his car and headed to Ghulam's.

The house had a porte cochere driveway, and we could get close to the front door. I wore my hoodie with a hat pulled low. I had my little pistol and told Curtis that he might hear one shot fired, but that it would only be for effect. While I was inside with Ghulam, Curtis would remain in the car. He pulled up to the front door, got out on the driver's side, and rang the doorbell, blocking any view of me. It didn't take long until Ghulam came out, and as Curtis engaged him in conversation, I got out and approached from the side.

When he saw me, his jaw fell.

"Fadi, Fadi." I shook my head slowly from side to side. "You look like you've seen a ghost."

He glanced at the pistol in my right hand.

I clenched his arm with my left. "Seems you and I need to go inside and have a little tete-a-tete." I could see the fear in his eyes. "That's French for a chat."

He and I went inside while Curtis got in his car.

Once inside, I pushed him into a chair. "Since you know me as Bruce Wayne, fine with me that we keep it that way. What you should know, however, is that I'm a retired assassin, but I gotta tell you, thus far, retirement ain't all it's cracked up to be, thanks to you. Like the two attempts on my life." I again shook my head, feigning disappointment. "First order of business, I know you have a gun in the house, so let's go get it."

He gave me a surprised look and started to speak. "I do not have a gun . . ."

But before he could finish, I shot the Tiffany lamp that was on the table next to him. The shot was loud, the lamp shattered, and I think he peed in his pants.

"Next one goes in your kneecap." I started to lower the barrel.

"All right, all right, all right." His fear was intense. He got up and walked over to his desk.

As he opened the top right drawer, I pointed the gun at his head. "Now, very carefully, lift it out and set it on the desk, and sit in that chair."

He did as told. The gun was out of reach.

I settled into a chair beside him. "Apparently you didn't listen to my warning at the club." I let him think about that. After a moment, I continued. "Two things I really hate, Fadi: liars and child abusers. You lied to me about Frick and Frack, and then you lied about 'shortcrotch.' I told you I would put him in a body bag and then come and find you. So here we are, you with a gun with your fingerprints all over it, which the police will find in your hand, along with a small hole in your right temple, and me, an innocent victim who was forced to protect himself." I smiled at him.

He didn't return the smile.

"Alive, you're guilty of two counts of attempted murder, where a conviction will render a life sentence. Now, just for the hell of it, let's talk about child abuse." I stared him down. "I know everything about your housekeeper operation: recruiting, transport, the contracts, the threats, the punishments, the buyers, the payments, the bank accounts onshore and offshore, tax evasion, money laundering, blah-blah-blah. What I hadn't found out on my own, I learned from Hafeez Saeed and Mr. Silva, and yes, he's alive."

His visage was a mix of emotion, from surprise to anger.

"You, Fadi, are one naughty boy. Your partners have turned against you, and their plea bargains are the carrots. You get the stick."

He hung his head, having nothing to say. He knew he was finished.

Time for a stay of execution. I poked the bear. "Let's say old Fadi wants a carrot too, maybe a little revenge. And let's say you could provide some solid evidence against Hafeez. And let's say my attempted murder charge only goes against Silva. Would that interest you?"

He reached for the life raft. "How about the other charges?" he asked, with hope.

I shook my head. "Human trafficking is a federal crime," I replied. "I have no say."

His head bowed.

"But for my offer, I need a response now."

He didn't answer. I grabbed my phone. "Feebees will be here in six minutes."

Ghulam caved. "Hold on. Tell me what you want."

"Hold that thought, Fadi."

I called Curtis, who was just outside, and asked him to bring in my backpack. When he did, I asked him to set up the camera.

While he did that, I set paper and pen in front of Ghulam. "Start writing, Fadi. Don't hold anything back. I want every bit of evidence against Hafeez. Once you have that, everything against the operators in Galveston and San Diego. Hold back and the deal's off."

I called Jack instead of texting him. I did want him to be here for the recording. I then reviewed the opening statement I had prepared for Ghulam to read on camera. It started with the normal CYA language about freely making the statement, not being under duress or threat, and so forth. That would be followed by his reading the statement he was writing now.

Jack and Billy arrived. They put Ghulam's gun in a ziplock bag. Billy stared at the remains of the Tiffany lamp and then looked at me.

I shrugged my shoulders and said, "Accident." I told him to watch Ghulam while I stepped outside with Jack, where I filled him in on what happened, and then we called Tommy.

Jack and Tommy agreed that from their point of view, Ghulam's statement and evidence, as well as what Hafeez had already provided, should be sufficient evidence for convictions. And there was Marta, Ilana, and who knows how many more. I felt no guilt in foisting Ghulam and Hafeez while playing them against each other. The carrots I was offering them were certainly weak, and both would spend a long time in prison for money laundering and tax evasion, with human trafficking being the MacGuffin.

Tommy gave Jack the contact information for Eduardo, Tommy's guy in the Caymans. Jack had secured all of the official paperwork needed to arrest Hafeez and bring her back, as well as what the bank needed to confiscate the account, minus some rather generous bank fees and expenses. Jack claimed that the Bureau could reap some goodwill collateral by earmarking those funds for the victims, like Marta and Ilana.

Jack had reserved a room at a beachside motel for tonight and would meet Eduardo tomorrow and prepare for Monday morning. Eduardo was surveilling Hafeez now. Her Argentinian friend was supposed to meet her tonight as well, though in the "large photo" of things, he was a nonevent.

Still, Tommy, the magician, had some more good news. "I have a client, a young fella, who owns a security company that does contract work for the DOD," Tommy said. "Last year, he discovered that he was missing almost seven million dollars. He was having trouble with the who and how these funds were being siphoned off. He called me, and within two weeks we solved the puzzle. It involved his CFO and two foreign vendors. Complicated deal, but my client was elated and quite generous. Told me he was still indebted. In any event, he has a new girlfriend, and when I suggested he take her to Grand Cayman for a couple of days, he jumped on it. Bottom line, his Lear Jet 40XR will leave Atlanta for Georgetown when Jack arrives, around six this evening, and return on Monday with Jack and his female guest."

Jack picked it up after a pause. "I gotta tell both you guys, outside of tying the knot with Jenny, I haven't been so exhilarated in decades," he said with a near-effusive sentiment. "You guys are the best. You have no idea." He had been in a dark hole.

I jumped in before it became uncomfortable. "Yup, gitten-er-done. Barging ahead and doing the right thing. Screw the red tape. Kinda like those three amigos. 'We don't need no stinking badges.'"

We giggled.

"I'm thinking about the follow-up. Billy can handle getting Ghulam to the FBI office in Atlanta. I want to go see my daughter-in-law's sister, the award-winning journalist, swear her to confidentiality, and get her moving on this breaking story. Jack and I can follow Billy to Atlanta, and I'll take Jack to the airport."

We agreed. I then called Carol, dangled the bait, and told her I would see her tomorrow.

CHAPTER 57

G hulam's statement was more than I expected. Most was redundant, stuff we already knew, and of course, the expected blame throwing and redirect, but one piece of information was significant. One of the customers, a very wealthy guy in New York who had former ties to Hafeez, had a housekeeper disappear. The guy, according to Ghulam, was a substantial political contributor. We would find out from Tommy that he was on the CIA's radar for business affiliations in both Russia and China. In any event, he was also tagged as a woman abuser. Ghulam claimed that at one point, his housekeeper disappeared. Hafeez had apparently met with him, made some kind of financial arrangement, and replaced the old with a new girl. The one who disappeared was never heard from again. Ghulam was certain that there was foul play and that Hafeez was complicit. Tommy would pass that bit of intel on.

After the statement and the video were completed, we went past my place, I grabbed a bag, and the two cars left for Atlanta.

Riding with Jack was enjoyable, but a bit of a mixed bag. He was in a good place these days, looking forward to retirement with Jenny and his family, several of which were estranged, but he had gone through a rough five to six years.

Jack had been one tough cookie. He had a high IQ and had brought an element of intuition to the Counter Intelligence Corp that resulted in several tactical victories for the infantry. He had a touch of "crazy" however, and on those rare occasions when our team engaged the "Cong," he was Audie

Murphy incarnate. He had earned his Bronze Star. The FBI had recruited him with zeal, and his stock rose until he crossed the new, rather opaque line that had been quietly and surreptitiously drawn by the "politically correct" brain trust. Even though his actions had saved the lives of six agents, that fact was dismissed, and soon afterward, so was Jack. His teammates all supported him, but the "star chamber" held firm. His fall from grace was quick, as was his transition from "bender" to depression. His wife left him, his son blamed him, and he slid down the rabbit hole.

If left unattended, depression can become an unrelenting and recreant assassin that, much like plaque in our blood vessels, builds scar tissue on the soul, wounds that never show on the body, but are more devastating than anything that bleeds . . . dark and hopeless. We can all make it through adversity, unless you don't see an end.

Tough love works. There's just not enough of it anymore. The new world says it's abusive . . . even illegal. I look back, and not only am I glad that my parents kicked my ass when I deserved it, but I can clearly measure the results. Jack would have jumped off a bridge without it. Jenny kicked his ass, and then kicked it again. Then she told him to get some humility and drag that black-and-blue raggedy ass, with his hat in hand, back to the Bureau. He did. They made an exception. He got his swagger back, with an upgrade of depth and wisdom.

"You know, Woody, as much as humility is now a part of my character, this opportunity you and Tommy have created for me can send me into retirement on a chariot of fire. I want the respect, Woody." Jack's new humility was evident.

"When this goes down, you'll be the man, Jack," I replied.

"I know better," he said. "Wish I'd had your humility and strength a long time ago."

"I genuinely prize my anonymity, Jack. My life is easier, safer. Kind of like, if I don't own anything, no one can steal it. Know what I mean?"

"Yeah, I get it, but I'm a small-time phoenix. I just want to get back to where I was, in a different way. You know what I'm saying."

"I do, Jack. Indeed, I do."

CHAPTER 58

South of Atlanta, we called Billy. He was copacetic and would go directly to FBI HQ while Jack and I would split off and head to the private airfield. When we got there, we called Tommy's client. His name was Trelawny Barker, but he went by Buddy. I could understand why. Buddy sent an official to the gate with a pass that allowed us to drive to his jet.

We got out, and as Buddy descended down the plane's cabin staircase, he said, "Hi, Jack," and laughed. "Say that on a commercial plane, and you get arrested!" he bellowed and laughed again. Could have been scripted. "I'm Buddy." He extended his hand.

Jack introduced himself and then me.

"Welcome aboard. Friends of Tommy are friends of mine." Buddy seemed genuine, handsome, and smooth.

We looked to the top of the stair, and a facsimile of Bo Derek appeared and smiled at us. I was waiting for the beat of Ravel's *Bolero* to start.

"Gentlemen, meet my friend, Marnie." Buddy swung his arm up to Marnie, like Ed Sullivan did when he introduced the Beatles.

We waved. I wondered if Jack might want to trade places. C'est la vie.

Jack and I stepped aside. Jack said he would call with an update after he met with Eduardo tomorrow. We shook hands. He gave me a collusive grin and nodded toward Marnie. I gave him the bird, smiled, and waved to Buddy and Marnie before leaving.

CHAPTER 59

Since I wasn't meeting Carol until tomorrow, I had time on my hands. For the hell of it, I drove past the Arabian Knights. What a dump. I wasn't much of an artist, but I could put that sign painter to shame. No cars, no business, no Hafeez. The store would be empty in a month.

I checked into a Holiday Inn and grabbed a handful of brochures, Chamber of Commerce promotions, and decided to check out the city. After sightseeing for an hour, I had had enough. Tall buildings, tons of traffic, short tempers, little tolerance—the usual urban circus. I double-checked the directions to Carol's and concluded that Atlanta would be a great place to catch up on some sleep. When I walked into my room, my cell buzzed. It was Tommy.

It seemed that both the CIA and the FBI were interested in the New York customer. As an afterthought, Tommy added the IRS. The CIA for his foreign business dealings, the FBI for the missing girl and the Hafeez connection, and the IRS, well, they were always looking for money for any reason, and this dude fell under the umbrella of "person of interest." Tommy giggled when I told him about Buddy and Marnie.

"He's an ass bandit," Tommy said. "What can I say? But he's a straight shooter, having fun with his well-earned affluence."

"Echoes of the past, huh, Tommy? But without the affluence."

"Learjet 40XR or 1962 Dodge beater. What's the difference, Woody? All relative."

"Ain't that the truth. Let's talk tomorrow." I signed off, went downstairs, grabbed a sandwich, took it to my room, watched a National Geographic documentary on endangered elephants, got pissed off at poachers, and went to sleep.

CHAPTER 60

I got to Carol's at 10:00 a.m. Carol and her husband, John, had two kids, a boy and girl, about the same age as Sonny's twin girls. John was in the backyard building what looked like a tree house, more of a platform, about six feet off the ground, in one of those trees indigenous to Georgia. John was a good man, successful and solid. The kids were happy and lovable.

They hugged me, and after fifteen minutes of family time, Carol and I went to her office. She had photos and awards over her desk. She appeared to be excited about this story, while most empathetic with the topic. I started from the time of my first suspicions and brought her to the arrest of Hafeez, which would take place tomorrow. We talked for over an hour.

"This is a major story, Woody. National scope. I truly appreciate you bringing it to me. I'm torn between anger and sadness. I assure you that you'll see both in my presentation." Carol shook her head slowly.

"I wanted you to be prepared when the story breaks after the raids, but until you get the green light from me, it remains strictly confidential."

"My lips are sealed."

On the drive back to Jekyll Island, I went over the things that could go wrong, and there were many. Most of the potential roadblocks to justice were hidden in the legal complex, the chasm between justice and the law. That, however, was out of my hands.

When I was halfway home, Jack called. His hookup with Eduardo went well. Seems Hafeez's white knight from

Argentina arrived, and the two were keeping a low profile. Jack and Eduardo were all set for tomorrow morning. He added, with a chuckle, that he figured Marnie had formed a crush on him on the flight down to Grand Cayman. I told him I was going to call Jenny, and he just bellowed. We were anxious for the arrest.

I turned on the radio. There had been more shootings. Predictably, the politicians blamed it on the guns, not the assholes who pulled the triggers. Like blaming God for the drunk driver who kills the busload of children. They give no thought to the army of responsible gun owners who provide a deterrent to crime and murder. They seem unaware of the fact that if I decide I want to burglarize or shoot someone, with two hundred bucks in my pocket, I can get an illegal gun in any urban city in the country within three hours, anytime I want to. They're blind to the fact that the miscreants are licking their chops, waiting for the political idiots to remove the Second Amendment, and seemingly, law enforcement, and in the process, the only threat to their crimes. And for the victims, and future victims, they aren't supposed to defend themselves, their families, or their property? No, to the politicians, the shooters are the victims. Once again, laws without enforcement are impotent.

It seemed to me that most of these shootings were related to power, money, or hatred. The quest for power hasn't changed since Cain and Abel. Same for money, be it drachmas or gold. But are we seeing an increase in hatred? It's always been as prevalent as love, but somehow, those two have yin and yanged it to a standoff. Today, it appears that hatred has taken the lead. James Baldwin said, "I imagine one of the reasons people cling to their hates so stubbornly is because they sense, once hate is gone, they will be forced to deal with pain." Fear and pain will do that. Blame is for many an elixir, a replacement for self-analysis. Who and what can turn the tide?

News always seems to take me to a bad place. I turned on a

country station that was playing old country: Hank Williams, Hank Snow, Patsy Cline, and Ray Price. I mellowed out. Reality sucks. Give me the time of Martha White's Self-Rising Flour and Dreamsicles and Clarabell the Clown. I don't think I was an earthling before. If I was, I was a sailor on one of the tall ships or a Greek philosopher wandering the streets of Athens, but I do think I will come back. When I do, I will either be a porpoise or a sea gull. Neither of them hates; they just see and do cool things.

When I pulled into my driveway, I was beat. I did the only thing that made any sense. I grabbed a Sam Adams and a two-week old pack of Marlboros, sat on the patio, adjusted my 'tude, and talked to my Great Spirit, offering gratitude for my life. I slept like a baby.

CHAPTER 61

The bank didn't officially open until 8:00 a.m., but Jack and Eduardo arrived outside at 7:30. The bank manager had agreed that once Hafeez and her sidekick had filled out the paperwork for withdrawal of the funds, Jack and Eduardo, who would be sitting in an adjacent office, would come in and confront.

At 7:50, a cab pulled up, and Hafeez got out, as did a sixties-looking dandy with a goatee and a Panama hat. Quintessential caricature. Soon after they entered the lobby, Jack and Eduardo followed. The bank manager's office had plenty of glass. The perps were seated and digging into the briefcases they had brought. Jack and Eduardo sat in the contiguous office for about ten minutes. They heard the manager's door open.

He entered their space, looking most professional. "They've filled out the request to close the account," the manager stated to Jack. "We have both signatures, and they insist on good funds. It's all on the desk. I'll remain outside unless you need me."

Jack thanked him as he walked into the office. He sat at the desk while Eduardo shut the door. He looked at both of them. He saw anger in the eyes of Hafeez and fear in the dandy. Jack said nothing as he studied the paperwork on the desk, which included passports.

After an extended silence, Hafeez asked, with anger and impatience, "What the hell is going on?"

Jack just looked at her and stared before responding. "You know, just like Eddie Fisher and Richard Burton, I was an

Elizabeth fan. And like Bogie, a Hepburn fan. Seems you're a twofer."

Hafeez said nothing. Eduardo snickered.

Jack then turned to Panama Hat. "And you, sir, represent a major conundrum. There's a guy who lives on Jekyll Island, Georgia, with the same name, but he looks much different than you. You have much more . . . savoir faire than the other Fadi Ghulam." He let that percolate.

The man twitched, and his eyes bugged.

Finally, Jack continued. "Okay. Silly me for playing games. Let me get to the point. I'm Jack O'Brien, special agent of the FBI. First, I shall deal with you, Mateo. Are you aware of the consequences for someone convicted of false impersonation for purposes of bank fraud? And are you familiar with what happens to someone who alters a passport?"

Goatee Man shook his head.

"Perhaps not," Jack said, "but here's the deal. You'll go with my colleague to the room next door and provide him with a statement. Full disclosure, Mateo. If I'm satisfied with your statement, I will magnanimously let you cab it to the airport and return to Argentina. If not, the local gendarmes will not be so generous. What say you, Mateo?"

Mateo looked at Jack, looked at Hafeez, stood up, and left with Eduardo.

Jack turned to Hafeez, whose head hung down. "And you, Ms. Saeed, you're a horse of a different color. My friend and colleague, Woody, thinks you're a very naughty girl. He's anxious to talk with you. So where are we at? I propose you come back to the States with me, cooperatively, and we see where the chips fall."

"And if I don't?" she said.

"Well . . . as I implied to Mr. Mateo, the Cayman police frown on such things as bank fraud, drug money, sex trafficking money, passport fraud—and the thing is, one may rot in their horrible little jails for three years before they even look at court. Never know, a hotshot lawyer might save your bacon in the Georgia legal system. I, however, have a private jet to Atlanta that I need to catch, so I'll have the bank manager call the cops if you prefer."

She stared at the floor.

Jack got up to head for the door.

"I'll go back, but I have conditions," she stated.

Jack just laughed and reached for the door handle.

She stood up, defeated, and said, "Come on, let's get the hell out of here."

Jack and Eduardo agreed that Mateo's statement was as condemning as they could expect, considering the source. They also agreed that he was far less a criminal than he was a fool. He'd served his sentence.

They put Hafeez in Eduardo's car and turned to Mateo. "*Adiós, amigo*," they said, drove away, and left him standing on the curb.

CHAPTER 62

The morning was balmy. I had a jug of Highlander Grog coffee as I walked my backyard. In addition to the coffee smell, there was fragrance in the air. I had kept my interest in gardening close to the vest. Admittedly, it was my own misplaced protection of my image. Not insecurity, mind you, just an old-school perception of the manly man. I had looked up the shrubs and flowers, even planted a few. The scents were soothing. Fragrant tea olive, anise, confederate jasmine, Clematis Snowdrifts, and of course, excel lilacs. I was really beginning to like this place. I was also deflecting. Nervous energy, waiting to hear from Jack. Finally, at nine thirty, my cell buzzed.

"Hey, Woody, Jack here, and I got Tommy on the line. Saves me from having to repeat. First off, it went well. Hafeez is on the plane, charming Buddy, probably asking if he has a parachute she could use and if he would fly over Cuba. And by the way, Woody, I think I saw Marnie winking at me." Jack was in high spirits.

"Chicks will always take pity on dirty old men, Jack," I said with a chuckle.

"I suppose. Still, the illusion keeps me young and vibrant. Something about a legend in my own mind."

"Well, you are a legend, Jack," I said in support.

"Okay, kids. Did you get all the docs we need, Jack, and control of the account?" Tommy interjected.

"Got it all, Tommy," Jack said. "And Eduardo is a keeper. Good man."

"How about her lover boy?" I asked.

"Seems his commitment to Hafeez was a bit shallow. Ephemeral type." Jack described Mateo's reaction and anxiety to skip town as quick as possible. "I'll send you guys a copy of his statement. Not earthshaking, but still, more damaging evidence for the prosecution."

"Be still my soul, be still, the love he bears is brittle," I added.

"Poor old Hafeez. She really does deserve better. How's the social life in prison?" Jack chuckled. "Hey, guys, I'm getting the wave from Buddy. Gotta' go. I'll call from the FBI office in Atlanta. By the way, Tommy, Buddy is terrific." Jack signed off.

Time to call Curtis.

"Hey there, Curtis, there's a cool little bar near the marina, Doogie's, so let's meet for a margarita this afternoon. Would that work? Just heard from Jack and want to bring you up-to-date."

"I'll be there at two," he said enthusiastically. "Anxious to get your update."

I went to the marina at noon, threw the kayak in the harbor, and got an enjoyable workout. I spent some time studying Ghulam's speedboat. It was an abandoned floating haunted house. Needed to be sanitized and reimaged. I wondered if it would become confiscated property that would go to auction. I had an interest. Maybe Jack could get me a deal. I pictured my kids and grandkids cruising. Maybe Marylyn would want a ride.

That reminded me to call her with a status report. "Good afternoon, young lady," I said. "Lots has happened. I could be talked into a cocktail at a restaurant of your choice, if you're inclined." I found myself to be anxious.

"Sorry, who is this again?" she asked.

"Woody," I responded, air seeping out of my tires.

"Woody who?" she replied, but she couldn't muffle her giggle.

A silence ensued.

"I hate 'gotchas' when I'm the receiver. You'd better watch your back, Ms. Ottesen."

"I've been waiting with bated breath for your call, Mr. Woodward. How about six thirty at the Surf? Know where that is?"

"How about I pick you up around six, and you can show me?"

"Perfect. See you then."

I grabbed a small table on the porch of Doogie's, and when I saw Curtis's car pull in, ordered two margaritas. "You're looking mighty handsome, Dr. Red Crow," I said, with a certain elation in my voice.

"Okay, I'm not an idiot," he said with skepticism. "What's going on with you?"

"Nothing really," I replied. "Just got a dinner date is all." I tried to tamp down my excitement.

"I see," he said with a big smile. "So how is Marylyn?"

"Who said it was Marylyn?"

"Like I said, I'm not stupid."

"Whatever," I said, sounding dismissive. "I have a professional responsibility to let her know what has happened."

"In the old days, that's what a telephone was for." He paused. "In any event, how did it go with Jack in the Caymans?"

I gave him a full account.

"Seems there will be an empty table at the club, so from my perch, all that remains is for Jack to coordinate the raids and round up the girls and the bad guys. That about right?"

"Sounds about right, my friend," I said. "Lots of good news for the victims, and the fun will just begin for those bad guys. My daughter-in-law's sister will make a big splash with this story. Really ruffle some feathers. There will be a lot of clean-up as well. *But*, what's happened here will send a strong message to anyone else thinking about trafficking in sex." I looked at the water for a long time, thinking about those girls and how their dreams had been ruined.

"Fact is, you deserve a medal, Woody." Curtis spoke with deep sincerity.

"Thank you, Curtis, but know that I don't want any of the sunshine. I do want Jack to be redeemed and to ride off into retirement on a white horse, and I do want Tommy and his company, Coeus Intel Services, to receive lots of exposure. I want my anonymity and my privacy. My days of glory are long past, and giving me glory would only bring me grief."

"You weren't born for a quiet life, Woody. There's a new adventure out there waiting for you, maybe just a seed right now, but it'll burst through the ground and blossom at your feet. If I'm fortunate enough, I'll be a part of it. You're my Ponce de Leon."

I saw Curtis's eyes start to water and turned away. I'll never be comfortable in such situations. "We may be the first comedy slash investigation team in history," I said, trying to deflect.

"Like Inspector Clouseau and Woody LLC?" Curtis jibed.

"Something like that."

We smiled.

"I really am hoping that these raids will commence in the next several days," I said. "After that, you and I will go to that restaurant you mentioned and have the classic French bouil-labaisse, and celebrate."

"Les Appentis, absolutely, and it'll be my treat." Curtis threw his hands in the air.

CHAPTER 63

I had a date. Sounded weird. Kids have dates. My daughter has dates. My daughter's dad doesn't have dates. WTF? I wondered if my Mennen had reached its expiration date. Funny. Still, I'd make sure the tags were off my shirt.

I shaved, showered, dressed. White shirt, gray pants. Mennen still smelled okay, and so I headed for Marylyn's place. I was a couple of blocks away at five minutes to six, so I pulled over. I thought I should probably be a little late, as I didn't want to appear too anxious. I pulled up at ten after six and rang the bell. Marylyn looked stunning in a white shirt, blue necklace, and navy slacks. I smiled.

She cocked her head and gave me a rather cherubic smile back. "Hi, Woody, I'm glad you're late."

"Hi, Marylyn. Why's that?" I gave her a quizzical look.

"It tells me that you like me," she said, turning to grab her purse.

"Can't say I understand that," I replied, genuinely confused.

"Well . . . if you had been here at six, it would imply that this is strictly business. You know, the punctual thing. Being appropriately late, on the other hand, sends the message that you didn't want to appear too eager. And if by chance you had been on time and needed to pull over and wait for a bit, well then you really do like me." Her smile was genuine, and sweet.

My look had to be that of a deer in the headlights. Finally, I responded. "Are you some kind of psychiatrist or something?"

"Oh, no, Woody. Just women's intuition. And you're so . . . sweetly naïve, at least when it comes to women."

We walked to the car.

I was trying to form some sort of self-protective response, but gave up. I spoke, my eyes on the road. "Okay. Full disclosure. One, I do like you. Two, I was early and pulled over. Three, I feel naked and embarrassed. And four . . . " I looked at her. " . . . Are you satisfied?"

"Oh, yes." She tittered as she grabbed my arm and laid her head against my shoulder.

Her perfume was alluring. I felt a burst of euphoria. I always knew exactly what to say and do. In this case, I had no clue.

She directed us to the Surf. It was sunset time, and we sat at a table overlooking the water, quiet and romantic. She ordered a scotch. I ordered a Manhattan. There was a crystal ball with a candle in it. We clinked our glasses.

"You look very pretty." I fumbled with my words, but spoke with sincerity.

"And you look especially handsome, Mr. Woodward."

We were quiet for almost a minute.

"Now what?" I asked. My visage cried out that I was a lost puppy.

Her laugh was so genuine and infectious that my anxiety, like a wisp of smoke, disappeared, and we laughed together for a long time, starting and stopping again. We both knew the games had ended. The mines were defused, and the posturing was kaput. The laughter said everything. Words weren't needed, and the walls came tumbling down. After that, we were "easy like Sunday morning."

I told her all about our ambush of Ghulam, his arrest, his statement, and escorting him to Atlanta. I told her about Jack and Billy and Tommy's client Buddy. I told her about my meeting with Carol and the budding story that would expose the whole operation. I told her about Jack and Eduardo, the Cayman bank, securing the account, and how they had caught Hafeez red-handed, had arrested her, and had flown her back to Atlanta. Finally, with a twist of levity, I told her about Mateo.

"Shakespeare might have had some fun with that love story," she quipped.

"I'll be talking to Jack and Tommy tomorrow, but all of the miscreants should be rounded up in the next few days. You'll be most happy to hear that a portion of the funds from the Cayman account will be set aside for the girls, the victims."

She turned her head away in a failed attempt to mask her emotion. "I know you pushed for that, Woody. Thank you."

I wasn't very good at the "aw-shucks" routine. "Team effort, kiddo." I immediately regretted the trite reply. I never said *kiddo*. I didn't even like the word. I would be so much more comfortable if no one ever again gave me a compliment.

Of course, the Surf had a surf-and-turf dinner special for two with a bottle of champagne. It was nummy. We took our time. Eventually, I paid the bill.

"We shall have two snifters of cognac at my place," Marylyn declared.

We sat together on her couch, sniffing the snifters.

"Let's dance, Woody." Marylyn got up and went to an old turntable, where she pushed a button and a 33 rpm record dropped down to the voice of Johnny Mathis. "I'm as helpless as a kitten up a tree." Really?

As we danced to "Misty," it dawned on me. "Now I know you like me!" I looked into her eyes.

"And its déjà vu all over again, so I'll play . . . Why's that?" she answered in a soft, sexy voice.

"You had that song all set up. Not John Fogerty or the Six Fat Dutchmen. No ma'am, the always romantic Johnny Mathis."

"Yup. And I even considered Tony Bennett and 'The Second Time Around,' but I went with more subtle."

We looked at each other with knowing smiles, and then we kissed.

"Next time, when this nasty business is over, we're going to do this again, but I just might keep you here for the night." She set that bar with a flirty smile.

"Never say anything to me that you don't intend to follow through on, Ms. Ottesen."

"Never do, Mr. Woodward." She leaned her head against my shoulder, and we danced through "Chances Are."

We kissed again when I left.

It took me a while to fall asleep. *Sweetly naïve*, huh? The truth can be cruel. For the second time in the past few hours, I said aloud, "Now what?"

CHAPTER 64

J ack and Tommy were on the phone early the next day. Ghulam and Hafeez were in chains, so to speak, and the logistics for the FBI raids were being set up, which included names, addresses, flights, timing, multiple legal issues, and mucho coordination. They would commence at 7:00 a.m., day after tomorrow. Jack promised to call us at his first opportunity. The anxiety was palpable. We signed off. I called Curtis and brought him up to speed. I had done everything I could. I let go of my control.

So what now? I had a lot of shit I wanted to do before the bugler finally played taps for me. I was going to be cremated, so for all I cared, those carnivorous worms could starve to death, but the good news was that I would be surrounded by soldiers.

I was already beating the odds as, last I heard, the average lifespan in America was seventy-eight years. So say the insurance actuaries, who are downers and don't make the top ten list of guys I want to drink beer with anyway. I suppose in some circles, those guys bring something to the party. In any event, average life expectancy in Japan is eighty-four years. Wonder if I moved there, would I automatically get another six years?

Death didn't scare me. It was part of the gig. You can't

really live until you lose your fear of death. And what is truly living? We are what we think, and most people are hardwired in what they think. Conditioning mostly. The mantra of self-help groups is *know thyself*. It may have been Lao Tzu who said, "Knowing others is wisdom, knowing yourself is enlightenment."

David Foster Wallace once lectured that it is hubris that creates blind certainty, "the close-mindedness that creates the arrogant prisoner who eventually doesn't even recognize that he is locked up." It's a fact of human nature that "we believe that we are the absolute center of the universe." We might try to deny it, and we don't talk about it because it's socially rejected, but the fact remains that for most people, it's our default setting. "The thoughts and feelings of others have to be communicated to us while our own are urgent, and dominate our lives." But it's not just self-absorption, but absorption. Awareness, consciousness, and choice, the paths to intellectual freedom. The mind may be a loyal servant, but it can be a terrible master.

A long time ago, I was having a beer and burger at the VFW in Saint Paul. I was sitting next to an old Korean War vet who had retired from the railroad. For whatever reason, our discussion got philosophical, and I asked him the age-old question, What is the meaning of life?

He looked at me with those eyes of age and wisdom. "Kind of a dumb question, if you ask me. I figure, you're born, and God or one of his angels spins a big wheel with numbers one through a hundred. Where it lands is how much time you got. You're using the wrong preposition, young fella. What you really want to know is, what is the meaning *in* life, not *of* life. Puts the ball in your court. Since that's totally up to you, choose well."

Wisdom can come from unexpected places, though sometimes it can be opaque.

Each of us can consciously decide what has meaning in

our lives. Choose money and status, and you'll not only never be truly happy, but you'll never have enough. Worship your body, beauty, and sexual allure, you'll always feel ugly. Worship power, you'll feel weak and afraid, and if you worship your intellect, you'll feel stupid and fraudulent. And despite the relativity of these truths, it's not so much that they're bad, it's that they're unconscious. Therein lies the lesson for which I offer my own gratitude, and for me, it isn't that I wouldn't lose the lessons from time to time. It's that I would come back to them. We're either part of the universal solution . . . or not.

Once again, my mind had wandered off, like a child, without permission. You'd think I was used to that by now.

When I awoke the next day, my first thought was that the day needed fill. Fie on me. Patience and anxiety had wrestled each other throughout my life, and the penalty had always been lost time. Yesterday was a canceled check, and tomorrow an IOU. Now, today was a precious commodity I swore to cherish each time I'd thought I'd seen my last. The number was finite, all of equal value. The big moments are rare, and in the end, it's the collective of the small ones that we remember. And so, today, my fill would become my full.

A young woman, Shauna Niequist, put it well.

Your life, right now, today, is exploding with energy and power and detail and dimension, better than the best movie you have ever seen.

She also said,

This is life in all its glory, swirling and unfolding around us, disguised as pedantic, pedestrian nonevents.

I believe some see these as only mundane and redundant. She had more to say:

You have stories worth telling, memories worth re-membering, dreams worth working toward, a body worth feeding, a soul worth tending, and beyond that, the God of the universe dwells within you . . . You are more than dust and bones . . . and you have been given today.

I took the kayak to a beach on the north end of the island. I pushed myself hard, absorbing the sand and the shore, the waves and the trees, the flowers and the rocks. Another kayak passed me, and the paddler waved. I wondered whether he had a wife and children, and what his next disappointment would be, and the tragedy he would encounter, as he surely would. I beached and swam and fell on the warm sand, exhausted physically, and to some extent, emotionally. I was in the world. The world was in me. Pantheism was the divine, and when the surrealism had passed, I put the kayak on the car and went home, where I poured a glass of wine and read *The Face of a Nation* by Thomas Wolfe, lost in thoughts of long ago.

Still, a white haunting moon, a dreamlike phoenix of memories came from somewhere, long-buried coffins, repressed but not uncomfortable visions and visages, helter-skelter through the mist of forgotten days, the timeless iconoclasm of reality, my first shattering of the innocence of my youth.

CHAPTER 65

Military command centers throughout history have encompassed as many eerie similarities as differences, with commanders and minions scurrying around issuing and following orders. Ivar the Boneless surveyed his inventory of swords and axes on a sheet of vellum, his wooden desk strewn with the bones of turkey legs and grape seeds, just before he invaded York some thirteen hundred years ago. Churchill's bunker desk was covered with teacups and crumpet crumbs as he and his brain trust studied Overlord maps almost eighty years ago. So it was with Jack at FBI central in Atlanta: underlings manning computers, cameras, and headsets; latte cups and yellow MacDonald's breakfast wrappers cluttering desks and furniture.

The biggest difference, however, was that today there would be no combat. There should not be a shot fired. Search warrants had all been issued. The "housekeepers" would be rounded up, and the interview process was in place, their testimony being the imperative component for convictions. The kingpins in Galveston and San Diego would be arrested, and the armies of combatants would be the legal beagles in a battle of words and paperwork between the "end users," their legal reps, and the government.

At seven eastern time, the twelve locations along the seaboard would be visited by an agent and a local law enforcement representative. An hour later, the exercise would be repeated in Texas, and in California an hour after that.

By seven forty-five, the first reports were in. Two of the

so-called johns were missing, allegedly out of town on business. The others had been served, including the New York guy, a suspect for a missing girl, and close connections to Hafeez. The girls would be transported to Atlanta, where they would be interviewed. Jack had instructed his agents to have a quick preliminary discussion with each of the girls and report their initial findings and opinions back to him.

These reports were an interesting mix of responses, but generally seemed to confirm his suspicions. Collectively, the girls were scared. They weren't sure who were the good guys and who were the bad guys. Most thought they were being arrested as illegals. Most also seemed grateful for being rescued, but two of them said they were "happy with their jobs." It could be Stockholm syndrome.

Still, that could be a bugaboo. There was no doubt that there was substantial evidence that crimes had been committed and that convictions would follow. At the same time, Jack could see that there would be a mountain of lawsuits, and these perps had the resources to bring in the heavyweight lawyers and big-name firms. This mess would take months. The FBI legal team would be on overload. The good news was that it would be a real blow to the human trafficking trade, and numerous innocent victims would be freed.

It wasn't until around ten that Jack could sit back and take a break. Galveston and San Diego had gone smoothly from the logistics side. The girls were all headed to Atlanta, papers were in order, and the hornet's nest of attorneys was buzzing in both cities. With appropriate relativity considered, Jack could intuit how Ike must have felt at some point on D Day when he sat down for a coffee break. Time to bring Woody and Tommy up-to-date.

CHAPTER 66

When my cell rang, I figured it was Jack. The time was 10:06, about what I had expected. Jack pulled Tommy into the conversation from his end.

Jack sounded beat. "Hey, guys, first off, I would label this exercise as successful. From the standpoint of tactics, logistics, and execution, it was nearly flawless. Counting Ghulam and Hafeez, there are four perps who will go to prison, and the whole operation has been closed down. The fallout will be a clusterfuck, however, with the perp employers. Big legal fees on the horizon." Jack proceeded to fill in the details. "I really won't have anything of substance to pass along until the girls have been interviewed, the charges clarified, and legal department has solidified the exact nature of the crimes. That will take a while. I'm handing off the baton until those pieces have been completed." Jack's voice held an element of relief and resignation.

"Hell of a job, Jack," Tommy offered.

"Ditto," I added.

"Never could have done this without you two," Jack stated. "I'm most grateful, and you guys deserve credit."

I followed up on that. "I've got no interest in credit and celebrity bullshit. There's no benefit to me. Both of you guys, however, can get some real benefit from this. I'll make sure that Carol does that in her story."

"Wish I had your humility, Woody," Jack said. "One caveat for Carol: be sure to clarify the spider web of potential litigation and defamation claims that will pop up. I wouldn't use many names until the smoke has cleared."

"And both of you, don't hesitate to call me with any delicate issues that are sure to surface," Tommy said. "So what do you get out of this, Woody? You were the epicenter."

"You guys need to come down here and take me out for a steak. The adventure and reuniting with you two has been its own reward." I thought for a few seconds before adding, "One seed I will plant with you, Jack, is that if Ghulam's speedboat ends up in an auction of confiscated assets, keep me in mind."

"You got it, pardner," Jack responded. "When I have more, I'll be back to you guys." Jack signed off.

I grabbed my coffee and sat outside. The letdown was probably to be expected. It had always happened after a mission. Move along, little doggie.

I called Marylyn first. She was chipper and most happy about the news. She was anxious to call Marta and Ilana. We agreed to reconnect and have another dinner date. I told her I would look forward to that. Our exchange was free-flow and comfortable.

Next, I called Curtis. He was anxious to hear what happened. I told him it was a long story, best related over sea bass and white wine. He pushed hard. I deflected. All would be disclosed at six at the club.

"Yeah, yeah, okay. See you then."

I was reminded of Pavlov's theory when I walked into the dining room. A woman was sitting in Hafeez's chair, at her usual table, the woman's back to me. Turned out to be a single female golfer on her iPad. We see what our brains tell us we're supposed to see. I felt relief in a silly way. It was good to see Curtis.

"Hey, mi amigo," I said with a smile. "You look healthy and happy."

"I can't disagree, Woody," Curtis said. "It kind of feels

like our adventure is done. Little bit of relief, little bit of loss. You're an unsung hero. So, what now?"

The redundancy of that question was coincidental.

"First, however, I'm chomping at the bit to hear the story," he said.

So I told him. "Aside from the legal issues, things turned out well. I'm so happy for those girls and pleased that justice will be served."

We clinked our glasses of a white wine that Curtis had ordered.

After a bit, Curtis asked me an unrelated question. "Woody, if you won the lottery, what would you do with the money?"

"That's an easy answer, Curtis. Take care of my family, like college funds for my grandkids, and then give most of it away. It would be a real hoot giving it to needy people and places. And how about you, Curtis? What would you do?"

There was a long pause.

Curtis looked at me for a while, then he smiled. "Pretty much the same, Woody. Only difference is, I don't have family left, so I would give it all away. And yes, that would be a hoot."

Another long pause before he spoke again.

"You know, I wish we would have met a long time ago. We're kindred spirits. Then again, perhaps we were meant to meet late in life. You know, that karma thing."

"To everything, there is a season," I said.

"Ecclesiastes Three or the Byrds?" he replied.

We shared a laugh.

Curtis raised his arm, and the waiter came over. He looked at me.

"We'll follow your script, Woody." Curtis looked up at the waiter. "Two sea bass and a small carafe of Chardonnay."

The waiter smiled and nodded, then headed off toward the kitchen.

Curtis gave me a quizzical look. "I've never asked you this.

How does a born-and-bred Minnesotan end up on Jekyll Island, Georgia?"

I laughed out loud. "You know, Curtis, up until now, so it seems, you've had a decent opinion of me, to include my mental stability. I really don't want to change that." I grinned.

"Nothing will change that, Woody, but you can't just throw out a line like that and leave me in the lurch, so spit it out. I never judge a friend."

"But nobody knows, Curtis, not even my kids."

"I'm not your kids."

After thinking it over, I raised my pointy finger and said, "You're looking at magic. Mr. Pointy is both prescient and serendipitous." Then I told him.

He shook his head with a wide grin. "Now that, my friend, is quintessential folklore, and it so defines you. Do I assume that you don't regret the poetic, fickle finger of fate? And unlike Mr. Shakespeare, I find the double entendre to be an elevated form of humor."

"I do like it here, Curtis, for many reasons. I like the house and have over half a year left on the lease. I hope to renew it."

"Well, the next time you have a confidential discussion with the eminent Mr. Pointy, please express my gratitude."

We chuckled at that.

The food arrived. We enjoyed the meal, comfortable to where there was no need to talk just for the sake of talking.

Eventually, Curtis made the comment, "I'm on a panel of five this Friday that will be addressing a group of students at a small college about seventy-five miles up north. The topic is History's Greatest Frauds. We've picked our subjects, including people from Roman emperors to presidents. Mine is as a result of my papers and lectures. Few fraudsters are in this guy's league: George Armstrong Custer." Curtis looked at me.

"You know, Curtis, as a vet and a student of history, I know Custer is certainly one of the most embarrassing incompetents in US history, yet there are still parks, counties, and cities that bear his name. His lack of intelligence is documented. He was a duplicitous liar who lacked leadership skills, an egomaniac who showed no concern for the welfare of the men he commanded, a thief, an intense racist, and a murderer of unarmed women and children. It can only be money and politics that created his distorted image."

"Actually, it was his self-serving wife and a delusional general. But I'm impressed. I didn't know you were so well informed."

"I have a special interest in General Ulysses S. Grant, the Union commander and president who court-martialed Custer for corruption. If Custer had survived the Battle of the Little Big Horn, he should have been court-martialed and shot. Instead, they called him a hero. I think you got the winner of history's greatest frauds."

"So what's on your schedule, Woody? I'm most anxious to make our reservation and celebrate with the best French fare in Georgia."

"First thing I have to do is revisit with Carol so that she has all of the facts and caveats for her story. It could be a slippery slope from the legal perspective." I thought for a few seconds. "How about Saturday night?"

"Works for me."

When I got home, I called Carol. I gave her a brief synopsis, and we agreed to meet at a place between Atlanta and Jekyll. I was more tired than I thought and had no problem falling asleep after reading translated accounts about American Horse, Wooden Leg, Two Moons, Crazy Horse, Gall, and Sitting Bull, and the parts they played in late June of 1876.

CHAPTER 67

Ｗe met at a Saladworks about a two-hour drive from my place. Carol was into the diet and nutrition gig. Fine with me. I liked salads, especially those smothered with sausages and other high-calorie toppings.

I filled her in on everything that had gone down. I answered a pile of questions. This was a "big" story and the "ambulance chasing" journalists were already sniffing around the activity of Bureau agents.

This would be Carol's story, and the media would know it. She would have the facts, the data, the specifics, and the backstory from a "most informed and reliable, but unnamed, source." She would release the names of those arrested—Ghulam, Hafeez, and the two key players in Galveston and San Diego—but only allude to the "employers" who paid for the services. A full description of the girls, over thirty in all, their recruitment and such, would make for captivating reading. Carol was a pro and fully aware of the legal plight that would surround this exposure, and would write with appropriate delicacy and protection. She would now have access to all of the sources, including Jack, to make public the arrests before the media found out.

She would probably receive awards and recognition she hadn't dreamed of. "I don't know how I can ever thank you, Woody, but I'll think of something," she said with an ear-to-ear smile.

"What I want is for the world to know that the two heroes of this story are Jack O'Brien of the FBI and Tommy Nguyen, owner of Coeus Intel Services of Dover, Delaware. I need nothing else."

We hugged when we parted. I was done. I was ready for some alone time—well, maybe another one of those dates . . . with Marylyn. I wanted to read and do research. Oh, and play.

CHAPTER 68

"Let's meet at the club, and I'll drive," Curtis offered. He was calling from the library, finishing some article for a Midwest paper. "I'll be there at five forty-five. Our reservation is for six."

"Should I wear a beret?" I asked.

"Up to you." He hung up. No time for small talk.

When I got in his car, he was still flustered.

"Damn, deadlines. I had completely forgotten about that article."

"Hey, mellow out." I gave him a mild scold. "We're going to celebrate. No worries. No issues."

"Okay, done," he said quietly, morphing to mellow.

The parking lot was full. Made me wonder if there was a senior special or something. We got a booth near the window. I hadn't worn a beret. Didn't have one. But the waiter did. He welcomed us with a faux French accent that sounded more like Sergeant Schultz than de Gaulle. We ordered drinks and looked at the menu, which was as thick as the Obama health care proposal, and was in French. Weren't even pictures, so I pretended. Thing is, when you've implanted a food you want, you can't unimplant it. I was having the bouillabaisse anyway, so my ruse didn't matter. I suppose I could have called Tommy, ruined his cocktail hour, and asked for translation.

"How did your meeting with Carol go?" Curtis asked.

"*Très bien, Monsieur.*"

"Hey, when in Rome, do as the Parisians do," Curtis replied.

"It went well. The story will hit the Sunday edition

tomorrow."

Curtis raised his drink to mine. "I'll want to get the early edition. This is justice in action. Well done, my friend." Curtis seemed genuinely excited.

"Same back." I nodded. "And did you hang Custer from the yardarm?"

"He's now the most unpopular man in Georgia, though Ghulam could give him a run for his money by tomorrow evening."

The bouillabaisse exceeded expectations. Best ever.

I patted Curtis on the back. "I'm humbled," I said. "You're the real deal on connoisseurship, which might not be a word, but you get my drift. I see the most diverse company in existence in our future . . . investigation, comedy, and fine food. What do you think?"

"I think you've had one too many Manhattans."

"You really did pick a great place to celebrate, Curtis. What's with the name?"

"Les Appentis. In French, it means *the Shed*."

I was processing that when it hit me, like a fist to the mid-section. My mind was in a swirl. I suddenly wanted to get home.

"Woody, are you okay? You look like you've just seen Casper."

"Huh? Oh, nothing. Just remembered a chore I have to do when I get home." I paused. "I'm stuffed. No room for dessert. How about you?"

"You sure, Woody? The French pastry dish is to die for."

"Then how about I take one home, but you go ahead." I tried to keep anxiety out of my response.

"I'm with you. Midnight snack. Delayed gratification."

The waiter brought the tray, we each picked a pastry, and Curtis asked for the check.

On the drive back to the club, I tried to curb my preoccupation. I thanked Curtis profusely when I got out of his car. He went one way, and I kept telling myself I did not need a speeding ticket when I pulled out. I made it, and double-timed it through the front door and straight to my office.

My notes were on my bookshelf. It didn't take long to find the poem.

Voir la Lumiere Celeste d.l.a.,
See the Heavenly Light d.l.a.

In English, the corpus of the poem read:

When the fires of Hell precurse the fray,
Her golden hair will melt away;
Before she leaves and won't come back,
She'll find her treasure in 15 bric-a-brac.

I made a cup of coffee and put my figurative thinking cap on. I had concluded that not too many people had read the poem. It had been hidden in the archives, and too, a number of people who had read it probably dismissed it as being anything other than waggish. I now believed it contained the clues to DuBignon's treasure.

See the Heavenly Light d.l.a. My first thought had been that the poem was an ode to a girl, someone Christophe had known or fantasized about, but the idea that Heavenly Light was a metaphor for shiny gold made sense. I'd thought d.l.a. may have been her initials. One story had claimed that Christophe, while riding his horse, had passed a military man in a carriage with a female passenger that he had described as having "the face of an angel, with long yellow hair." Christophe was to have later said, "I am haunted by her face." But then, this was a man who was haunted by many faces. Did they meet again? Romance aside, I now suspected something very different.

I also recalled that Christophe had purchased building tools and materials for his personal use. It seemed he wanted to build some kind of cold storage facility for vegetables, various fruits, and certain crops, or maybe he simply wanted to hide something.

It was historical fact that British ships attacked Jekyll Island several times, with raids continuing even after the War of 1812 officially ended. Christophe DuBignon later testified "my house was plundered at four different times by said British." It was most likely burned as well: *the fires of Hell.*

Her golden hair will melt away. It's a well-known fact that gold will melt, but few people know that that will only happen at a temperature of over a thousand degrees Celsius.

Before she leaves and won't come back. Well, it could have been the woman with long yellow hair, or it could have been his family, but whoever it was, the message seemed clear: *Take the fifteen gold bricks with you.*

So what was d.l.a.? As of tonight, I was convinced that *L* stood for *les* and *A* for *appentis*, the shed. I found a French dictionary online and began scrolling down words that started with *D*. It didn't take long to find my answer: *dans*, meaning *in. See the Heavenly Light d.l.a.* could mean *See the shiny gold in the shed.* But the shed was basically gone, except for the foundation.

I knew what I needed. Tomorrow was Sunday, and the stores opened at noon. I needed a small, one-man, non-see-through tent; a flashlight; a cordless drill; and a specific kind of drill bit. I had a plan.

CHAPTER 69

A t ten the next morning, I drove out to the park, the old DuBignon estate. Even my iPod was fortuitous and uplifting as Nana Mouskouri sang "Turn on the Sun." I wanted to canvass the grounds in broad daylight, with people around. A half dozen tourists were walking the site and taking pictures. I was one.

I took some close-ups of the shed's foundation. There was still a three-to-four-inch wall of bricks covered with an ancient coat of tar, grass, and brush. There was little interest in that location. I saw what I needed to see.

I picked up the supplies I wanted at Walmart and drove back home. I checked out my equipment and studied the photos I'd taken. Ready to go. After that, I got on my computer and read all I could on the consequences for finding treasure on public and private land in Georgia. What the state's claim was on found treasure was unclear. Big surprise. They would get a piece of the pie under any circumstance, as I saw it. The taxes would dilute any trove for certain. Also, an investigation would be long and involved in tracing claims from descendants of the property. Lots of arbitrary allowance, lots of red tape and bureaucratic interference. I smiled at my conclusion. If by some chance I had located the nearly three-hundred-year-old search for Christophe's gold, I had the perfect plan. I returned to reality and managing my expectations by putting those thoughts on hold. For now, I would take a nap, as I wouldn't be getting much sleep in the coming hours.

At 2:00 a.m., I loaded my car and headed to the shed. There was a half-moon. Temperature was in the fifties. There were few cars at that time, and none around the park. I drove past to be sure that there was no security. I parked on a side street, grabbed my equipment, and took a circuitous path to the property. There was enough moonlight to set up the tent over the foundation, or at least part of it. In the enclosed space, I turned on my upright flashlight, put the long, thin bit in the drill, and started drilling from right to left, top to bottom. After the first nine holes, all old brick, the sound changed, as did the pressure, harder but smoother. This time, when I withdrew the bit, I removed the particles from the bit head onto a black cloth. Voila! The tiny particles sparkled. Christophe had to be laughing.

I filled all of the small holes with wet mud as a precaution and returned the appearance as it had been. I made a mental note of where the last hole had been made and calculated that the fifteen bricks would be contiguous, five rows of three bricks high. I put the cloth in my pocket, put the drill and bit in my backpack, turned off the light, came out of the tent, packed it up, and returned to my car.

When I got home, I studied the particles under a better light. No question, it was gold. I was exhilarated. It was a strange feeling, surreal, to say the least, but I had a vision, one of people dancing to a distant drum, of houses being built, and a community center, and a community of joy. It hit me hard. I was uncomfortable with the tears rolling down my cheeks. What the hell!

I went to the kitchen and opened the drawer with the old pack of Marlboros. I took a glass from the cupboard and put two fingers of Jose Cuervo in with a cube of ice. I sat in my chair, and as some ancient conditioned reflex, looked toward the ceiling and raised the glass. "Thank you, Great Spirit. I am part of the solution."

After a while, I went to Google. The price of gold was $1,284 an ounce. There are 439 ounces of gold in today's gold bars, so assuming my calculator worked, one gold bar was worth $563,676, and accordingly, fifteen times that number was valued at approximately $8,455,140. It was probable that gold bars two hundred years ago were bigger. I just stared at that figure, bottoms-upped my friend Jose, took one last drag on my cigarette, and went to bed. I had a really tough time falling asleep.

At eight the next morning, I called Curtis. "Hey, man. You have to come to my place as soon as you can."

CHAPTER 70

Curtis pulled into the driveway at a little after nine. I had coffee and a French pastry that I cut in half.

"Yesterday you asked me what I would do with the money if I won the lottery," I told him. "I said I would give it away. Well, Curtis, it's complicated, but I did, and I *am* prepared to give it away, with your help." I looked at his expression.

"Unlike you, Woody," he said, "I'm not very adept at the use of profanity. That's not a criticism, just an observation. Some people are just good at it. Some people fumble and stumble. I'm the latter. In any event, what the fuck are you talking about?"

I couldn't stop laughing. Finally, I replied. "At dinner, when you told me what Les Appentis meant, the fog cleared. I apologize, but I had to get home and confirm my suspicions. Turns out, I was right. I now have over eight million dollars to give away, with some not exactly legal work that needs to be done. But don't worry, it's the purist form of justice, the absolute right thing to do. But I would totally understand if you decline."

"Holy Mother of God, you need to be more specific."

And I was. I told him everything I had done and everything I had learned since our dinner.

"I'm having a hard time processing this," Curtis responded. "But you already know I'm in. What's your plan?"

"You need to get hold of the tribal chief of the Pine Ridge Reservation and a rep from the Native American Veterans group, and they need to get a solid SUV and drive here. I have the plan on how this can be done, and only a select few will ever know. Can you do that?" I was firm and obviously excited.

"My God. A saint should never be incognito. There will be stories of 'Saint Woody' for years to come. Let's do it. I'll make sure I do my part. You make life so exciting and worthwhile, Woody. This was meant to be." Curtis had the excitement of a child.

We ate the snack and drank coffee and talked about things that were and things to come.

After Curtis left, I got back on Google. I knew that Indian reservations were independent nations and that mineral rights and discoveries were tribal business. What I wanted to find out was whether history would confirm my opinion that there was gold or buried treasure on the Pine Ridge Reservation. Turns out, there were multiple stories dating back to the Gold Rush discoveries in the Black Hills about buried treasure. It was going to be imperative that the bars would need to be melted down before they could be cashed in. Otherwise, they just might be identified. I was beginning to feel a bit like a criminal, but then, guess I was one. There were some criminals I liked: Robin Hood, Willie "the Actor" Sutton, and D. B. Cooper. I still hoped he made it.

Time to wait for a response from Curtis.

It sunk in that like that rabbi and his hole in one, I could never tell anybody about this. What could be more of a character challenge? Rehashing the story with Curtis would lose its luster at some point. I could always fabricate friends, like Neil Diamond and Shiloh, but that too would be a watered-down version of reality. But of course, I wasn't a fan of reality anyway, so suck it up and move along, little doggie.

Curtis called just before dinner. They would be here in four days. I would have to get back to Walmart. I needed about three dozen bricks and some tar, as well as a couple of tools. Hell, who said crime couldn't be an innocent form of entertainment?

The best part of the next three days was a dinner date with Marylyn. This one had a unique twist to it. Now that I was becoming more engaged in the criminal life, innocent as it might be, what was one more little crime? Like stealing a boat, a criminal's boat.

The next morning, I took the kayak to the marina. The day was gorgeous. White candy-floss clouds drifted across the deep-blue backdrop with occasional long, straight lines and *X*s, the contrails of jet engines heading to and from London, Dublin, and places beyond. A national convention of sea gulls was apparently in process, and I watched the aberrant flight of a man-of-war heading out to sea. My favorites were the pelicans, divebombing and filling their pouches with wriggling fish, then swallowing them whole, circling, and giving it another go.

I pushed myself hard. I could see and feel the development of my upper body. This was good. What the hell. Life was good.

After putting the kayak on the car, I walked to where Ghulam's speedboat was docked. It had been abandoned and had a sad look to it. I looked around. No one watching, so I got on board. I spoke in a tender tone, "You look like you could use some exercise, old boy."

There was a box with a lock. I suspected the engine key was inside. If I cut the lock and replaced it with another, who would know the difference? What the hell. Another trip to Walmart couldn't hurt. Just start the engine and warm it up, no harm done. A guy named Ullman stated that "we are so clothed in rationalization and dissemblance that we can recognize but dimly the deep primal impulses that motivate us."

Nothing deep or primal about this innocent little impulse. I just wanted this lonely old scow to feel some TLC, that's all. On occasion, the Good Samaritan still comes along.

Bolt cutter cost me ten bucks, and the lock was three. Alms for the poor. I was on a hot streak. I had guessed right twice in two days: eight million in gold and an engine key in a box. What next, Madam Zorba?

The engine started on the first push and hummed like a bee. While it warmed up, I toured below deck. It was a real beauty. The thought struck me that a small grill and a cooler would fit nicely on the back deck, with two comfortable fold-ups, some soft music, and a pretty lady.

I turned it off, locked her up, and headed home, from where I was able to reach Marylyn. Dinner tomorrow was "perfect." I told her the location would be a surprise. I said we'd have a moveable feast. Clever, huh? I found myself humming an old Paul McCartney song: *Will you still need me, will you still feed me, when I'm seventy-four.* Okay, slight alteration.

When I got to Marylyn's, I was five minutes early. She answered the door and immediately looked down at her watch.

"First of all, yes, I'm early. Second, yes, I like you very much, and I'm just anxious for our date to begin. And third, get your ass moving. We have fun stuff to do. How'd I do?"

"Not bad. Know that on a second date, late is rude, and early means you couldn't wait to see me, so let's get going." She was ready for fun.

"I think you just made that up," I said.

She chuckled.

When I pulled into the marina, I could see some anxiety.

"What are you doing, Woody?"

"Stealing a boat."

"This boat has bad karma. I don't know."

"Well, the government owns it now. The wraiths are gone. The girls are free and starting new lives, and this is a new beginning. Besides, this boat is a sweetheart. She and I have had a nice chat, and she wants to show you that it was never her fault. She's asking for your forgiveness." I gave Marylyn a puppy-dog smile.

She thought about that. "Okay, I'll give her a chance, but that little speech of yours scares me. You're not going into politics, are you?" She waited for me to say something.

I started to giggle. "My answer to that is self-evident. I actually meant what I said, which eliminates me from running for public office. Capeesh?"

"Then I still like you. So what are we doing here?"

"You just go on board and find a comfy chair. I have scotch and soda, a good steak, a grill to cook it on, garlic toast we can heat in the oven, and a Caesar salad."

"Well, aren't you the romantic one?" She winked. "I can at least make the drinks, Romeo."

I started the engine, untied the leash, and motored out of the marina. Marylyn fixed the drinks and put charcoal in the grill, and we sat and watched the sun slowly settle in the western sky while we glided along the coastline.

The whole evening was a delight. Neither of us wanted it to end, so when I dropped her off, we didn't. We slept, on and off, in her queen bed that overlooked the Atlantic.

When I left the next morning, we kissed, and Marylyn gave me a mock serious look. "I believe that went well enough. Perhaps we should do it again sometime." Her visage was an exaggerated question mark.

I rubbed my chin, emulating deep thought. "It has possibilities. I'll have to think it over." I stuck out my hand to shake.

She slapped my hand in jest, called me an ass, then grabbed my cheeks and planted a big smooch.

Seemed life just kept getting better. Maybe someday I would tell her about the treasure.

CHAPTER 71

They would be arriving around four. They would be staying with Curtis, as a low-profile presence was necessary. They would come to my place, where we could chat and plan, as well as enjoy beers and brats. Curtis had not yet shared the specifics of the treasure and its value, only that there was a significant opportunity for the tribe.

In the meantime, I had gone to a building supply store. I wanted to find vintage bricks that could pass muster if they were ever uncovered. I also needed a close matching tar for the disguise. Finally, I needed the appropriate tools for removal.

Curtis's car pulled into my driveway at five thirty. He introduced me to Henry, the Oglala Lakota chief, and Clay, ex-marine vet who ran the Native American Veterans Assistance program on the Pine Ridge Reservation. We settled into the living room with beers and snacks and would wait to get the grill started until after the introductory discussion.

I began with the history. "Gentlemen, two hundred years ago, a musketeer named Christophe DuBignon settled on this island." I gave them the full monty for the next forty-five minutes. "Five nights ago, I played my hunch and beat the odds. I discovered the gold bars. I believe the value to be in excess of eight million dollars, and I've decided to give it away: one million to the veterans group you operate, Clay, and the balance to the Pine Ridge Reservation."

It was like a scene in a feature film. To say they were astounded would be minimizing. They looked at me, they looked at Curtis, they looked at each other, and they looked back at me. Clay bent over and put his face into his hands. I'm never comfortable when tough guys become sentimental.

The chief was more stoic, but his body language showed he had been moved. "We don't even know you, Mr. Woodward. Why us?"

"That doesn't matter, Henry. And please call me Woody. What we do have is some issues, legal and logistical. There is unequivocally no question about the ethical arguments, and I want those to be mine, no one else's." I proceeded to tell them about the issues surrounding treasure discoveries. "I believe my plan will work, and no issues will ever surface."

"It almost seems trite, Woody, but I'm at a total loss for words." Clay spoke with genuine emotion. "We don't get windfalls. We crawl and scrape for every meal and every home improvement and every dollar. We believe in angels, but they are angels of strength and spiritual support, never anything of this magnitude. We will owe you so much. What will you keep for yourself?"

"Clay, I have everything I need. This will be my greatest reward." I nodded with a sense of finality. "Now we shall have a victory meal of brats and chips and my favorite, orange Jell-O. As we eat, I'll go over the plan."

We bonded until 8:30, when they left. I would meet them at 2:00 a.m. at the park. Curtis and the chief would perform sentinel duty, while Clay and I would do the grunt work.

There was barely enough room for Clay and me in the tent. The work was more arduous than I had anticipated. The tar was resistant, but then it may have been a century or two older than me.

After a tough first hour, we had the bars free, but covered in black tar. I put them in the gym bag we had brought with the replacement bricks, signaled to Curtis, who took it away, and we started the rebuild. That took less time. We finished around 4:10. The artwork to restore the appearance was well done. Clay and I looked at each other and nodded agreement. Even the grassy brush looked undisturbed.

We drove to Curtis's place and inspected the booty. At almost $1,300 an ounce, we didn't want to do much scraping. We did enjoy a collective smile when we put a bar on the bathroom scale and found it weighed a little over thirty pounds. Even counting the weight of the tar, over two pounds heavier than today's bars. That's over $40,000 a bar. What, another $600,000? The numbers were making me dizzy. I quit doing the math.

I did share my research about the stories of buried gold on the reservation, in case there was ever a question about where it came from. That would be the story going into the new history books.

I had put some tar on a number of the new bricks, and we loaded almost forty bricks into the back of the SUV, with a bag of cement, a couple of trowels, and cementing tools, giving the appearance of a couple of guys going to do a job. This was simply precaution, should they get stopped for a broken taillight or some such. They knew to drive conservatively. They would leave at dawn.

When I left to head home, they hugged me for a long time, and really hard. When they thanked me for the third time, I ran my hand across my neck to signal enough.

I was dead on my feet. I jumped into the sack. I had no regrets, although I admit that the last vision I had before slipping into the deep abyss of slumber was that image you see in comic books of a bag of money, with wings, flying away.

No news was good news right up until Curtis called two days later with the message that they had made it. Once again, he was effusive with gratitude and prayers. I was relieved.

Once again, I was finished with my work. I wanted a break. Was I addicted to excitement? Maybe I needed one of those twelve-step support groups for excitement addicts. I don't know, and I'm too old and stubborn to care. Instead of worrying about that kind of bullshit, I let a thought come to mind: I hadn't yet opened that speedboat to full throttle. I wondered what top speed was. Hell, might as well go find out.

CHAPTER 72

The summer months always whizzed by like an arrow in flight. Memorial Day morphed into the Fourth of July, and the next day was Labor Day. Pissed me off. Luckily, it was still early, and the days were full of kayaking, dates with Marylyn, dinners with Curtis, and phone calls with family and friends, all of that underscored with reading and research for one million topics that gained my interest. And all around me, life happened.

Carol was the media darling of talk shows, news briefs, and late night. You could always weigh your success by the number of people and groups that hated you and disparaged you and wanted you to crash. Carol was a success. She called me often, mostly to express her gratitude. She hadn't figured out how she would repay me, since she couldn't make me a hero with her pen, but she would. I asked her please not to worry about that. She was already repaying me with her work.

I did have one call with Winston and Sam. They kind of scolded me for not telling them about my role in the sex-trafficking scandal. Of course, Sam did talk to her sister. I was "too old to be involved in things like that."

B. J., on the other hand, was rapturous. "All my friends say you're the coolest guy on the planet, Grandpa. Did you use the magic stick again?"

Seems I got my fifteen minutes of fame from the right place.

Mary Beth's call was classic Mary Beth. "I knew you were into some crazy shit, Dad. I knew you wouldn't tell me too.

Oh, and by the way, how's your new girlfriend doing?" She giggled.

I just shook my head.

Both Jack and Tommy were heroes, however. Jack was receiving recognition from both within and without the FBI. I saw him on TV on several occasions. He sent me a beautiful card as well. Tommy was turning down business left and right, bitching on every call how he would gladly trade places with me.

"Be careful what you wish for, my friend," I told him. "Should have told you that months ago."

The accounts of the girls were almost totally condemning of what had happened to them. Several kept quiet for reasons of fear or just wanting to put it behind them. Several were victims of Stockholm syndrome. They were becoming citizens and were being funded for education and jobs. Marylyn was simply ecstatic with those developments. Most of the dickheads that had used the girls were being punished in one way or another: the press, where it was appropriate, but even more lethal, by word of mouth. Lawsuits were flying around, but they always did.

Hafeez and Ghulam were behind bars, their money and assets confiscated, and they would be waiting for a while for the justice system to show up. Same for the two in Galveston and San Diego.

Both Jack and Tommy had let me know they would be coming to Jekyll to personally bring Curtis and me up-to-date and to have a celebratory dinner. They might bring their wives. On top of that, Curtis had heard from the chief, who said that within the next thirty days, he should have things in place and wanted to do the same with Clay, without wives, mostly because neither had one. I let Curtis know that I now had an open dance card and to just let me know. In the meantime, I went outside to play.

CHAPTER 73

S eventy-five, WTF?
I always tried to keep my birthday to myself. Never worked. If there was a surprise party or some such, I always figured it out, and pretended. I mean, really, just what a seventy-five-year-old dude needs: a big fat reminder that he's nearly dead. I would have to start looking out for the signs. Maybe I could disappear for a week. What the hell. Can't beat 'em, join 'em. Still had ten days.

Gallows humor. I think God is a prankster, at least I hope so in a world of hatred and destruction. The "Big Guy" needed comic relief like any other sane person. Among other things, I think he has a fast-forward button that he pushes from time to time. Those ten days went by in three. Tommy and Jack were coming, as were their spouses. Tommy's wife, Julie, was a riot. Had to be to put up with Tommy's bullshit, and I couldn't wait to meet Jenny, the drill sergeant. I was also anxious for everyone to meet Marylyn. It had to be coincidental that they would be here on my birthday. None of them knew that, so mum's the word.

A couple days before our dinner, Marylyn and I were lollygagging on Driftwood Beach, and I told her about all the players and the parts they had played in the takedown of the trafficking ring. I told her about our history, going back to Vietnam, and I told her about my more recent friendship with Curtis. That segued into a discussion about family.

"You and Mary Beth would get along far too well. I'd be odd man out and probably a victim to boot."

"She know about us?" she asked.

"She knows everything. I don't need to tell her. I suspect Jack's wife, Jenny, fits that mold as well."

"I must say that I'm looking forward to meeting all of them," she said with a cryptic smile.

The beach was full of kids and families and swimmers and shell searchers and dogs and sugar and spice and everything nice. These were the days we remember.

CHAPTER 74

The troops had arrived. They were staying at the club. Dinner was at six bells.

Other than a strong breeze, the sun was smiling on Jekyll Island. Clouds were racing across the sky and seabirds were doing acrobatic tricks. And my kids called, as did my brothers. Just another notch on the totem pole. Three-quarters of a century. To me, now entering middle age, like halfway home. Back to my safe place . . . delusion.

When I picked her up, Marylyn looked like a model, and she knew it. I did that wolf whistle thing, kind of. Like everything else, I couldn't whistle like I used to.

"Well, do I pass muster, soldier?" she asked.

"You went way past muster."

The dining room was packed. There was a table near the window where the others were already seated, having animated conversations. We joined the jocund milieu and went around the table, introducing Marylyn, hugging Julie, and shaking hands. When I came to Jenny, she stood up, and I extended my hand.

"Not a chance, big boy. You don't get off the hook with a handshake, so bring it in." She opened her arms for a hug. She looked up at me. "You must know that you saved my man. He was walking around like an old hound dog, hanging his head and thinking he was going to get a tin watch and a boot in the ass from the Bureau, when you came along and made him a hero. We're all aware that you avoid any credit, but like it or not, you're the hero."

I wasn't about to argue with this five-foot, two-inch stick of dynamite. I looked at Jack, who hunched his shoulders as if to say, "Sorry, but she's out of my control."

"Well then, I guess I'll just say that it's a great pleasure to meet you, Jenny."

She wasn't the six-foot Amazon I had expected. She hugged Marylyn as well.

I'm a true-blue introvert, at least according to Myers and Briggs, and thus not much of a social butterfly, but this meal was a gas. Even Tommy had us laughing after a couple Macallans. Curtis was quiet, but never lost that big smile and those laughing eyes. We ate family-style with a bunch of hors d'oeuvres and "sharesies" on the main dishes.

It was great fun until I returned to the table from a trip to the men's room. Shit! They were wearing little cone hats. There was a cake in the middle of the table, and they had presents. They sang happy birthday. Shit! Most of the other diners were watching, some singing, some clapping. Double shit!

"Okay, who knew it was my birthday?" I asked.

They all looked at Marylyn.

She hunched her shoulders with a *what can I say* look. "What? You think I go out with any dufus that comes along? I do my due diligence, Mr. Army Intelligence."

"We've been talking and planning with her for two weeks, Mr. Nothing Gets Past Me," Curtis said.

They all nodded.

I blew out the single candle, and we had cake. I opened the presents, gimmicks, and memorabilia.

Jack was last, and he handed me a small box. Inside was a key. "If you go on that speedboat down at the marina, there's a box with a lock on it," he said. "Inside that box is another key to start the engine to your new boat." He grinned.

They all smiled and clapped. I looked at Marylyn. Her surreptitious nod told me that no one else knew about our excursion. I looked at Jack, wonder on my face.

"Believe it or not, Woody, but this boat was not on the as-set manifest. License wasn't registered. It was not in anyone's name, so as far as the Bureau was concerned, it didn't exist. I've made a fake bill of sale, a fact that is of the highest confidentiality, but you can now register your new speedboat."

For the first time in years, I really was at a loss for words. This was a total surprise, and it made the birthday celebration worthwhile. Jack and Tommy were headed back home tomorrow. We hugged. I was effusive with gratitude.

"Well, aren't you a sneaky little shit," I said to Marylyn as we got in the car. I smiled a big, gracious smile.

"It's been fun for the past couple of weeks, Woody. It's so nice to meet this caliber of people. I don't think I've quite met anyone like Jenny. What a pistol. They all think the world of you. By the way, it was also fun keeping you in the dark, but a bit testier hiding our boat trip from Jack."

"Now I have this vision of you, Jenny, and Mary Beth together. Talk about three peas from the same pod. A most formidable triplex."

"Any time that could be arranged, I'm in." Marylyn grinned.

Two days later, I got a call from Carol. She wanted me to come to Atlanta for a final roundup on the story and a home-made dinner with her family. I agreed.

I had become quite familiar with the drive. It was comfortable and made easier by Art Pepper, George Winston, Gordon Lightfoot, hits from the '50s, and other favorites, as well as my planning session of one about upgrades to my new toy, a fifty-mile-per-hour speedboat.

John had taken the kids to swim class. Carol and I went over all of the developments that had taken place since the raids. She was far more informed at this stage than I on the status of all facets of the ongoing investigations. Justice was being served.

Carol had made a prime rib with all my favorite trimmings. The kids were a trip. Seems that kids intuitively liked me. Not totally sure why, but part of it was that I always talked to them like they were adults. John was a solid guy, and when dinner was over, he and Carol gave me a beautiful card with a $1,000 gift card to Cabela's.

I left early the next morning, and the drive home was full of visions about stuff I might buy at the outdoor sporting goods store, especially stuff that went with a speedboat, or maybe a two-person kayak. Marylyn could use a good workout.

Three weeks passed. Curtis told me he had heard from both the chief and Clay. They had a number of updates to show us. Most exciting developments. It had been six weeks, and they were ready to share them. They were flying to Atlanta, renting a car, and driving down to visit us within the next week or so. Apparently, there was one thing that needed to be completed before they left.

It took three full days to complete the work on my new boat, including a top-to-bottom cleaning, dry-dock work on the hull, fiberglass, plumbing, wood refinishing, polishing, and bringing in a high-test mechanic to check the engine. The last thing was to hire a local artist to paint the name across the transom. I wanted the name to relate to its acquisition, but in a subtle, tangential way. I settled on *Brick-A-Brac*, misspelling intended.

This time, the chief and Clay would stay at the club. We met at six. They were in high spirits, as was Curtis. They sat at a table for five, one empty chair. After the personal exchanges and getting caught up on the past six to seven weeks, Clay went into a description about how they had leased an electric furnace designed for melting metals, including gold, purifying and converting it to smaller, marketable ingots. He used terms like "flux" and "graphite casting molds." I listened with feigned interest, not wanting to dilute his enthusiasm in any way. Once that process was finished, he said, the value of the gold was just over $9.2 million. We all shared a victory smile. They had circulated opaque stories of discovering buried gold from over a century and a half ago. No names. No accounts.

The chief took over and brought out a scrapbook of pictures. It included the plans for a community center, a rehab center, school improvements, a scholarship program, a food market, and a wholesale warehouse for clothing and household necessities. Long-term housing development plans and drawings were the last item.

He emphasized the need for professional cost analyses and projections and a plan that was commensurate with the net proceeds. "One thing we knew that we needed was a top-end financial analyst we could trust. In addition to the interests of the tribe, there were several tricky and confidential issues to settle, so we leaned on Curtis for help. He introduced us to a perfect candidate, who will perhaps surprise you, but you'll see the wisdom after a full explanation."

Curtis patted me on the back as he got up and walked to what I recalled as the club reading room. When he returned, he was escorting my daughter, Mary Beth. I was surprised but not shocked. I stood and hugged her.

She looked at me, smiled, and shook her head. "Well, Father, I can't decide which disguise you wear best: Audie Murphy, James Bond, or Indiana Jones." She gave me that killer smile and sat down. "Whichever, you certainly do make life interesting." She then turned to Curtis. "Dr. Red Crow, would you be so kind as to order me a Grey Goose vodka martini, dirty, straight up, with two anchovy olives?"

"Yes, ma'am." Curtis walked to the bar.

The chief picked it up. "Our counselor, your daughter, has convinced us that we should take advantage of a strong stock market for part of our funds, about one million dollars, and between now and when those funds are needed, we should be able to do well, so we've opened an account. In addition, through some information that came to us from unnamed sources, we have set up three one-hundred-thousand-dollar college funds for your three grandchildren. When they're ready for college, they should be pretty healthy accounts as well."

I was quite moved, as Clay had been when we first met, and I struggled to hide it. Mary Beth knew it. Hell, she knew everything.

"The last thing we did, Woody, is we invested in a piece of real estate, a house actually. Your house, which we understand you like. In turn, we have a piece of paper we would like you to review. It's a lease. The lease is for one dollar a month rent for the remainder of your life, or until you wish to move. The tribe is your new landlord." The chief looked at me, evaluating my reaction. "We feel that our response to what you've done for us is our small gesture of gratitude, Woody. We know we can never truly repay your generosity."

I was having genuine difficulty processing this development. "I didn't expect anything like this, gentlemen. I'm truly overwhelmed. In the end, please understand that the greatest reward I can receive is seeing what you're doing for your people, with a biased emotion for the vets. I'm the one who is so grateful. And what you've done for me is the best-tasting frosting I could ever have on that cake. Thank you." I looked at all of them. "Two other comments: I owe you, Curtis, a debt of gratitude for your part, and . . ." I looked at my daughter. "You have selected the right adviser."

It was ten o'clock before we finished. It was a joyous session, as evidenced by our farewells.

Mary Beth turned to me. "I don't want to intrude, Pops, but if that second bedroom is available, I could use a place to crash."

"There's a couple of chicks in their twenties waiting for me to get home, but I'll call them now and tell them to come back tomorrow." I had a serious look on my face as I grabbed my cell to make a call.

My daughter's jaw dropped.

I threw my hands in the air in celebration as I said to her, "Gotcha! And that doesn't happen very often."

Everyone laughed and then laughed some more. Mary Beth laughed too.

Mary Beth followed me home in a snazzy yellow sports car, which she parked behind me in my driveway.

"My little tomboy is a Wall Street kingpin . . . or queen pin, or whatever the current politically correct expression would be." I put my arm around her shoulder and took her inside.

"And my father is a soldier, a crime fighter, *and* a soldier of fortune, all in one, at the ripe young age of seventy-five. So what do you want to be when you grow up, Woody?" That smile told me she had broken more than one heart.

"I have no interest in growing up. I know some grown-ups, and they're a tiresome lot."

We grinned at that.

"So it seems you've been plotting behind my back."

"Blame it on your friends. I was sworn to secrecy. Almost made me pinky promise. And, speaking of plotting, you find a two-hundred-year-old hoard of gold worth nine million dollars, steal it from the rich, and give it to the poor? I need to add Robin Hood to your résumé of characters."

"It was three hundred years, and I didn't steal it. I relocated it." I handed her a Sam Adams.

"So now, along with a hundred other people, I'm indebted to you for bringing me a million-dollar client. We pay big fees for that, you know."

"If one more person gives me one more thing, I'll sizzle 'em with my Zap. That's my walking stick taser."

"Well, just know that I truly appreciate it, Dad. Just as important, this account, and the college trust accounts, will be my pet projects. Don't you worry about them."

"You have my full confidence, my dear. You do need to know that if the truth ever did get out, that cache would be contested and I could end up in the pokey, so let's do that pinky-promise thing."

I offered my pinky, and we swore the secret.

"And one other thing. I want you to figure out a credible story to tell Winston and Sonny as to how I could afford those trusts for the kids. They'll have to know."

"Not to worry, Dad. I'll figure it out."

"Okay, so if you have time, we could take a ride on my new speedboat tomorrow, a present from the FBI."

She thought about that. "Why not? I'll head to Atlanta tomorrow afternoon and catch an early flight the next day." She paused. "So would it be just the two of us?"

I knew where she was going. "Since you seem to know every secret I have, I suppose I could ask a lady along who has become a friend."

"Friend, huh? More politically correct sophistry?"

"Think what you wish. You two are a lot alike . . . which is a scary thought. I'm a risk-taker, however, and will give her a call in the morning."

We finished our beers, hugged, and headed for sleep.

"By the way, Dad, you could be overpaying for this dump at a dollar a month."

"I was told a while ago that rent would be going up, so now

I'll be saving seventeen hundred and ninety-nine dollars a month. But you're right, it's still a rip-off."

Marylyn was excited about meeting Mary Beth. She had a meeting and would be tied up until eleven. She said she would grab three submarine sandwiches and meet us at the boat around eleven forty-five.

The connection was instantaneous. My fear of two felines going paw to paw was quickly extinguished. Now, would the two cats join forces and attack the sweet, cuddly golden retriever?

"I suspected he was seeing someone, just wasn't expecting someone so elegant," Mary Beth said to Marylyn.

"I think that silver-tongued gene was passed on. You're so sweet to say that, and I've been looking forward to meeting a financial icon who can advise me on overdraft prevention."

They laughed. Now, what direction would it take?

"Hope you know what you're getting into, Marylyn."

Here we go, I thought.

"Well, if you have a list of caveats, I could keep it in my purse."

"Boy, am I hungry for one of those pastrami submarine sandwiches," I said in a weak attempt to cut that discussion off at the pass. "How about you guys?"

I took the boat to deep water, where we trolled, took drinks from the cooler, and ate our food. The talk was benign and fun. There was a small breeze with lots of blue sky, blue water, and blue spruce along the shore.

"Brick-A-Brac," Marylyn said. "Interesting name, Woody. You misspelled it, you know."

"Yup, and here's the reason why," I replied. "Make people notice and want to fix it. Asymmetry will cause discomfort."

"That's rather cryptic," Marylyn said. "You want discomfort?"

"The study of human nature," I said. "Separate the stressful from the serene. A subtle life lesson is all."

"So, Dad, do I need to add Sophocles to your ever-growing list of alter egos?" Mary Beth chimed in.

"I believe that was Epictetus," I retorted.

"Way too heavy for me," Mary Beth stated. "What kind of birds are those?"

After mooring the boat, we said goodbye to Marylyn.

"Might be a keeper, Pops," my daughter said when she was gone.

"One day at a time, my dear. So far, so good. Let me know the story you come up with, and call me after you talk to your brothers. I'm sure they'll call me with both thanks and questions."

"Not a problem, Dad. I'll call you in the next few days, and thanks again."

We hugged before she left. I waved to my little girl. *Turn around and you're tiny, turn around and you're grown.* Life and I were smiling at each other. I was in a good place and didn't need an infusion of delusion.

CHAPTER 75

C urtis and I met for dinner at the club. It was as if the world
had stopped its rumble and settled into a more normal
state of placidity and quietude. On second thought, the world
is incapable of doing that, but maybe, at least for the moment, my little life could. I was also experiencing my normal
conditioned response to this state of affairs . . . Where was
the boogeyman? I knew he was there, maybe taking a coffee
break. *Hope it's a long one.*

Curtis might have been thinking the same thing. He put his
hands up in a defensive position. "*No más!* Let's take a break,
Woody. Push the pause button on excitement, at least until
I've reacquainted myself with my pre-Woody days of peace
and quiet." He gave a great guffaw. "No mistake, however, I
will look forward to our next adventure."

"I'm with you, Curtis. Let's ride the serenity wave until it
crashes on the beach. And speaking of the beach, you need to
ride with me in my new toy."

"That I could handle."

"I've been catching up on the news," I said. "Big mistake.
Think I'll continue on as an ostrich. The outside world has
become quite unattractive."

"If you're a patriot, the outlook is a bit foreboding," Curtis
said. "The changes are dictating a new direction, but one that
encompasses a threatening historical confirmation. As Lord
Woodhouselee said, democracies don't survive much over two
hundred years. We're past that."

"Thing is, Tytler said that when the cycle ends, it starts

over again," I said. "With all due respect for the fact that his prescient thesis was written over two hundred years ago, that isn't what normally happens, and it's not what's happening in America."

"Churchill said that democracy is the worst form of government, except for all the rest, but he was wrong as well," Curtis said. "If the people are free from oppression, are happy and prosperous, other forms make up *good* government: a benevolent monarchy, benevolent aristocracy or polity, the rule of many. These, as opposed to *bad* government: tyranny, oligarchy, and *bad* democracy, and that isn't just semantics. Communists are great fans of democracy, which they see as a tool to remove the rights of capitalists and the wealthy and to centralize power in the hands of government. Marxism is alive and well in our country as democracy morphs into socialism and then into a form of Communism. That's political evolution." Curtis was on a roll, reminiscent of a street lecturer with a gathering crowd. "You can talk about equality until you're blue in the face, but outside of equal rights, it doesn't, and can't exist. The political attempts to eliminate meritocracy might sound good to the masses, but their attempts to make everyone equal is a paradox, against the natural order of things, and can only be accomplished by treating people unequally.

"The socialist ideal, where everybody owns everything equally and wealth is shared, because of human nature will degenerate into oligarchy, and from there, usually into tyrannical control. The quest for power is man's strongest motivator. If you think those who possess that power will simply walk away, you're only kidding yourself.

"There are those whose goal is to achieve socialism by way of democracy, a clear foist. The so-called progressives have already polluted the Constitution and the institutional safeguards of our historic human rights." Curtis paused to catch his breath. "As I said, the direction the country is headed should give pause to a patriot, a term the progressives despise." Curtis was finished.

After a bit, I asked him a question. "Did you say your doctorate was in psychology or political science?"

"I do get a bit passionate from time to time, Woody. It's just that I risked my life, as did you, to protect our way of life. Not so sure I would do that today."

"You're singing to the choir, my friend."

Curtis and I were old school. We didn't hide it. We also knew that the younger generations were pushing us aside, some with a nudge, some with a club. They weren't aware that it was a mistake. There was a great deal of wisdom and experience that was simply being discarded, stuff that could be part of the new engine they were building. Most old-schoolers saw the futility and weren't interested in pushing rope and went to *solicited only* mode, and there weren't many solicitations.

Our dinner was upbeat. We shared our collective gratitude for the outcome of our adventures: so many better lives, hope, opportunity, and the reality of happiness. And too, a most meaningful friendship.

EPILOGUE

"The bottom line, Dad, is that every way I spin this thing, it's a clusterfuck, so here's the story. You and Curtis hit on a lucky lottery number. You both took a little piece, set up these college trusts, and gave the rest to the reservation. Sonny and Barb will be ecstatic and grateful and won't ask any questions. I don't have to tell you that they live in the merry old land of Oz, do I?"

"It's why everybody loves them," I replied.

"Then there's Winnie, who will want a forensic, but I can be a bullshitter, and I learned from the best, so, Mr. Mentor, dazzle him with artifice. I've set up the accounts and trusts. I'll need to get your signatures on some stuff, so I'll book another trip to Jekyll Island. Great fun for me, Dad. Maybe have a dinner with that *friend* of yours?" She giggled.

"Anyone ever tell you that you can be snarky?"

"Incessantly."

"You still beat up boys?"

"At every opportunity. Now go and play with your new toy, and for God's sake, stay out of trouble. Yeah, right. Talk soon." Mary Beth hung up.

I spent the day emptying my job jar: writing thank-you letters to Jack and the chief and Clay, registering my boat, and setting up tomorrow, when Marylyn and I would mosey around the island and head out to a Cabela's store to browse and spend my thousand bucks.

I still hadn't told her about my discovery. There would come a time. In the meantime, we would tour the old DuBignon estate before we went shopping. I wanted to check it out.

I supposed that someday, some newly named hurricane would beat up on Jekyll Island, but for the most part, the weather here was great. Today was no exception. My skinny old legs embarrassed a nifty pair of shorts and a seersucker shirt, while Marylyn sported a lightweight dress that flowed in the breeze. We could have been a couple of fun-loving undergrads from days long past.

There were a handful of cars, and several groups of tourists roamed the grounds. We did the same. The shed foundation looked just like it always had, ancient and overgrown. Near the plaque that welcomed visitors were three young, enthusiastic kids, maybe in their twenties. One was holding a metal detector. We stood near them, looking at what remained of the entryway.

The kid holding the metal detector turned and spoke to us. "Did you guys know that the guy who built this place was some kind of pirate? Rumor has it that he buried some gold a couple hundred years ago. Could be worth a fortune."

The other two joined us.

"So we bought this gadget." He showed it to us. "Never know. Today might be our lucky day." He gave us that *whaddaya think* look.

Marylyn and I looked at each other and hunched our shoulders.

I spoke. "Well, just know that the world is full of treasures, and when it's your time, you'll find them. Or, just maybe, they'll find you."

THAT'S ALL FOLKS

CPSIA information can be obtained
at www.ICGtesting.com
Printed in the USA
BVHW080046220921
617192BV00009B/999